Journal of the

American Psychoanalytic Association

KT-223-387

Vol. 43

No. 4

1995

International
Universities
Press, Inc.
59 Boston Post Rd.
Madison, CT

Editor	Arnold D. Richards
Associate Editors	Lawrence Friedman
	Glen O. Gabbard
	Henry F. Smith
	Phyllis Tyson
Editorial Board	James Barron
	Cecile Bassen (associate)
	Fred Busch
	Steven Cooper
	Scott Dowling
	Gerald Fogel
	Richard P. Fox
	Arnold Goldberg
	Stuart T. Hauser
	Axel Hoffer
	Dorothy E. Holmes
	Judith Kantrowitz
	Jane Kite (associate)
	Nathan Kravis (associate)
	Peter J. Loewenberg
	Elizabeth Lloyd Mayer
	William Meissner
	Humphrey Morris (associate)
	Paul H. Ornstein
	Joy D. Osofsky
	David L. Raphling
	Alan Z. Skolnikoff
	Robert L. Tyson
Former Editors	John Frosch (emeritus)
	Nathaniel Ross (associate)
	Harold P. Blum
	Theodore Shapiro
Consultants	Lolafaye Coyne (statistics)
	Linda Goettina (library)
Manuscript Editor	Michael Farrin
Administrative Board	Lawrence S. Chalfin
	Stephen K. Firestein
	David M. Hurst
	Marvin Margolis
	Arnold D. Richards
	Judith S. Schachter

Bernard L. Pacella, M.D.
President of the American Psychoanalytic Association
1992–1994

Journal of the

JAPA 43/4

American **P**sychoanalytic Association

Vol. 43

No. 4

1995

TRIBUTE TO BERNARD L. PACELLA   957

Opinion

THE FATE OF RELATIVES AND COLLEAGUES IN THE AFTERMATH OF BOUNDARY VIOLATIONS   959

Plenary Address

Howard Shevrin
IS PSYCHOANALYSIS ONE SCIENCE, TWO SCIENCES, OR NO SCIENCE AT ALL? A DISCOURSE AMONG FRIENDLY ANTAGONISTS   963

Lawrence Friedman, Wilma Bucci, Arnold Goldberg, William I. Grossman, Paul E. Meehl, Robert Michels, Richard C. Simons, and Mark Solms
COMMENTARIES   986

Howard Shevrin
AMAGANSETT REVISITED   1035

Scientific Papers

Salman Akhtar
A THIRD INDIVIDUATION: IMMIGRATION, IDENTITY, AND THE PSYCHOANALYTIC PROCESS   1051

Robert M. Galatzer-Levy
PSYCHOANALYSIS AND DYNAMICAL SYSTEMS THEORY: PREDICTION AND SELF SIMILARITY   1085

Glen O. Gabbard
THE EARLY HISTORY OF BOUNDARY VIOLATIONS IN PSYCHOANALYSIS   1115

Michael I. Good
KARL ABRAHAM, SIGMUND FREUD, AND THE FATE OF THE SEDUCTION THEORY   1137

Milton Viederman
THE RECONSTRUCTION OF A REPRESSED SEXUAL MOLESTATION FIFTY YEARS LATER   1169

Book Reviews

PSYCHOANALYSTS TALK by Virginia Hunter
reviewed by Joseph Reppen   1197

WOMEN ANALYZE WOMEN by Elaine Hoffman Baruch and Lucienne J. Serrano
reviewed by Martha Kirkpatrick   1201

THE EGO AND ANALYSIS OF DEFENSE by Paul Gray
reviewed by Evelyne Albrecht Schwaber   1208

THE USE OF THE SELF by Theodore J. Jacobs
reviewed by Michael G. Moran   1214

THE MISUSE OF PERSONS: ANALYZING PATHOLOGICAL DEPENDENCY by Stanley J. Coen
reviewed by Paul A. Dewald   1216

PSYCHOANALYSIS AND ETHICS by Ernest Wallwork
reviewed by Edwin R. Wallace, IV   1221

BETWEEN HERMENEUTICS AND SCIENCE by Carlo Strenger
reviewed by Donald P. Spence   1229

THE MIND AND ITS DEPTHS by Richard Wollheim
reviewed by Barnaby B. Barratt   1233

PSYCHOANALYSIS AND THE SCIENCES by André Haynal
reviewed by John E. Gedo   1236

HIERARCHICAL CONCEPTS IN PSYCHOANALYSIS: THEORY, RESEARCH AND CLINICAL PRACTICE edited by Arnold Wilson and John E. Gedo
reviewed by Milton Viederman   1239

Letters   1247

Contents of Volume 43   1255

Bernard Pacella's terms as treasurer and then president of the American Psychoanalytic Association are but the most recent evidence of his commitment to the field of mental health. Trained in pediatrics, child and adult psychiatry, and child and adult psychoanalysis, he has been a full-time research psychiatrist at the New York State Psychiatric Institute and chief of child psychiatry at Columbia University College of Physicians and Surgeons. With Eugene Barrera, he conducted the first neurological and neurophysiological studies in the U.S. of the effects of electroconvulsive therapy on the brain. He was a charter member of the American Electroencephalographic Association and headed the EEG department at the Psychiatric Institute.

It was when Margaret Mahler arrived in the United States and became consulting child psychiatrist at Columbia that Pacella's career took a new turn. At her urging, he resigned his full-time position to devote himself to psychoanalysis, child psychiatry, and child analysis, and began analytic training at the New York Psychoanalytic Institute. In the years that followed, his career continued to be strongly influenced by Mahler. He worked closely with her as colleague and friend and served for a number of years as president of the Margaret Mahler Psychiatric Foundation. He published a number of papers on dream process, including some in which his background in neurophysiology led him to raise questions about the compulsory nature of dreaming, and a paper on the concept of the primal maternal matrix, a precursor of recent interest in "the tether."

During his tenure as treasurer of the American Psychoanalytic Association, Pacella was a primary figure in reviewing Central Office operations and arranging the purchase of new offices. As president, among his major achievements was the organization of the Committee on Societies as a means of keeping local societies informed and encouraging discussion and involvement at the local level and the formation of the Steering Committee to coordinate the workings of the Executive Council Committees and the Executive Committee. Pacella holds the deep conviction that we must take seriously our task as mental providers, and that our primary concern should be the effective and efficient delivery of mental health care, all the while adhering to sound analytic principles.

Donald Meyers

THE FATE OF RELATIVES AND COLLEAGUES IN THE AFTERMATH OF BOUNDARY VIOLATIONS

At the beginning of his now notorious "The Unknown Freud," *New York Review of Books* essayist Frederick Crews names names in the Emma Eckstein and Horace Frink debacles, two of the most obvious and scandalous boundary violations in Freud's history and thus that of psychoanalysis. Most modern analysts have been made aware, belatedly but with no uncertainty by now, of the details of these rare lapses. Both episodes begin with a sort of supervisory hubris—Fliess's with Freud, Freud's with his patient Frink—and end in disaster or near disaster for the patients involved. In the latter of these transgressions, Frink's marriage to his rich patient Angelika Bijur at the advice of an uncharacteristically avaricious Freud, the calamities extended beyond the consulting room and the dyad of analyst and analysand. Frink, pushed forward by Freud to become twice in the 1920s the New York Psychoanalytic Society's president, sank into a psychotic depression after his patient bride quickly divorced him. While he made repeated suicide attempts, both his wife and his patient's first husband, devastated by the betrayals, deteriorated and died.

There are many other stories like this one, as we sadly know—mostly unwritten stories in which the spouses of transgressing analysts and analysands plunge into despair and the alcoholism and suicidality that so often accompany overwhelming loss and disillusionment. But what of the impressionable and vulnerable children of such parents, the parents who, once esteemed and trusted, have cast themselves into the role of pariah or into simple oblivion? About them and the impact on their lives little has been chronicled. Often enough, the psychoanalytic cautionary tale concludes with the gullible patient who has been victimized and the admired psychoanalyst who has ruined his career. The consequences for the nonconsenting adults and children whose lives have also been compromised remain matters for the collective imagination. These are stories that, officially at least, we like to forget.

And what of the effect of boundary violations on colleagues, particularly those who find themselves charged with the therapeutic care, if not of the transgressors themselves, then of those hurt by them? Clinging to idealizations for dear life, the life of their profession and their conviction in it, institutes and the individuals in them typically hushed up discomfiting affairs like these while continuing to kowtow to the very authorities who let them down. Thus, for example, all three institutes in New York City found themselves under the aegis of brilliant but supremely entitled sexual boundary violators. Only recently, and in the most circumspect and veiled terms, have the students and analysands of these luminaries begun to come forward and confide their dismay over the clay feet of their fallen idols. Long winking at indiscretions, the peers, analysands, and supervisees of these men for years made the most scupulous and often unrealistic demands for a generalized abstinence and unwarranted self-denial on the part of their own students—on the third and fourth generations on whom the sins of psychoanalytic forefathers were thus visited. Indeed, the simmering and inexpressible rage incurred as a result of this duplicity and oppression may be partly responsible for the contemporary revolt against ego psychology, and for the yielding of theoretic authoritarianism to a pluralism that borders on anarchy. But that's another complex story in its own right.

In the meantime, no psychoanalytic discussion of boundary violations is complete without attention to their impact on the more or less innocent bystanders cut down by the ill-considered and selfish actions of their spouses or parents, analysts or patients, whose individual treatment contracts these victims were neither privy nor party to. Where it falls short of utter destruction, the effect on families and, less poignantly perhaps, on psychoanalytic communities has most often been to encourage patently defensive overidealizations, ego-deforming disavowals of truth, and decades of hazy submission and stasis. In focusing, here as elsewhere, in our observations about the analytic process, exclusively on the single analytic relationship, we ignore what most of us know firsthand—its far-reaching and potentially dangerous reverberations in the concentric circles of the immediate interpersonal surround and the enveloping society in which families and institutions are embedded and in which individuals grow up. Thus, boundary violations constitute collective traumas that live on in the psychic and political lives of generations to come.

Seen in this larger social and historical context, the complex ethical dilemmas posed by treatment transgressions, sexual and otherwise, also demand consideration. At present we have few mechanisms in place with which to safeguard the greater public from abusive and therefore incompetent practitioners—not only the patients, that is, who fall into their hands, as if blindly, but the otherwise unprotected dependents of both participants, individuals who have never had any say in the matter at all. Soon enough, I suspect, professional liability suits will be leveled not only by disgruntled former patients at their imperfect psychotherapists but by family members whose lives have miscarried as a result of such abuses of power.

John Munder Ross
243 West End Avenue
New York, NY 10023

HOWARD SHEVRIN, PH.D.

Is Psychoanalysis One Science, Two Sciences, or No Science at All? A Discourse among Friendly Antagonists

When I was invited to give this plenary address I surmised that people would be interested in learning about my research. The invitation also offered the opportunity to place my research in the broader context of research in psychoanalysis, a complex and even controversial subject. What you will hear is my attempt to present that context in the form of a discourse among friendly antagonists. My research will be introduced at an appropriate point so that its relevance to the larger picture of research in psychoanalysis can be evaluated.

THE FRIENDLY ANTAGONISTS

On a rainy August afternoon, somewhere near Amagansett, three psychoanalysts gather in the summer home of Professor di Sapienza, an academic colleague who is a psychologist knowledgeable in the philosophy of science.

Dr. Case is a staunch believer in the primacy of the clinical situation as the bedrock of psychoanalytic science.

Plenary Address, American Psychoanalytic Association, New York, December 17, 1993.

This presentation has benefited from suggestions made by its many helpful readers, including members of my clinical research team—Drs. James Bond, Linda Brakel, and Richard Hertel—who patiently read through version after version, and members of my laboratory research group—Drs. Scott Bunce, Steven Hibbard, Michael Snodgrass, and Philip Wong. I am also especially grateful to Dr. Richard Simons for his encouragement; Dr. Donald Kaplan for his reckless confidence in me (how I wish he could read it now!); Dr. Louise Kaplan for her fine sense of form; Dr. William Grossman, who steered me in the right direction from the start and then helped me arrive at my destination; Aliza Shevrin, who knew how to help me "slide by" my obsessiveness; and last, Mrs. Beverly Knickerbocker, who tirelessly redid and redid a manuscript that was not so much written as constructed—I will miss her.

Dr. Sample, a careful and sophisticated thinker, although as convinced as Dr. Case of the centrality of the clinical situation to psychoanalysis, is seriously concerned about its scientific foundations and a believer in the necessity of systematic research, albeit limited to the clinical situation.

Dr. Link, noted for his efforts to build interdisciplinary bridges to other sciences, believes that a comprehensive theory incorporating the insights of the clinician and recent research in related fields will serve to broaden and deepen psychoanalysis and increase its acceptance among skeptical scientists.

Professor di Sapienza has an ulterior motive in inviting her friends to her home on this rainy afternoon: She has finally decided to stop being so kind to her psychoanalytic colleagues, to be so ready to listen without criticism to their admittedly fascinating but empirically and systematically anecdotal effort at science. She has always secretly been convinced that fundamentally psychoanalysis is not really a science, but is nevertheless an important rational enterprise. She is prepared to have it out with her colleagues as a first important step in her plan to write a telling critique of psychoanalysis and a recommendation as to its true place among intellectual pursuits.

FIRST MEETING

Di Sapienza: Thank you all for coming. As I mentioned to each of you over the phone, what better way to spend a rainy afternoon than to get together and discuss matters of mutual interest? I asked each of you to come prepared to discuss your view of psychoanalysis as a science. To some this is an old chestnut, to others it is a burning question, and to still others it matters not at all. What I would like to invite you to do first is for each of you to state your position as succinctly as possible in this first go-around. After each of you has stated your point of view, we will then see where we are and if there is reason to continue further. I would like to invite Dr. Case to begin.

Case: My position can be put simply, and I believe it constitutes a classical view of psychoanalysis as a science sui generis. The psychoanalytic situation is the locus not only of discovery but also for testing hypotheses. The data of psychoanalysis can *only* be obtained in the psychoanalytic situation. Past efforts to investigate psychoanalytic phenomena in the laboratory, or in the field, have largely failed because they cannot duplicate the phenomena or benefit from the full richness of the theory. The debacle of so-called repression research in the 1940s is a telling and grim reminder of how all such misguided efforts must fail. I maintain that the sheer growth, the dynamism, and the actual results of psychoanalysis are themselves proof of the validity of psychoanalytic propositions. There is no need to discount the experience worldwide of thousands of psychoanalysts who agree on fundamentals derived from their practice: the role of the unconscious, transference, resistance, the discoveries of infantile sexuality, and the central role of conflict. On the basis of phenomena brought to light by psychoanalysis, as Brenner has demonstrated (1982), the richest, most complex theory of the mind in conflict has been forged. Moreover, a science can be qualitative and empirical (that is, nonexperimental) and yet be lawful and capable of proof within the domain of its application. Take the example of geology for long periods of its development. Other sciences are certainly welcome to select from among our findings and hypotheses and see how they are relevant to their own domain of application. Only the psychoanalytic method itself can inform us about what goes on intrapsychically and, by way of reconstruction or construction, what the nature of earlier intrapsychic experience was like.

My conclusion, therefore, is that psychoanalysis is indeed a science in its own right, with its own domain of application, phenomena, discoveries, theories, and criteria of proof, and I would be more than happy to provide at some later time more detailed evidence in favor of my position.

Di Sapienza: Dr. Sample, I would anticipate that you have a thought or two about what Dr. Case has just propounded.

Sample: With the greatest respect for Dr. Case's forthright presentation of a classical view of psychoanalysis as a science, I would like to argue for a significantly modified version of his position. Certainly I agree that psychoanalysis is a science in its own right; however, I am much less sanguine than Dr. Case concerning the psychoanalytic situation as a locus for testing and proving hypotheses. In the clinical literature, composed mainly of case reports, often the criteria of proof cited by psychoanalysts amount to a list of positive instances. But what philosophers of science refer to as *enumerative inductionism* does not constitute proof. Edelson (1988) reminds us of the turkey who comes to believe that 364 days of well-fed contentment is a guarantee of immortality. Positive instances, no matter how many, will not suffice. The need is to meet the criterion for *eliminative inductionism,* which requires that the *absence* of a given factor be correlated with the *absence* of its consequent. Seldom if ever do we find this criterion met in the psychoanalytic literature, nor does one often encounter the discipline involved in formulating alternate hypotheses and submitting them to proof.

Further, psychoanalysts practice a method based on certain presuppositions for which the procedure or the method itself cannot provide proof. These two presuppositions can be stated quite briefly in Freud's own words: "When conscious purposive ideas are abandoned, concealed purposive ideas assume control of the current of ideas, and . . . superficial associations are only substitutes by displacement for suppressed deeper ones" (1900, p. 531). What independent evidence can be found in support of these presuppositions—the first having to do with a causative psychological unconscious, the latter with the crucial role played by such transformations in consciousness as displacement, reversals, and symbols as the presumed complex effects of unconscious causes? At this stage, perhaps little, yet scientists often work productively for years without examining their methods and presuppositions. For the longest time, chemistry assumed that something like molecules existed, though they could cite no independent proof. It just made too much sense to assume it. So, immediate examination of these presuppositions is not urgent, but they should be recognized as assumptions, ultimately in need of independent proof.

Much more urgent is to deal with the clinical situation in a more systematic way by introducing the usual essentials of the scientific method: controls, reliable measures, and above all testing of alternate hypotheses so that the criterion of eliminative inductionism can be met. The need is for sophisticated outcome and process research devoted to the psychoanalytic situation.

Although I would not rule out in principle relationships to other sciences, the pursuit of these relationships is at this time premature—concepts that can "bridge over" to other sciences are lacking and will likely remain so for some time to come.

I conclude that psychoanalysis as a science has not yet achieved its fullest flowering but is capable of benefiting from a more rigorous application of scientific method to the phenomena obtained within the psychoanalytic situation.

Di Sapienza: Well, Dr. Link, it's your turn. I know you depart radically from the positions just outlined by Drs. Case and Sample.

Link: You are exactly right. In my opinion, Dr. Sample's position encounters three serious problems, two of which apply also to Dr. Case's position. First, they both narrow the purview of psychoanalysis to the clinical situation itself as the locus of scientific inquiry. As a result, they sell short the powerful theories developed by psychoanalysts constituting what psychoanalysis has to say about the mind itself, its biological roots, its development, and, in short, the implications of these theories for other sciences. Reiser (1984, 1990) has explored some of these possibilities in two recent books. Second, Dr. Sample's position advocates enlisting all psychoanalytic scientific resources in the service of psychotherapy research, which, while necessary, is inherently limited, as I will try to show. Finally, by relying only on psychoanalytic data, Dr. Sample ignores his own acknowledged need for independent evidence for psychoanalytic presuppositions, which he has quite concisely identified, while Dr. Case does not seem to be concerned with this problem at all.

As a consequence of these three problems, Dr. Sample's position, while shrinking psychoanalysis to the limits of a purely applied science, requires at the same time that it perform as a basic science. This is not possible. We should recognize that psychoanalysis is really two integrally related but separate sciences: an applied clinical science and a basic science of the mind. As an applied clinical science, it must be concerned with treatment outcome and process, the limits of its applicability, and the training of clinicians. But at the same time it must be recognized that insofar as it is an applied science it applies a body of knowledge and theory—based on certain presuppositions or assumptions—to a given patient's emotional disorder. It is the task of the psychoanalytic basic science of the mind to raise up this edifice of knowledge out of clinically derived insight, systematic, experimental, and nonexperimental research, and bridge building to other sciences. This task requires drawing upon the findings of these other sciences and their methods for convergent, as well as potentially contradictory, evidence. The optimum relationship between an applied and a basic science requires a separation of methods and at least of some of its investigators while maintaining an active commerce between the two.

I conclude that psychoanalysis has in reality always been two sciences—an applied science and a basic science—but they have through the long history of psychoanalysis been confounded so that the advantages and power of each have been vitiated. Let us finally recognize that psychoanalysis is really composed of two sciences, separate them, and keep them creatively interacting.

Di Sapienza: Perhaps you were all expecting that I would remain in the role of interlocutor, but I suspect that I will now surprise you by advancing the argument that psychoanalysis is not a science at all but rather is a rational but distinctly nonscientific enterprise. You have all assumed that psychoanalysis must be a science, either by nature or by fiat, if it is to hold its head up among intellectual disciplines and be taken seriously. This need not be the case at all. Teaching and governing are both rational enterprises with worthwhile goals involving bringing about change in individuals or in society at large, and yet are not sciences, neither applied nor basic. Nor are teaching and governing to be confused with hermeneutic science; neither teaching nor governing requires exegesis of a text or following rules of textual interpretation, but are quintessentially rational human enterprises dedicated to bringing about change in one form or another. Efforts to convert teaching and governing into applied sciences continue to fail, even though educational theoreticians and political scientists may offer theories and findings from time to time that can be of some limited use.

A rational enterprise such as teaching, governing, or psychoanalysis must be distinguished on the one hand from applied science, and on the other from an art, though it draws upon both and may erroneously be confounded with one or the other. Neither teaching nor governing nor psychoanalysis are basic sciences, or sciences in any true sense, but they are important rational enterprises conducted by rational change agents with highly valued goals. For teaching, the goal is to assist individuals to acquire knowledge and skills. For governing, it is to provide the greatest good for the greatest number. And, for psychoanalysis, it is to assist an individual to acquire self-knowledge and self-mastery.

Psychoanalysis as Science

Why is psychoanalysis not a science? The problem is not in the need to be rational and systematic. All human pursuits require a modicum of rationality and discipline. The problem resides in the nature of the subject matter, the practitioner, and in the nature of the goal. Teaching, governing, and psychoanalysis share as their subject matter humanity itself, albeit from different perspectives. Human beings, both individually and in groups, are complex, changing, growing, deceptive, and unpredictable. The practitioner is a human being also, to whom the same considerations apply.

It is this relationship between two human beings—each complex, changing, growing, and highly individual—having the goal of bringing about change that makes it necessary to resort to what I will call *improvisation*, or inspired guesswork. The reason I referred to teaching, governing, and psychoanalysis as rational *enterprises* is to emphasize that each requires action rather than simply contemplation. By action I mean making decisions that affect people's lives. In view of the sheer complexity of the circumstances—its constantly changing, evolving character—each action must to a significant extent be different and suited to highly specific circumstances. It is in this sense that these rational actions must be considered improvisations. To those who would say that guesswork is also part of science, my response would be that what are initially guesses can be tested under similar conditions, whereas this cannot be the case for teaching, governing, or psychoanalysis.

Why is psychoanalysis not an art? Artists work their will on relatively inert material lacking a will or purpose of its own, nor is their aim to transform the material for its own sake, but rather to serve their own ends. When people refer to psychoanalysis as an art, what they seem to mean is that there is a technique or a set of guidelines as to how to proceed with an analysis, rather than referring to *creating* a work of art. To attempt the latter as a psychoanalyst would simply be hubris.

My conclusion is quite different from all of yours. Psychoanalysts are to be congratulated and respected for valiantly taking the Socratic admonition to "know thyself" beyond the limits of the purely philosophical and cognitive to incorporate the rest of the human psyche and, further, to aim at bringing about significant changes not only in self-knowledge but in self-mastery. As such, they are in the special and elite company of teachers and governors who in their own ways attempt to facilitate the growth of mastery and human satisfaction. It is unworthy of the nature and goal of psychoanalysis to require that it be a science, either applied or basic. The criteria of science when applied to psychoanalysis curb and hamper its ability to perform what it alone can accomplish as a rational human enterprise. The often heard complaint of psychoanalysts that research findings are of little help to them can best be understood in this light. It is not that the research is meaningless; it is simply irrelevant.

I would like to propose that we not wait for another rainy day but meet at this same time next week. I propose that you each present a more fully worked out statement of your position and that we then have a go at each other.

SECOND MEETING

Di Sapienza: Welcome. Again, I would ask Dr. Case to begin.

Case: I will argue and provide evidence in favor of the sufficiency of the clinical situation for a full-bodied science of psychoanalysis. But I will start with the flat statement that psychoanalysis is neither a purely clinical nor an applied science, and certainly not a practical enterprise like teaching or governing. In the strictest sense, psychoanalysis is a science in its own right, using a unique method enabling the psychoanalyst to get in touch with phenomena that no other method can deliver.

Psychoanalysis is not a clinical science in the usual sense, because its method is inherently *investigative* as well as ameliorative. Psychoanalysis, for example, does not provide a medication whose ameliorative action is based on principles and knowledge derived from some presumably more basic science like biochemistry. Rather, the investigative method of psychoanalysis in its own right aims to disclose the principles and knowledge upon which the cure depends, as well as to create the conditions for that disclosure. This point is of decisive importance. The psychoanalytic method, properly employed, *elicits* as well as *elucidates* the phenomena of interest. The patient's resistances and transferences, although always potentially present, are drawn forth by the operation of the method so that these resistances and transferences can be experienced by the analysand. The psychoanalytic method is not simply a telescope or microscope making something visible that is already there; it is more like an alembic in which materials are transformed, distilled, and fractionated, or, if you like, analyzed. For these reasons, no other science can be "basic" to psychoanalysis, because only the psychoanalytic method both elicits and elucidates the phenomena of interest. For these reasons, no further "proof" is necessary—the rightness or wrongness of the results are apparent to analyst and analysand, much as one knows when one has recovered the right name after a brief search. You do not need someone else to tell you that the name is right or wrong. In fact, you are the only one who *can* decide that. Psychotherapy research at best only gilds the lily, while research requirements such as recordings and sampling destroy the organic integrity of psychoanalysis. The psychoanalytic method is *not* a series of inspired improvisations, but requires systematic application and rigorous attention to the unfolding of the process, a process that is subject to the discipline of a method. For *all* these reasons, I maintain that psychoanalysis is a science sui generis. It is neither an applied science requiring adjunctive proof or the elucidation of its underlying principles by a more basic science, nor a nonscientific yet rational improvisational enterprise.

Di Sapienza: After that brilliant cadenza, Dr. Sample, it is your turn.

Sample: As a science sui generis as described by Dr. Case, psychoanalysis will not, I'm afraid, stand up to scrutiny. Its unique method has serious limitations, and other methods must be applied to the clinical data to make up for them.

To start with one obvious yet important point: the data of psychoanalysis are not public. A sine qua non of any science is that its data be fully available to other interested scientists. Although Dr. Case makes an eloquent argument for the uniqueness and power of the psychoanalytic method, how do we know that it is always practiced as preached? Despite elaborate procedures for evaluating the quality of psychoanalysis practiced by our graduates, these procedures depend almost entirely on examining analyst summary reports of their cases—an inadequate substitute for the data themselves. Of course, this is the very same problem we have with published case studies. Although some may balk at this, it is only through audio and video recordings of an analysis that a public record of the data can even be approximated.

But having a public record is only the beginning. Certainly, for one, the limitations of these audio and video data as a full record must be acknowledged. Much of importance obviously goes on in the minds of analyst and analysand that is neither spoken nor visible. Nevertheless, the recordings, though they do not present, for example, the analyst's fantasies or conjectures, are a real record of a significant portion of the analytic data and should not be sniffed at. Aside from the need for public data, one can also wonder if it is so clear that the method works as Dr. Case has described. Again, "rightness" to analyst and analysand is a purely subjective, as well as private, criterion. The analyst in effect tells his scientific colleagues: "Take my word for it. This is what happened in this psychoanalysis."

We must heed and respond to Grünbaum's searching critique of the psychoanalytic situation as the locus of hypothesis testing. How can we respond to his assertions that suggestion cannot be ruled out as a contaminant, and that correctness of interpretation cannot be demonstrated by therapeutic gain, the so-called tally argument?

Suggestion can be ruled out only by an examination of a public record. The critique of the tally argument can be answered only by developing methods that can assess correctness of interpretation independent of treatment outcome. Fortunately, methodological and empirical advances in psychotherapy research have been made on both these counts. Let me illustrate with two research findings. I offer these illustrations as examples of methodological solutions to the problems stated; no agreement with the theories employed in the research is required in order to appreciate the strength of these methods.

Weiss and Sampson (1986) have developed a method for identifying, in advance of treatment, certain pathological beliefs. They have been able to show that when the analyst addresses these pathological beliefs, the patient improves.

Based squarely on the central psychoanalytic conception of transference, Luborsky and coworkers (Luborsky and Crits-Christoph, 1990) have developed a way of inferring reliably the presence of what they refer to as a Core Conflictual Relationship Theme

(CCRT). When these themes, formulated in advance and thus independent of their therapeutic effect, are worked with interpretively in the treatment, the outcome is more likely to be favorable. These psychotherapy researches point to the right path to follow if our data are to be public and some of our basic hypotheses confirmed.

I would conclude, in agreement with Dr. Case, that the clinical situation can and should be the locus of scientific investigation and proof, but that additional, clinically based research methods are necessary to provide that proof. Although other sciences may provide converging evidence, they are not essential to investigating psychoanalytic hypotheses best studied in the psychoanalytic situation itself.

Di Sapienza: Well, Dr. Link, we are ready to hear from you.

Case: I would like to hear how any science can be basic to psychoanalysis. I hope you will cite chapter and verse.

Sample: Yes, in particular about bridge building to other sciences.

Link: I will try to satisfy you, but you will need to bear with me as I will have to go into some detail. But first some comments on Dr. Case's and Dr. Sample's positions. Dr. Case raises for me a fundamental question: Can any science be unique and sufficient unto itself? My answer is an emphatic no. The constraint on this uniqueness is to be found in its underlying presuppositions. Every science must assume some things to be true in order to get on with its work. These presuppositions may turn out to be true or false, with fateful consequences for the science.

I must take issue with Dr. Case on another point. It is not logically feasible that independent evidence in favor of psychoanalytic presuppositions of such central importance to psychoanalysis as a causative unconscious making itself known indirectly and through various transformations can be found within the psychoanalytic situation. Other independent methods are required.

I must also take issue with Dr. Sample's position. First, the psychotherapy researches he cites are based on the same presuppositions as the psychoanalytic method itself and thus cannot provide independent evidence for these presuppositions. Further, these researches do not explicitly and systematically incorporate distinctions between conscious and unconscious, or take into account the occurrence of transformations. For example, in the Luborsky research a consciously stated wish is taken at face value; the possibility that the wish may be a reversal, displacement, etc. is not considered. Thus, the Core Conflictual Relationship Theme method does not incorporate significant elements of the psychoanalytic model, though there is much of importance that it accomplishes.

I would also take issue with Dr. Sample's position that bridge building and collaboration with other sciences is premature. One can find out how premature it is only by undertaking the task. Otherwise, what criteria can one rely on to identify in advance whether the time is ripe for bridge building and collaboration?

And this leads me to another quite important consideration, touched on by Dr. Case when he recalled the dismal efforts of researchers in the 1940s to demonstrate the existence of repression. To be relevant and probative, research must incorporate the essential elements of the psychoanalytic model based on the two presuppositions previously described. If the research intends to deal with such clinical concepts as defenses, transference, and conflict, it must provide that its method take into account unconscious as well as conscious processes, transformed as well as transparent contents, by which I mean presumed "substitutes by displacement," as well as presumed direct effects of unconscious causes, as in a telling slip. If the research intends to address these two basic presuppositions, it must demonstrate how it can do so independently of the clinical method based on these presuppositions. Research of this nature, to succeed, must either discover new consequences of these presuppositions independently arrived at, or provide evidence of what underlying factors or preconditions cause them. I will describe an example of each later on. These criteria constitute a tall order, but in my judgment define what I mean by a science basic to psychoanalysis. It is not at all difficult for me to sympathize with Dr. Case's position in light of these admittedly demanding criteria that successful psychoanalytic research must meet. I also very much sympathize with Dr. Sample's position on psychotherapy research, because the task the psychotherapy researcher faces is a formidable one and the successes he cites must be judged against the exacting standards that must be applied. On the other hand, if we can become explicitly aware of the extent of the task and of its absolute necessity, we are in a much stronger position to know what we need and to judge what we have accomplished.

Now for the research. You will need to judge how relevant the findings are and how true to the essentials of the psychoanalytic model and its presuppositions. I will, of course, try to make out a case for both.

I will draw on two pieces of research conducted by Shevrin and colleagues at the University of Michigan (Shevrin et al., 1992, in press; Snodgrass et al., 1995). I will be selective and, I hope, concise and reasonably clear, but I will go into sufficient detail so that you can judge for yourselves whether the research accomplishes the ends I envision.

I argued earlier that a psychoanalytic basic science should address the fundamental presuppositions of our clinical method while remaining true to the essentials of the psychoanalytic model. I would quickly add, and then try to defend, the proposition that a true basic science of psychoanalysis can do both—contribute importantly to support fundamental propositions and remain true to the psychoanalytic model, without, I stress, itself being a psychoanalysis.

In the first study I will describe, Shevrin and colleagues invented a method drawing on three sources: (1) the psychoanalytic clinical method, but not as applied to a psychoanalysis; (2) cognitive laboratory methods involving subliminal and supraliminal procedures; (3) a psychophysiological method based on obtaining brain responses to these sub- and supraliminal stimuli (Shevrin, 1988; Shevrin et al., 1992, in press). A brief word about each and then how they fit together. The subjects for the study were mainly patients within the neurotic range suffering from social phobias. Subjects were evaluated by experienced psychoanalysts. Each evaluation observed three essential aspects of the psychoanalytic clinical method: (1) a series of in-depth, unstructured interviews were conducted in which both content and process were addressed; (2) an account of the complaint and relevant history were obtained, with attention paid to the manner in which the patient engaged in the evaluation; (3) initial transferential and resistance issues were noted and where indicated addressed as a further source of diagnostic information. The essentials of the psychoanalytic clinical method was here employed for diagnostic but not therapeutic purposes. Pace Dr. Case, the interviews were also audio recorded and transcribed. A team of three analysts and one psychodynamically trained clinical psychologist then studied the verbatim transcripts, and each arrived at a psychodynamic formulation, including the patient's account of his presenting complaint, the patient's own understanding of the complaint, and hypotheses concerning the underlying unconscious conflict causing the complaint.

But this was not the end of the clinicians' task. They were then asked to select words or brief phrases used by the patient that conveyed the patients' conscious experience of the complaint, but also words and brief phrases that, in the clinicians' judgment, expressed in derivative form the hypothesized underlying unconscious conflict. These words might be drawn from anywhere in the protocol—reported memories, dreams, fantasies. This research application of the clinical method follows exactly the essential steps of the clinical method: (1) obtaining the basic clinical data in a psychodynamic manner (as I have just previously described); (2) organizing them into psychoanalytically relevant propositions by applying the psychoanalytic model and its presuppositions. It departs from the usual application of the clinical method in two ways that do not, however, subvert the clinical method: (1) in place of developing interpretive statements offered to the patient, words and brief phrases are selected that would be incorporated in such interpretations; and (2) in place of new clinical data usually obtained following interpretations, physiological responses are instead obtained to the words selected.

Once the words have been agreed on, the research subjects move from the consulting room to the laboratory. There the words selected are presented to the patient in a tachistoscopic viewing box. Initially the words are flashed so quickly that they cannot be seen consciously; thereafter they are presented slowly enough so that they can be. In brief, this constitutes the cognitive sub- and supraliminal laboratory method. Its importance, however, is critical to the research: it is only through the subliminal presentation of the stimuli that an operational method for investigating the *descriptive* unconscious can be achieved. No inference from the patient's conscious communication is required in order to demonstrate that the stimuli in question are indeed unconscious. They have been rendered so by the subliminal method itself. Whether or not they are *dynamically* unconscious will then emerge as a finding determined by the fate the different types of words undergo when presented subliminally and thereafter supraliminally. But more of this a bit later.

Psychoanalysis as Science

Each time a word is presented either subliminally or supraliminally, a brain response is obtained that is electrically recorded for future analysis. On the basis of extensive work in Shevrin's laboratory and elsewhere, there is good reason to expect that brain responses related to the subliminal stimuli will be obtained (Barkoczi et al., 1983; Brandeis and Lehmann, 1986; Libet et al., 1967; Kostandov and Arzumanov, 1977; Shevrin, 1973; Shevrin et al., 1969, 1970, 1972; Shevrin and Fitzler, 1968a, 1968b; Shevrin and Rennick, 1967).

The use of brain responses is of special methodological importance as well as of substantive interest in its own right: These responses are the new consequences following from the presupposition of a causative psychological unconscious; they would constitute discoveries that support the validity of that presupposition while building a bridge to another science, neurophysiology.

In the research these brain responses are analyzed into sequences of time-frequency features (Williams and Jeong, 1989). When applied to the data this mode of analysis yielded significant patterns or sequences of five brain frequencies at specific points in time, not too dissimilar from a melody—which is, of course, no more than a sequence of auditory frequencies called notes. When these sets of five time-frequency features are analyzed, striking differences emerge. When the unconscious conflict words were presented *subliminally*, the time-frequency feature analysis showed they are associated with each other. When the same words were presented *supraliminally*, the brain responses failed to show them as associated. If I can put it in these terms and get away with it, what the brain/mind "knew" unconsciously, it seemed not to "know" consciously, but only for the words related to the unconscious conflict as selected by the clinicians beforehand.

Let me tell you briefly about one subject, a young man of twenty suffering from a public eating phobia. The clinical team agreed that the underlying unconscious conflict was oedipal in nature, with prominent negative oedipal elements. The phobia was related to the regressive homoerotic wish to submit to an oral phallic attack and the great fear of it. The words for the conscious experience of the symptom were plain enough from his account; they were words such as cafeteria, swallowing, nauseous. A primary source for words related to the unconscious conflict derived from a disturbing dream

977

in which he was stabbed by a close male friend, John, with a sword that was thrust upward through his throat while he was lying on his back. As he told the dream to the interviewer, he felt a sensation in the same throat muscles that would tense up and inhibit his swallowing in a public eating place. The telling of the dream was itself a revealing transference communication. It is also notable that John was the same friend from whom he had taken a girlfriend away; once having done so, he lost interest in her, a pattern he had repeated with several friends. He had in fact taken the same girl away from John twice, given her back each time, and each time returned to a close younger brother relationship with John in which much carousing without women occurred. Some unconscious conflict words selected were *John, stab me, on my back* from the dream, as well as several words like *massaging muscle* and *men hugging*, drawn from elsewhere in the protocol and derivatives of the hypothesized regressive homoerotic position.

When the brain time-frequency features were analyzed in greater detail, it turned out that there was one pattern for unconscious conflict words and another for conscious symptom words. For the unconscious conflict words, the highest and lowest frequencies traded places in the five-note "brain melody" as a function of consciousness; subliminally the *highest* frequency was early, the *lowest* frequency later; this order was reversed supraliminally. For the conscious symptom words, subliminally it was the *lowest* frequency that occurs early and the *highest* frequency later; the reverse of this order was found supraliminally. The "brain melodies" for conscious symptom and unconscious conflict words were *inversions* of each other. When one goes up, the other goes down, and it all depends on whether they are related to consciousness or not. The temporal organization of neural processes differs dramatically as a function of consciousness and conflict.

To summarize, the research—based in part on the psychoanalytic clinical method, but conducted in such a way as to test the presupposition of a causative psychological unconscious—resulted in the discovery of unique patterns of brain responses supporting the validity of that presupposition while at the same time potentially building a bridge to neurophysiology.

The second experiment I would like to tell you about speaks to the second presupposition: that unconscious causes are revealed through manifest expressions, or transformations of the content of these unconscious causes in the form of displacements, superficial associations, and symbols.

Let me begin with an old but useful saw in the form of a question: When is a cigar a cigar, and when is it a phallus? When do we judge that the patient is really talking about cigars or that he is really talking about phalluses? Or, in technical terms, when do we have warrant to infer from conscious communications that the explicit communication is really about something else that is stirring unconsciously.

From a cognitive psychological standpoint, the problem can be recast, interestingly enough, as a question of categories: When is a cigar mainly categorized with other smoking items, and when is it mainly categorized with phallic objects? Shevrin and colleagues posed two questions: (1) Would the principles of categorization be different unconsciously as compared to consciously? (2) Would the presence of unconscious conflict make a difference with respect to these principles? (Note how the research incorporates the essentials of the psychoanalytic model by including distinctions between conscious and unconscious, unconscious conflict, and categorical transformations.) The research in progress I will describe concerns only the first question at this point. The words to be categorized were entirely conflict-neutral and the same words were given to all subjects. Two principles of categorization were played off against each other: categorization on the basis of similar relationships *among* attributes and similarity of *individual* attributes. For example, a whale is a mammal because of complex relationships among such attributes as giving birth to live young, nursing, evolutionary history, etc; it also shares a number of attributes with fish—fins, living in the ocean, etc. One might consider the latter basis for categorization as superficial and even misleading in the light of our fuller knowledge. In the experiment, you shall see that these two principles are played off against each other with provocative initial results.

Suppose the word *pea*, presented initially either sub- or supraliminally, is paired with one of four words presented supraliminally only—*spinach, carrot, emerald, ruby*. In both conditions, sub- and supraliminally, each of these four words is presented twice with *pea*; once with the question *vegetable?* and once with the question *green?* The question *vegetable?* requires categorization on the basis of complex relationships among attributes—i.e., edible, form of plant, etc. The question *green?* requires categorization on the basis of a single attribute, color. The subject is to respond yes or no as quickly as possible to the question by pressing the appropriate button. How will the previous presentation of the word *pea* affect the time to answer the categorizing questions, and will it make a difference if *pea* is sub- or supraliminal—that is, if the categorization of *pea* with each of the other words is prompted unconsciously or consciously? Note that *spinach* is both a vegetable and green; *carrot* is a vegetable and not green; *emerald* is green and not a vegetable; *ruby* is neither. Thus, these four words cover the four different relationships possible with *pea*, for the two types of categorization. In the experiment, fifteen such sets of words were presented.

Categorization turns out to be different sub- and supraliminally in an interesting way: When *pea* is subliminal, categorization by single attribute, in this case *green*, is much faster than when *pea* is supraliminal. The answer *yes* to the question *green?* for *emerald* is made much faster sub- than supraliminally—in fact, much faster than to the multiple attribute question *vegetable?* for either *spinach* or *carrot*. Subliminally prompted categorization appears to favor single attributes over complex relationships among attributes—the whale as fish rather than as mammal. To go back to cigars and phalluses: when an unconscious cause is at work, it is the shape of the cigar, a single attribute, that is more likely to be used as a basis for categorization, while in the absence of an unconscious cause it is the complex relationships among features—made of tobacco, capable of being smoked, etc.—that provide the basis for categorization.

Since these results are based on conflict-neutral words, it is possible that categorization by single attribute is the way categorization works *unconsciously*, and that more dynamic unconscious processes "use" the principles already available unconsciously rather than introducing new ones. Additional experiments will need to address this question.

The research provides independent support for the second presupposition of the psychoanalytic method, that unconscious causes are inferred from so-called displaced and substitute formations. This might now be restated as follows: unconscious causes are revealed through properties, such as color or shape, that are superficial or inessential and that are often unrelated to the function or customary meaning of the items. It is these superficial associations that constitute the basis for unconscious categorization. In fact, Freud borrowed the term "superficial associations" from the psychologist Wundt as a way to characterize primary process displacements. This new evidence suggests that even neutral stimuli are categorized through what appear to be superficial attributes when the categorization goes on unconsciously.

To summarize, the second experiment identifies an underlying cause or precondition of the second presupposition having to do with substitute formations. The underlying causes are differences in categorization, a basic psychological and not uniquely psychoanalytic process, and thus the second presupposition is shown to be related to the psychology of categorization, another potential bridge.

As I have tried to illustrate, other sciences *can* be brought into creative interaction with clinical psychoanalysis. The first experiment demonstrates that other sciences, in this instance neurophysiology, can be basic insofar as they discover new consequences of psychoanalytic presuppositions, thus providing independent convergent evidence for their validity. The second experiment demonstrates that other sciences, in this instance cognitive psychology, can be basic by identifying preconditions for these presuppositions and in so doing increase our understanding of their nature.

Case: As I listened to your exposition of these experiments, and I know that you cannot do them full justice, I must confess I am reminded of those complicated Rube Goldberg devices for opening a door, when all you really have to do is turn the knob. Yes, you can open the door with a Rube Goldberg device, but why do it that way? Your arguments about presuppositions are a bit overdrawn. What if I were to say that they are reasonable generalizations based on clinical evidence and not assumptions at all? Also, I am not convinced that the so-called clinical method in the first experiment does incorporate the essentials of the psychoanalytic model. Only a psychoanalysis can do that. Yet, the brain results are fascinating. What exactly they are about, though, is not so clear. I am sure that more research is on the way and we will one day hear about it.

Sample: It's a long way from brain responses to a psychological process, especially one as complex as the dynamic unconscious related to unconscious conflict. How do these intriguing brain frequencies translate into psychological meaning? At best, these are correlations across the great divide separating mind and body. You have not proposed any bridging concepts. I don't yet see how "time-frequency" features and "brain melodies" help us much in this regard. As best as I can see, the results you have cited do provide some convergent evidence on the basis of independent methods for certain basic presuppositions. But the methods and measurements do not yet define the essential intervening steps.

Link: Most new scientific methods when they are first created seem laborious and indeed can seem rather like a Rube Goldberg contraption. The first computers were massive and filled entire rooms; now they can fit on your lap. But those early mammoth computers embodied for the first time significant principles of lasting importance. But when you claim, Dr. Case, that rather than being presuppositions these propositions are really empirical generalizations, you have in fact demonstrated how presuppositions arise in the first place—from usually unsystematic observation or even prejudice. But no matter how these propositions arise, it is logically necessary that they be independently confirmed and their place in the larger scheme of scientific understanding situated (Brakel, 1994). As for Dr. Sample's admonition concerning the failure to specify the links intervening between brain and mind, I respond by saying that a bridge isn't built in a day. Nevertheless, I think it would be correct to assert that Shevrin's research has sunk piers on either side of the great divide Dr. Sample refers to and that these piers are in fact across the way from each other so that we at least know where the span should be erected and even some hint concerning the nature of the bridging materials—patterns of brain frequencies and principles of categorization.

Di Sapienza: Now it is my turn. I have listened intently to all of your arguments. Ironically, I can advance my position that psychoanalysis is not a science at all, albeit a valuable rational enterprise, by citing in turn each of your own objections to the other two positions. Dr. Case has already dismissed psychotherapy research as unnecessary meddling in the psychoanalytic process. He has argued forcefully against any science being basic to psychoanalysis because the psychoanalytic method is, in his view, a unique *investigative* method through which whatever is basic can only be discovered and tested in the psychoanalytic situation. Dr. Sample points out eloquently that Dr. Case is forced to defend a science without truly public data and without independent means to demonstrate the probative status of its hypotheses. He scores against Dr. Link by asserting that science can progress for years without paying attention to its method or presuppositions. In any case, he argues that efforts to develop fruitful interactions between psychoanalysis and other sciences, basic or not, are premature. Dr. Link argues against Dr. Case's position that psychoanalysis is a science sui generis because admittedly it is based on presuppositions for which we need independent support and against Dr. Sample's reliance on psychotherapy research as short-sighted and sorely limited by its failure to incorporate essential elements of the psychoanalytic model.

Let me now confront you with the inescapable implication of your obvious standoff: You can't agree on exactly what way psychoanalysis is or can be a science, because in fact it isn't a science at all.

Case, Sample, and Link: No!

Di Sapienza: No matter how loudly you may all shout "No," it will not make it so. I have heard interesting argumentation and intriguing experimental results, but I have yet to be convinced how it all hangs together. Quite otherwise, you seem hardly to have in any way modified your individual positions in the light of what you have heard. It seems rather to me that you will leave this room reinforced in your own opinions. You will carry on with your analytic practices convinced, perhaps rightly, that you bear the future of your profession in your hands. Dr. Sample's handful of psychotherapy researchers will ply their recondite trade on the few fully recorded psychoanalyses available, and talk to each other while bemoaning the lack of interest of their clinical colleagues. What Dr. Link's basic psychoanalytic scientists will do is beyond me. I doubt whether they will have anyone to talk to; perhaps their fate is to talk to themselves and, like Beckett's Krapp, obsess over their pretty results with increasing despair.

If I cannot convince you to chuck overboard this superfluous scientific baggage, about which pieces to keep you cannot in any way agree, and take your rightful place in the ranks of the powerful agents for rational change in our society, then you must put your heads together and arrive at some mutual understanding. If psychoanalysis is in fact a science, and if it is as sturdy and self-reliant as Dr. Case insists, and as ready for closer systematic scrutiny of its data as Dr. Sample believes, and as rich in its conception of the human mind and as capable of benefiting from the methods and findings of other sciences as portrayed by Dr. Link, then perhaps some day you *could* convince me of the scientific status of psychoanalysis, if—and this is a big if—you can deliver the goods. Although for the reasons I have already given, you have not yet convinced me, I do believe you have much to offer to each other. The first bridges I would build are those connecting your different positions.

Case: I suppose it is worth a try. I have certainly enjoyed these interchanges, though I must confess I retain a bit of skepticism about where it will get us.

Sample: As long as it doesn't hold us back from what really needs doing. There might be some gain if in fact Dr. Link's optimism about bridge building is warranted, as perhaps the research he cited suggests.

Link: I have myself been excited by this opportunity to see the diverse pieces of the analytic puzzle laid out so clearly. I would like very much to see how we can put these pieces together and, if need be, find the pieces that are still missing. The rich intuitive skills and theoretical grasp of the experienced analyst, the careful, systematic attention to the nitty-gritty of the clinical process practiced by psychotherapy researchers, and the power of bringing to bear different and complementary methods to psychoanalytic issues by experimental scientists all working together holds forth the promise of scientific progress.

Di Sapienza: The time is getting late. Perhaps next summer we can meet again and see what the intervening year has brought to light. Thank you and good luck!

REFERENCES

Barkoczi, I., Sera, L., & Komlosi, A. (1983). Relationships between functional symmetry of the hemispheres, subliminal perception and some defense mechanisms in various experimental settings. *Psychologia*, 26:1–20.

Psychoanalysis as Science

BRAKEL, L. (1994). On knowing the unconscious: lessons from the epistemology of geometry and space. *Int. J. Psychoanal.*, 75:39–49.

BRANDEIS, D. & LEHMANN, D. (1986). Event-related potentials of the brain and cognitive processes: approaches and applications. *Neuropsychologia*, 24(1): 151–166.

BRENNER, C. (1982). *The Mind in Conflict.* New York: Int. Univ. Press.

EDELSON, M. (1988). *Psychoanalysis: A Theory in Crisis.* Chicago: Univ. Chicago Press.

FREUD, S. (1900). The interpretation of dreams. *S. E.*, 4/5.

KOSTANDOV, E. & ARZUMANOV, Y. (1977). Averaged cortical evoked potentials to recognized and non-recognized verbal stimuli. *Acta Neurobiologica Experimentalis*, 37:311–324.

LIBET, B., ALBERTS, W.W., WRIGHT, E.W. & FEINSTEIN, B. (1967). Responses of human somatosensory cortext to stimuli below threshold for conscious sensation. *Science*, 158:1597–1600.

LUBORSKY, L. & CRITS-CHRISTOPH, P. (1990). *Understanding Transference: The Core Conflictual Relationship Theme Method.* New York: Basic Books.

REISER, M.F. (1984). *Mind, Brain, Body: Toward a Convergence of Psychoanalysis and Neurobiology.* New York: Basic Books.

———— (1990). *Memory in Mind and Brain: What Dream Imagery Reveals.* New York: Basic Books.

SHEVRIN, H. (1973). Brain wave correlates of subliminal stimulation, unconscious attention, primary- and secondary-process thinking and repressiveness. *Psychological Issues Monograph 30*, 8(2):56–87.

———— (1988). Unconscious conflict: a convergent psychodynamic and electrophysiological approach. In: *Psychodynamics and Cognition*, ed. M.J. Horowitz. Chicago: Univ. Chicago Press.

———— BOND, J.A., BRAKEL, L., HERTEL, R.K. & WILLIAMS, W.J. (in press). *Conscious and Unconscious Processes: An Experimental Investigation Based on Convergent Psychodynamic, Cognitive, and Neurophysiological Methods.* New York: Guilford Press.

———— & DICKMAN, S. (1980). The psychological unconscious: a necessary assumption for all psychological theory? *Amer. Psychol.*, 35:421–434.

———— & FRITZLER, D. (1968a). Brain response correlates of repressiveness. *Psychol. Reports*, 23:887–892.

———— ———— (1968b). Visual evoked response correlates of unconscious mental processes. *Science*, 161:295–298.

———— & RENNICK, P. (1967). Cortical response to a tactile stimulus during attention, mental arithmetic and free associations. *Psychophysiology*, 3:381–388.

———— SMITH, W.H. & FRITZLER, D. (1969). Repressiveness as a factor in the subliminal activation of brain and verbal responses. *J. Nervous & Mental Dis.*, 149:261–269.

———— ———— ———— (1970). Subliminally stimulated brain and verbal responses of twins differing in repressiveness. *J. Abnormal Psychol.*, 76:39–46.

——— ——— ——— (1972). Average evoked response and verbal correlates of unconscious mental processes. *Psychophysiology*, 6:149–162.

——— WILLIAMS, W.J., MARSHALL, R.E., HERTEL, R.K., BOND, J.A. & BRAKEL, L. (1992). Event-related potential indicators of the dynamic unconscious. *Consciousness & Cognition*, 1:340–366.

SNODGRASS, M., SHEVRIN, H., BRAKEL, L. & MEDIN, D. (1995). Qualitative differences in the principles of organization in conscious and unconscious categorization. Presented to American Psychological Society, New York, July 1, 1995.

WEISS, J. & SAMPSON, H. (1986). *The Psychoanalytic Process: Theory, Clinical Observations in Empirical Research.* New York: Guilford Press.

WILLIAMS, W.J. & JEONG, J. (1989). New time-frequency distributions: theory and applications. *IEEE Transactions.* CH2692–0000, 1243–1247.

2021 Vinewood Boulevard
Ann Arbor, MI 48104

COMMENTARIES

Introduction: Lawrence Friedman

How scientific is psychoanalysis, and what sort of research is relevant to it? Today's harsh public scrutiny and bare-bones health financing bring new urgency to the old question.

For his plenary address to the American Psychoanalytic Association, Howard Shevrin has devised a playful and powerful teaching device that allows the reader to hold in imagination all four of the principal conflicting beliefs regarding psychoanalytic research. Shevrin's dramatic dialogue renders clearly visible the elements of the controversy, which are then measured against fascinating examples taken from his own research.

We have added another seven voices to Shevrin's four, and from all of these it is likely that readers will first identify their own position, then come to question it, and finally discover positions they had never thought of. They may also find that arguments about scientific status have a way of picking out shades of meaning within concepts (such as the unconscious) that might otherwise have gone unnoticed.

Psychoanalysis as Science

Wilma Bucci

The action takes place at the home of Dr. Nomological Network, in a newly renovated loft building in Soho, during the Labor Day weekend. We first meet Drs. Hermeneut and Philo. They enter a large elevator, decorated like a Victorian bird cage. Dr. Philo speaks first.

Philo: Haven't seen you in a while; where have you been? I felt sure *you* would have been invited to those soirees (*spoken with a deeply rolled* r) of di Sapienza's in Amagansett. I of course never leave the city in the summer.

Hermeneut: Who is di Sapienza?

Philo: I'm not surprised you haven't heard of her. She thinks of herself as something of a philosopher of science. My colleague, Dr. Link, who apparently has some interest in her ideas, has told me that she views psychoanalysis as a rational (sic) enterprise—comparable to teaching or governing—whose subject matter is humanity, and which is dedicated to bringing about adaptive change. It is distinguished, in her view, from applied or basic sciences, which require replication and systematic testing, and quite different from your kind of work, Hermeneut. It is also distinguished from art, in that psychoanalysis works with material that has a will and purpose of its own, while the artist works with inert material, which she transforms in the light of her own aesthetic vision.

Hermeneut: Enough, I get the idea. Perhaps di Sapienza can justify her view that education and government are rational enterprises, though I would expect someone who lives on Long Island to know better. However, I must say that she seems mired in a predeconstructionist conception both of art and of my work. I have much more I could say about her ideas, as I am sure you do, and this is all very interesting, but haven't we been in this elevator quite a long time? I believe our position in this shaft has not changed. Is there some meaning for this? (*They begin to look around them.*)

The scene shifts to the lobby of the building. Entering together are Dr. Brain and Dr. Mind. They notice an "out of order" sign near the elevator, infer that it is not working, and decide to take the stairs. Mind speaks.

Mind: Times have certainly changed, for us to be invited to the same gathering. It used to be that anyone who was interested in one of us would have ignored the other, and I was generally not invited to respectable scientific meetings, anyway.

Commentaries

Brain: We can thank our host, Dr. Nomological Network, for bringing us together. (*They ring the bell and enter his loft, which is in the process of construction.*)

Network: I assume you know why I have brought us together today. You have seen the report of the intellectual extravaganza organized by di Sapienza in Amagansett. Of course, I'm not surprised she failed to invite me; she might have had to read something written during the past half century to know about my role. Anyway, I never leave Manhattan in the summer. I wouldn't have given the whole event another thought, but it seems to have aroused some general interest in the field, and I think we have an obligation to continue the discussion so as to present a more balanced view.

I'd like to talk first about the presentation of Dr. Link, and we can talk about Case and Sample when the others arrive. As a cognitive scientist interested in psychoanalysis, what do you think, Mind? By the way, I hope you don't mind (*he chuckles softly*) my calling you Mind. I admire your "coming out," although I imagine you still make some psychologists and philosophers of science a bit uneasy, particularly those who have not accepted the cognitive revolution.

Mind: Of course it is largely because of you that I have been able to "come out," as you put it, as Bucci (1989, 1993) has discussed.

Network: Thank you. I do not like to grumble, but I do sometimes wish that more people understood that, from the perspective of science, mental representations and processes have the status of theoretical constructs, which are defined through links to other concepts, and through operational indicators, events that may be jointly observed. Psychological constructs have the same theoretical status as particles, dark matter, the big bang, and life in the Bronze Age; all are constructs, defined within, may I say, a nomological net. All sciences depend on the construction of such a theoretical framework. I assume Link understands this, though he did not see fit to cite me directly.

It is obvious that the mental representations *of other persons* must always be inferred; each of us does that constantly, in intuitive, at times unrecognized, ways. Science recognizes the need for systematic development and validation of such inference. If only people appreciated the power of my approach in this respect. Subjective meanings can indeed be part of a scientific theory, once a theoretical framework has been set up, within which concepts may be defined and systematic inferences made; subjective experience cannot be part of a scientific enterprise without such a framework. The failure to develop systematic definitions for experiential terms has contributed to a splitting of psychoanalysis from the scientific field, and has even drawn some leading psychoanalytic researchers to follow in the direction of Dr. Hermeneut. (I wonder where he and the others are, by the way; oh well, perhaps they are walking down the garden paths.)

Mind: You are preaching to the converted here. The application of your approach to mental representation and information processing is the day-by-day work of the cognitive science field. We recognize that nomological networks in the social sciences differ from those in the physical sciences in that the hypothetical constructs and correspondence rules are far less systematically defined, and we are working to remedy this; but the status of our theoretical constructs and the principles of our scientific approach are the same as for all science. I agree that it would have helped Link's argument to have cited your work, and I will certainly discuss this point further today.

Brain: (*To himself*) I'm sure you will.

Mind: (*Ignores interruption*) First, however, I need to tell you that Bucci (1989, 1993, in press) has expanded the cognitive domain to incorporate *emotional* information processing in the models of mind, and to account for the processes and functions with which psychoanalysts are concerned. I am convinced, as she is, by the need for this reformulation of cognitive science (although I must say that not all cognitive scientists are). Many emotion theorists, such as Lang (1994), Mandler (1984), and Scherer (1984), take a similar position. So let me ask that you now recognize me as Emotion-Mind. Emotions, like mental processes, as they figure in a scientific theory, are hypothetical constructs, defined in terms of other constructs and in terms of observable behavior, within a theoretical framework or, as we say now, a nomological net. "Rage" and "fear," "happiness" and "love"—all are constructs in this sense. This does not diminish their emotional meaning, but allows it to be studied in a systematic and productive way.

Network: I accept the correction, Emotion-Mind. But now what about the work of Dr. Link?

Commentaries

Emotion-Mind: I applaud Link's attempt to integrate psychoanalytic concepts with cognitive ones. However, I believe his call for two separate psychoanalytic sciences, one basic and one applied, is misguided, and indeed reflects his not acknowledging your role, Network. Psychoanalysis is neither "two sciences" nor even "a science." It is an aspect of scientific psychology, the aspect that concerns the interaction of mental, emotional, and somatic functions in an interpersonal context. Psychoanalysis was the first cognitive science (Baars, 1986; Erdelyi, 1985), but fell into the trap of focusing on certain types of cognitive-emotional contents without accounting for their integration within the overall functioning of the human organism. Interestingly, this is the same trap into which many cognitive psychologists have also fallen, from the opposite direction, in attempting to account for cognitive functions out of the context of emotional and somatic ones. The theoretical framework for psychoanalysis must emerge from a general psychological model that accounts for the interaction of cognitive, emotional, and somatic processes. A systematic account of pathology and of the process of change in treatment may then be developed within that general framework (Bucci, 1993, in press).

Brain: You've already taken up so much time here that I will not have time to outline my approach. That's okay, it's your show, Emotion-Mind, but let's at least try to be clear about the relationship between us. May I say first that the scientific approach that you outline applies to neurophysiology as well as to cognition and emotion. Neurophysiological, like cognitive constructs, are hypothetical entities, defined conceptually within a theoretical framework in terms of their relationship to other neurological constructs and defined operationally in terms of observable events. In other words, I am as much a construct as you.

Network: What you say is very important, Brain. Each theoretical level chunks the functional system in a different way, and each is needed to account for interactions in its own domain. Scientists do not use computations involving particles to study the forces that will enable them to build a rocket to the moon, although the action of particles is involved in all physical systems. As we can see, what we have is not a "mind-body problem" but a set of different types of theoretical relationships—among constructs of mind and emotion, their neurophysiological substrate, and somatic-visceral events—as Bucci (in press) has discussed. While psychological theories are not *reducible* to neurophysiological ones, we of course agree that the two levels must ultimately be *translatable* or mappable onto one another. The research of neuropsychologists such as LeDoux (1989) has provided promising and fascinating physiological data concerning the type of interaction between brain and body that is intrinsic to psychoanalysis, and that we study on a psychological level. We also need to remember—as I am sure you both are aware—that theories do not account for other theories; they account for observable events. Thus a theory of brain does not account for a theory of emotion or mind; each accounts in its own way for certain observable events.

Emotion-Mind: I couldn't have said that better myself. I am sure you will agree, Brain, that physiological theories will necessarily take a back seat to psychological ones, in this enterprise of developing a theory of cognitive and emotional functions, which may be applied to the data of the psychoanalytic process. We require psychological models to account for the psychoanalytic process, although we know, on another level, that physiological functions are involved in all mental and emotional ones.

Here is another twist for you to chew on (since our host has not yet seen fit to provide more concrete nourishment). We should recognize that neurological observations themselves may constitute observable data that provide evidence for a psychological theory, just as behavioral evidence may provide evidence for neurological theories. The former is precisely what Shevrin is doing in his experimental paradigm. He is not linking neurological and cognitive *concepts*; he is using neurological observations—along with behavioral ones—as evidence concerning psychological propositions.

Network: Can we move on now to discuss Shevrin's experimental work, as Link presents it. What do you think of Shevrin's research, Emotion-Mind?

Emotion-Mind: I must say that his results are so elegant and complex that one is first somewhat awestruck. Nevertheless, one may find reason to cavil—not to mention quibble—about certain points, in spite of the beauty of his experimental work.

Brain: (*sotto voce to Network*) Perhaps *because* of it?

Emotion-Mind: (*ignores Brain*) There seem to be some inconsistencies in his findings, though of course this may be a problem in

Link's presentation. One possible inconsistency seems worth mentioning. At one point Link says that when unconscious conflict words were presented supraliminally, "the brain responses failed to show them as associated." Later, however, he says, "For the unconscious conflict words, the highest and lowest frequencies traded places in the five-note 'brain melody' as a function of consciousness; subliminally the *highest* frequency was early, the *lowest* frequency later; this order was reversed supraliminally." In other words, "The 'brain melodies' for conscious symptom and unconscious conflict words were *inversions* of each other." The latter formulation, of a systematic inverse organization for unconscious conflict words when presented supraliminally, is quite different from absence of association, and does not seem readily accounted for by Shevrin's theory.

The results of Shevrin's experiment on principles of categorization are also fascinating. There are many questions and problems about this interesting research paradigm and its findings, some of which may arise because of the superficial nature of Link's presentation. Shevrin's results suggest that unconscious categorization is dependent on properties such as color and shape, which he characterizes as "superficial and inessential," whereas conscious classification is more likely to favor what he terms "complex relationships among attributes." Thus, for example, association to a single attribute, such as *green*, is faster when the word *pea* is presented subliminally than when *pea* is supraliminal. Also, for subliminal presentation, associations to single attributes are faster than to complex categories such as *vegetable*. We would then like to know how speed of response varies for different category types in *supraliminal* presentation. Link implies that supraliminal presentation would favor association to multiple attribute categories such as *vegetable*, but does not provide evidence to support this. This point would be important in building a consistent model of subliminal vs. supraliminal organization.

Along these lines, I would also like to mention that Bucci's multiple code theory (1993, in press) would place Shevrin's results in a more general cognitive framework. From her perspective, properties such as color and shape are not at all "superficial" or "inessential," but are the ways in which the nonverbal representational system is organized; this organization plays a crucial role in the process of symbolizing emotional experience. Organization into higher-order categories, such as *vegetable* or *plant*, is a function of the verbal symbolic system; it is a different type of organization from that which obtains in nonverbal systems, but not necessarily a more essential one. Viewing the categorical distinctions in this more general, information processing framework opens specific questions as to how subliminal processing may operate to favor nonverbal and subsymbolic processing systems, which were not addressed by Shevrin or Link.

This brings us to the basic issue of how we view the overall organization of the human emotional information processing system, and leads to the more general questions that I have about Shevrin's work. The major information processing architectures today, including symbolic and parallel distributed processing models, are based on aspects of mental structure *independent of their accessibility to awareness*. Similarly, within the functional rather than architectural approaches, cognitive scientists focus on distinctions that are independent of level of awareness, such as procedural vs. declarative memory, and episodic vs. semantic memory. It is also true that cognitive scientists today are interested, more than ever before, in systematic memory functions that are implicit, operating outside of awareness, and have raised new questions about the construct of consciousness and its characterization within a scientific model (Uleman and Bargh, 1989). From this perspective, they are beginning to tease apart the complex relationships among various functional dimensions that have been customarily assumed to covary, such as awareness, intention, automaticity, and control.

On the basis of current research, we must recognize that the construct of the unconscious can no longer be assumed as necessarily associated with pathology, regression, infantile thought, and wish fulfilling fantasy. From the psychoanalytic perspective, we may also note that the causative psychological unconscious, as defined and tested in Shevrin's paradigm, does not derive from either the topographic or the structural model of the psychic apparatus. In assuming accessibility to awareness as the major determinant of mode of cognitive processing, Shevrin appears to follow the topographic model. However, in relying entirely on verbal stimuli, he assumes linguistic organization in the unconscious, which is obviously at variance with the topographic formulation. Thus, his work cannot be said to test any existing psychoanalytic theory, though it yields results that seem of considerable interest to the psychoanalytic approach.

From either the basic cognitive or the psychoanalytic perspective, it seems crucial that we systematically formulate the model of the mental apparatus that we are testing, in order to understand the meaning of the empirical results. If there is indeed a causative *linguistic* unconscious, as Shevrin's work would indicate, the systemic implications of this within psychoanalytic theory need to be traced. If processing dimensions other than accessibility to awareness are more basic, as many cognitive scientists claim, the implications of these must be traced as well.

The doorbell rings. It is Dr. Qual.

Qual: Sorry to be late. I was trying out some alternative paths. By the way, I noticed a light flashing by the elevator and pounding coming from there. I wonder if someone would like to verify that observation.

Network: I will investigate; why don't you carry on? You probably all know Dr. Qual and his methods of discovery-oriented qualitative research. (*Exits*)

Emotion-Mind: We were just talking about Shevrin's work, which Link discussed at di Sapienza's happening—to which of course none of us was invited.

Qual: I wasn't surprised not to be asked. I rarely am included anywhere, although things have been getting a bit better lately, with respectable psychologists like Elliott (1994) and Mahrer (1988) speaking up for me. Of course, I never leave the city in the summer. I have quite a lot to say about the discussions at the di Sapienza meeting, but I am a bit out of my element in talking about laboratory research methods. Can we turn instead to the work of Drs. Case and Sample? I believe that Link does not sufficiently value the psychoanalytic situation as a research context, and therefore . . .

Emotion-Mind: I agree with you completely; that is part of the point I have been trying to make. Psychoanalysis is a part of scientific psychology, neither a separate basic science nor an applied science, although we may, of course, expect that clinically useful results will emerge from psychoanalytic research. Link appears to deny, or at least to downplay, the basic scientific potential of systematic psychoanalytic process research, and classifies this instead as applied research. In the context of current cognitive science, I would have to argue against this view. Cognitive scientists today have moved away from their initial reliance on laboratory experimentation and computer modeling to a recognition that most complex mental functions (at least those carried out by protoplasmic information processors rather than transistorized ones) need to be studied in naturalistic or quasi-naturalistic contexts. They are "discovering" research methods such as "protocol analysis" (Simon and Kaplan, 1989), which are strikingly similar to techniques that analysts and psychoanalytic researchers know (Bucci, in press). Of course, cognitive scientists fail to recognize the roots of protocol analysis in the psychoanalytic technique of free association, just as they fail to recognize their debt to psychoanalysis in a more general sense.

We need to use our strengths, not deny them, if we are to make a contribution to scientific psychology, and also to provide a systematic basis for addressing clinical questions. In contrast to Link's position, my claim is that the psychoanalytic situation provides a controlled, naturalistic research context ideally suited for testing the propositions of a general theory of emotion and mind. In the context of a consistent psychological model, measures developed by Luborsky (Luborsky and Crits-Cristoph, 1990), Weiss and Sampson (1986), Dahl (1988), Perry (1993), Bucci (1993), Mergenthaler (1992), and other psychoanalytic process researchers may be understood as operational indicators of significant mental and emotional constructs. By this means, it is also possible to define the nature of pathology and the goals of treatment, and to identify and evaluate mutative factors in the treatment in systematic ways.

Qual: That is very interesting, but . . .

Emotion-Mind: If I may make just one final point. While I agree with Dr. Case and Dr. Sample that it is important and quite feasible to carry out systematic research in the therapeutic context, I must also agree with Dr. Link that experimental research will contribute as well to the development of psychoanalytic theory. However, I cannot say too often that . . .

Qual: Apparently not . . .

Emotion-Mind: As I was trying to say, this approach requires that concepts as examined in the experimental setting have the same meaning as these concepts as clinically understood. The debacle of the experimental studies of repression in the 1940s, to which Case refers, occurred precisely because the process of repression, as studied in the laboratory, was quite different from the psychoanalytic concept of repression. We have seen a similar theoretical problem in the implicit characterization in Shevrin's work, of the unconscious as including linguistic components.

Unfortunately—and this brings me to a disagreement with Dr. Sample—the same problem arises for clinical concepts as studied in much psychotherapy research. For example, the clinical concept of *transference* is defined operationally as a Core Conflictual Relationship Theme in Luborsky's terms, as a judgment of disguised allusions by the patient to the relationship with the therapist by Hoffman and Gill (1988), and as a frame structure by Dahl (1988). In the absence of a systematic general theory, we have no way of knowing to what extent these concepts correspond to one another, much less to the notion of transference as clinically understood. Both experimental and psychotherapy process studies may potentially contribute to our understanding of psychoanalytic concepts, but only provided these are systematically defined in a theoretical framework or nomological net. Your type of research may contribute to the nomological net as well, Qual, do you not agree?

Qual: Yes, but . . .

Emotion-Mind: It seems to me that Link's critique of Case's and Sample's work ignored some new developments and possibilities, including qualitative research methods. Of course, that is partly because Sample himself does not tell us very much about the power and flexibility of single case designs. From a scientific perspective, the problem with the traditional case report is the absence of a public record that can be examined by observers other than the two participants, not the intensive focus on a single case. Spence (1993) has discussed possible ways to build checks and balances into the case report method. Fonagy and Moran (1993) have summarized a variety of scientific single case research designs, including qualitative as well as quantitative methods. Dr. Qual, you have hardly spoken; perhaps you would like to tell us about some of these new techniques.

Qual: Thank you; you are too kind.

Just then Network returns, with Philo and Hermeneut.

Network: I'm very sorry about your being trapped. But did you not see a sign that said the elevator was out of order, and another that said what to do in emergencies?

Heremeneut: We weren't sure about the meanings of those signs.

Philo: It doesn't matter; we were deep in conversation.

Hermeneut: I need a drink.

Network: I am a terrible host to have you all here for so long without offering you anything. I have a complex Meritage from California, which I have been saving for this occasion; may I offer you some?

They all drink and discuss the wine for a while, each in his own way. Qual seems eager to resume their previous discussion of science.

Qual: I am glad to have Dr. Hermeneut here; I have been wanting to speak with him. I may have more in common with him and, in one sense, with Case, than perhaps the rest of you do. I know that some of you are unlikely to remain quiet long enough for me to explain the qualitative approach. However, I suggest that it might be useful for Case to become aware of the possibilities of this paradigm; he and his colleagues may be able to systematize their observations using my techniques. Qualitative research focuses on the development of systematic means for analysis of the type of observations that have been made intuitively. The goals of qualitative research include identification and description of relevant variables and dimensions, and discovery of relationships among them. We rely extensively on narrative descriptions and text interpretations, and systematically incorporate the perspective of the observer, his problems and concerns, and his relation to the subject matter, in developing our category systems.

Of course—and Case would need to recognize this—such techniques do not obviate the need for public records or for shared observations, but make such verification more than ever necessary. The fundamental principle of good qualitative research is what Campbell and Fiske (1959) called "triangulation": using converging data from multiple sources. The possibility of public and replicable observations constitute the sine qua non for qualitative research, as for all scientific research. At the very least, this generally requires recordings that permit a public record of a treatment; we cannot depend on the single report of a privileged observer, whose own involvement is complex. Along these lines, an excellent example of qualitative research is the study by Eisenstein et al. (1994), which included analyst, patient, and multiple observer reports. Much of the work of psychotherapy process researchers, including identification of clinically meaningful variables, and development of scales, category systems, and rating procedures, may be seen as within the qualitative research paradigm. Only after the qualitative studies have been done to identify and define relevant variables, dimensions and categories, can systematic and meaningful quantitative designs be developed.

I certainly recognize the problem of intrusion of observers into the therapeutic relationship; one could argue that therapies that are taped are a distinct and unrepresentative set. Of course, one could make the same claim concerning any supervised treatment. This is an interesting dilemma but, I claim, a soluble one within the qualitative approach. Recognition of the impact of the observer on the phenomena being observed is central to the qualitative research paradigm, and techniques are available to account for this. In general, the treating analyst needs to be vigilant for derivatives of the recording, and to address these in the treatment; the research needs to examine the emergence of these derivatives and their vicissitudes in the treatment process.

Emotion-Mind: I agree with you completely as to procedures. At certain stages, we must use research techniques that are oriented toward discovery rather than hypothesis testing, and must build the nomological network interactively in this way. However, I see your approach not as a separate paradigm but simply as a stage in creative scientific thought. If we are clever enough, we can develop research designs that account systematically for the impact of the observer. For example, one could ask an analyst to begin a long-term treatment taking detailed process notes, then later to begin recording, and carry out systematic comparisons of the material in the different phases of treatment and in the two methods of recording. If you do your work systematically, Qual, you could become one of us.

Qual: Thanks a bunch.

Network: I know I missed part of the conversation while I was attempting to locate Philo and Hermeneut, but I think I can infer the major concepts from what I have heard. I will also try to integrate what we have said here with the proceedings of di Sapienza's group. We need to develop a general theoretical framework within which basic clinical concepts, including the nature of pathology and the process of change in treatment, may be defined. This needs to be a framework of general *psychological* concepts applying to all types of contents, not psychoanalytic contents alone. Assuming the concepts of the theory are systematically defined, in terms of one another and in terms of observable indicators, observations of language, behavior, and somatic expression in naturalistic contexts, such as the psychoanalytic sessions beloved of Sample and Case, as well as observations in the experimental contexts used by Link, will all serve to build the nomological net. Qualitative as well as quantitative research designs contribute in their own ways. Neurological data may also be used as evidence for cognitive and emotional events, as Shevrin has done. I notice Brain has not spoken for a while, but I can see that he is registering what is being said.

Brain: I understand that you are talking here about a psychological model, and a neurological theory does not explain the psychological one. Theories explain data, not other theories. Your theory is not reducible to neurons, but operates on a different level. I will just say that the neurological theory also predicts and explains observations of language, behavior, and somatic events, and in some cases perhaps better than the psychological models we have today.

All speak at once. Philo becomes somewhat aggressive at this point.

Philo: None of you has made a clear statement about the epistemological and ontological status of psychoanalytic propositions and the probative value of psychoanalytic data. In addition, I am not at all convinced by Network's, Emotion-Mind's, or even Brain's cavalier disposal of the mind-body relationship. We cannot turn away so easily from issues of translatability and reducibility. We also need to address issues of explanation, prediction, and clinical inference, not to mention transduction, construction, reconstruction, and deconstruction.

Emotion-Mind, Brain, and Qual (in unison): Be quiet and let us do our work.

These three walk together to the window. Hermeneut sits quietly in the corner, holding his wine up to the light. Philo continues to formulate his arguments. Network sits and listens to him for a while, then joins the three at the window, observing the passing scene.

Commentaries

REFERENCES

BAARS, B. (1986). *The Cognitive Revolution in Psychology.* New York: Guilford Press.

BUCCI, W. (1989). A reconstruction of Freud's tally argument: a program for psychoanalytic research. *Psychoanal. Inq.,* 9:249–281.

———— (1993). The development of emotional meaning in free association. In *Hierarchical Conceptions in Psychoanalysis,* ed. J. Gedo & A. Wilson. New York: Guilford Press, pp. 3–47.

———— (in press). *Psychoanalysis and Cognitive Science; A Multiple Code Theory.* New York: Guilford Press.

CAMPBELL, D.T. & FISKE, D.W. (1959). Convergent and discriminative validation by the multitrait-multimethod matrix. *Psychol. Bull.,* 56:81–105.

DAHL, H. (1988). Frames of mind. In *Psychoanalytic Process Research Strategies,* ed. H. Dahl, H. Kaechele, & H. Thomae. New York: Springer Verlag, pp. 51–66.

EISENSTEIN, S., LEVY, N.A. & MARMOR, J. (1994). *The Dyadic Transaction.* New Brunswick, NJ: Transaction Publishers.

ELLIOTT, R. (1994). Rigor in psychotherapy research: questions in search of appropriate methodologies. Paper presented at the meeting of the Society for Psychotherapy Research, York, England.

ERDELYI, M.H. (1985). *Psychoanalysis: Freud's Cognitive Psychology.* New York: W.H. Freeman.

FONAGY, P. & MORAN, G. (1993). Selecting single case research designs for clinicians. In *Psychodynamic Treatment Research,* ed. N.E. Miller, L. Luborsky, J.P. Barber, & J.P. Docherty. New York: Basic Books, pp. 62–95.

HOFFMAN, I.Z. & GILL, M.M. (1988). A scheme for coding the patient's experience of the relationship with the therapist (PERT): some applications, extensions, and comparisons. In *Psychoanalytic Process Research Strategies,* ed. H. Dahl, H. Kaechele, & H. Thomae. New York: Springer Verlag, pp. 67–98.

LANG, P.J. (1994). The varieties of emotional experience: a meditation on James-Lange theory. *Psychol. Rev.,* 101:211–221.

LEDOUX, J.E. (1989). Cognitive-emotional interactions in the brain. *Cognition & Emotion,* 3:267–289.

LUBORSKY, L. & CRITS-CHRISTOPH, P. (1990). *Understanding Transference: The Core Conflictual Relationship Theme Method.* New York: Basic Books.

MAHRER, A.R. (1988). Discovery-oriented psychotherapy research. *Amer. Psychol.,* 43:694–702.

MANDLER, G. (1984). *Mind and Body.* New York: Norton.

MERGENTHALER, E. (1992). Emotion/Abstractness Patterns as indicators of "hot spots" in psychotherapy transcripts. Society for Psychotherapy Research, Annual International Meeting, Berkeley, CA.

PERRY, J.C. (1993). Defenses and their effects. In *Psychodynamic Treatment Research,* ed. N. E. Miller, L. Luborsky, J.P. Barber & J.P. Docherty. New York: Basic Books, pp. 274–306.

SCHERER, K.R. (1984). On the nature and function of emotion: a component process approach. In *Approaches of Emotion,* ed. K.R. Scherer & P. Ekman. Hillsdale, NJ: Lawrence Erlbaum, pp. 293–317.

SIMON, H.A. & KAPLAN, C.A. (1989). Foundations of cognitive science. In *Foundations of Cognitive Science*, ed. M.I. Posner. Cambridge, MA: MIT Press, pp. 1–47.

SPENCE, D. (1993). Traditional case studies and prescriptions for improving them. In *Psychodynamic Treatment Research*, ed. N.E. Miller, L. Luborsky, J.P. Barber & J.P. Docherty. New York: Basic Books, pp. 37–52.

ULEMAN, J.S. & BARGH, J.A. (1989). *Unintended Thought.* New York: Guilford Press.

WEISS, J. & SAMPSON, H. (1986). *The Psychoanalytic Process Theory: Clinical Observation and Empirical Research.* New York: Guilford Press.

Derner Institute
Adelphi University
Garden City, NY 11530

Arnold Goldberg

One of the very first meetings of the Chicago Psychoanalytic Society that I attended as a fledgling candidate was highlighted by a presentation by Howard Shevrin. I remember none of what he said but of late that is a common enough condition of mine that it bears no connection to the excellence of his paper. But I do remember that Merton Gill rose to say something provocative about science and psychoanalysis, and I clearly remember Shevrin's plea not to divide science into two modes or forms: the Geisteswissenschaften and the Naturwissenschaften. Since I could then neither spell nor comprehend those words, I was mightily impressed with both Shevrin and Gill, and remain so to this day. Now, however, I have improved somewhat both in my spelling and my comprehension, and my respect for Shevrin remains undiminished. It remains so not only because of his continued and productive research, but also because he has kept alive those knotty questions of the proper position of psychoanalysis in the scientific community—questions that too many of us dismiss or disregard or secretly hope someone will one day solve and explain in simple, easily spelled terms. To be sure, these are primarily philosophical questions, and Shevrin's plenary dialogue is properly to be read as a discussion among philosophers who aim not so much to resolve questions as to create a state of wonder and bewilderment. And so I finished reading this plenary dialogue with a condition quite similar to the one with which I left that earlier meeting in Chicago. I think the best way to describe that condition is one of worry. However, I do believe and hope that that is the ideal condition for most practitioners of psychoanalysis, and so I did not feel at all burdened by the task of discussing this paper.

I worried about the paper for just a little while, because I think I rather quickly saw it as a snare: a trap for the philosophically unprepared. Though there seemed to be a conversation among three persons staking out positions for the consideration of the scientific status of psychoanalysis, I soon sniffed out a fourth party to that discussion—Howard Shevrin himself. And what he never told us, in this argument about whether or not psychoanalysis is a science, is just what a science is. Shevrin, in his presence in the background, seems to know; and in this bit of knowledge he joins with all of those other critics and friends of psychoanalysis, from Adolf Grünbaum to Robert Wallerstein. They all claim to know what science is, and I confess that I do not. They therefore are at a tremendous advantage in arguing about and determining whether psychoanalysis can properly join the ranks of science, because of my ignorance as well as the sophistication of Shevrin's discussants. Like the naive listener at a gospel meeting, I do believe! But, sadly, I seem to agree with the last person who has spoken and so am a pushover for each of Shevrin's clever protagonists.

However, not only can I spell somewhat better these days, but I have also developed a bit of competence and confidence in avoiding snares and traps. If indeed we subscribe to one or another definition of science, then I fear we shall all be befuddled and confused by the positions offered by Shevrin up to and including the presentation of his elegant research, which, I guess, is offered to show us a way to a form of freedom. But my own position, radical as it may seem at first, is that any claim to know what science *really* is is born of arrogance and presumption. That is to say that it is arrogant to assume that there exists any single, agreed-upon definition of science, and so it is fairly easy to answer the question of Shevrin's title. Let me buttress my own radical opinion with a quote from the philosopher Hilary Putnam (1987): "this appeal to the scientific method is empty. . . . there is no such thing as *the* scientific method. Case studies of particular theories in physics, biology, etc. have convinced me that no one paradigm can fit all of the various inquiries that go under the name of 'science' " (p. 72). Thus, I claim, like a good rabbi, that everyone is right and justified. But this is not to say that simply everything goes. Being right and correct flows essentially from a tradition, which comes from a community of scholars with shared procedures and a common vocabulary. And each of Shevrin's speakers represents a single tradition that for him or her claims an unspoken definition of science; but each such definition is different while still able to enjoy a status of correctness.

Psychoanalysis cannot be forced into a definition it is unable to qualify for, and no one is licensed to tell us what science is, because science simply is not one thing. Shevrin's article demonstrates three traditions of scientific pursuit. I suspect that none of them properly is relevant singularly to psychoanalysis, which certainly has a need for its particular scientific tradition to be clarified. However, that clarification is not presently available to analysis. It is not sui generis, which means it is like no other, and that precious state cannot be claimed until we know of all the others. Nor need it fulfill the criteria of "eliminative inductionism," another demand of opinion rather than of fact; nor is it two sciences. All of the friendly antagonists of Shevrin miss the point, because they start at the wrong place and/ or subscribe to an implicit doctrine forced on us by many philosophers of science who are now (see, e.g., Feyerabend, 1981) seen to be simply in error about the nature of science. In truth, we today have a golden opportunity to stake out a new definition of psychoanalysis as science. We await a philosopher who will undertake that task while not chastising us for not being what someone else wants us to be. Alas, none of the people involved in the conversation was qualified to be that person.

REFERENCES

FEYERABEND, P.K. (1981). Problems of empiricism. *Philosophical Papers*, Vol. 2. Cambridge: Cambridge Univ. Press.
PUTNAM, H. (1987). *The Many Faces of Realism*. LaSalle, IL: Open Court.

180 N. Michigan Avenue
Chicago, IL 60601

Commentaries

William I. Grossman

In his skillful and entertaining tour de force, Shevrin calls for an integration of approaches to gathering and collating information for the development of psychoanalytic theory. His dialogue morality play deftly outlines four positions on the problem of whether psychoanalysis is a science—basic, applied, or both—or can become a science by means of research techniques. He addresses the question of whether the treatment setting of psychoanalysis is by itself a means of scientific observation, or instead must be supplemented by modifying its methods and/or importing data from other fields. That is, can psychoanalytic theory be proved by a scientific method of observation consisting of the therapeutic setting, experimental methods outside that setting, or some combination of methods? His discussion and critiques of therapeutic psychoanalysis and psychotherapy research as sources of observation for the development and support for psychoanalytic theory serves as a background for presenting his own research.

By presenting these issues in the form of a debate, he demonstrates that much of our discussion on these matters emphasizes critiques, limitations, and differences among approaches. Such critiques can be supplemented by developing ideas on the ways diverse approaches to the acquisition of knowledge can be integrated, and the information gained by each method can be used to construct a multifaceted picture of mental function. I believe his paper, by pointing out what each method discussed can and cannot do, points the way to the utilization of various sources of data in formulating a psychoanalytic theory with some testable inferences.

It is readily apparent that the various pithily summarized positions refer to different notions of what psychoanalysis is, and are determined by different immediate interests and goals. These interests are different aspects of the conglomeration of concerns that are all referred to as "psychoanalysis." Shevrin's paper not only helps us to see the range of interests that term covers today, but also points to the need to clarify the relationship beween the kinds of things learned clinically and through research—that is, the nature of psychoanalytic knowledge.

The particular concerns and points of view presented have to do with proving fundamental psychoanalytic assumptions, demonstrating the operation of a specific clinical phenomenon by experiment, supporting the self-validating aspect of the clinical situation, and—finally—the role in society of psychoanalysis as a quasi-institution. However, there are other interests that come into play in traditional psychoanalysis. Among these are the role of developmental conceptions and developmental observations in clinical work, and ways of validating particular interpretations in any ongoing analysis. Although any of these areas of interest might appear at first to belong to one of the others, I believe they do not fit neatly into any of them. The characteristics of any psychoanalytic interest under discussion will determine what assumptions, observations, and data are essential to it and available. For these reasons, any discussion of whether psychoanalysis is or isn't anything can make sense only if the specific aspects of psychoanalysis, the interests and goals, are specified.

The question of whether "psychoanalysis" is a science is difficult because of these complexities, but also because of changing ideas about the essentials of science and scientific theory construction. Much of what is said in this paper mingles discussions of what constitutes proof with considerations of method on the way to conviction based on decisive experiment. The paper understates the point that much work acknowledged as science does not involve decisive experiments or exploration of fundamental concepts. I will return to this issue later, after reframing the positions summarized in the paper.

Each of the participants in Shevrin's encounter group appears to mean something different by "psychoanalysis." Their opinions may be summarized and interpretively elaborated by the following formulations.

First, according to one view, the term "psychoanalysis" refers to the clinical situation, which is said to be a science in itself. This means that the clinical situation is the *source* of hypotheses, the *test* of hypotheses, and the *proof* of hypotheses. The resulting generalizations, which are derived from and apply to the clinical situation, are considered to be generally valid descriptions of mental function. The argument suggests that "analytic method" is, in a sense, a technology, the only method capable of producing the observed results and having its own rationale. According to this view, the data are unique and cannot be tested elsewhere. Other observations and formulations may be consistent with those made in the clinical situation, which is not, however, dependent on them for its validity. This view asserts that the goals and procedures of therapy and research are compatible. (See Freud [1912] pro and con on this matter.)[1]

Second, "psychoanalysis" is regarded as a set of concepts *derived from* the clinical situation and the theory referring to it. These concepts can be studied experimentally in isolation so that they can meet the requirements of science for an experimental science with public data of observation to be examined by others. This would be a science of psychoanalysis that would test, prove, or modify the working ideas of the clinician. This assumes that "psychoanalysis" is a theory (or perhaps alternative theories) that can be stated as a set of propositions, with potentially publicly presentable, supporting, repeatable data, that excludes alternative hypotheses.

Third, "psychoanalysis" consists of two sciences, one basic and one applied. According to this perspective, the clinical method itself, or aspects of it, can be a source of data and hypotheses to be correlated systematically and publicly with behavioral and physiological data. Basic propositions of psychoanalysis can be tested and proved, establishing a basic science from which other propositions of psychoanalysis can be examined and demonstrated. Since according to this view *clinical* psychoanalysis is *applied* science, we might assume that the basic science may be useful in clinical psychoanalysis. This approach would depend on a chain of interpretations from clinical or quasi-clinical observations to arrive at something to be correlated with physiological data.

Fourth, there is something called "psychoanalysis" and it is a "rational enterprise," a helpful activity in which experience and judgment are useful. It is not a science because it does not have the recognized characteristics of science. From this point of view, no comment is made about the scientific aspects of the research discussed, presumably because they are not yet sufficiently integrated, encompassing, or demonstrably relevant to be considered "psychoanalysis"—i.e., the whole field.

I share the view, assigned by Shevrin to Professor di Sapienza, that the desire to say that "psychoanalysis" is or isn't a science is an issue of social prestige and, I would add, a matter of epistemological

---

[1]"One of the claims of psycho-analysis to distinction is, no doubt, that in its execution research and treatment coincide; nevertheless, after a certain point, the technique required for the one opposes that required for the other" (p. 114).

preference. Such a question leads inevitably to some decision about the definition of a science. This is related to the role of group psychology in science as a social institution. As such, the definition is often another covert argument about social acceptability. In any case, my position in what follows is that "psychoanalysis" is a term covering too many more or less scientific, or unscientific, activities, interests, and points of view to be characterized by a single term like "science."

In each position, including di Sapienza's, a different area of activity is called "psychoanalysis," implying that in some way the limited area described represents the whole of psychoanalysis. The series consisting of rational enterprise/clinical situation/clinical science/basic science, starts with rational social concerns and ends with fundamental laboratory science.

This series might be described as going from a focus on the most general view, social interests, to the narrowest, most basic concepts and laboratory science. This last, of course, is a subject of social interest without having that interest as its subject. The series cannot really be said to go from less basic to more basic, or from more complex to simpler. The reason is that each position is concerned with working out a different set of problems. They are all interested in *psychoanalytic ideas* from some angle, but the subject matter of their inquiries is different. For each area of inquiry there is a different set of basic assumptions for its working conceptions and methods. They are equally complex in their efforts to solve the problems they have set out to study, and in their relation to their version of psychoanalytic theory.

A similar point may be made with respect to different theoretical approaches to, or so-called schools of, "psychoanalysis." That is, those who practice according to any one approach observe in a way somewhat different from that employed by those following another approach. Some aspects of the clinical material that are regarded as valuable from one point of view are considered indifferent according to a different model. Any thorough and systematic attempt to compare two approaches in order to clarify the ways they overlap and are different would be difficult, although there have been some interesting efforts to do so (see Bernardi, 1989). However, we don't have a systematic canon of psychoanalytic theory because it is difficult to give an adequately detailed account of any one version of psychoanalysis. This makes it difficult to describe the relationships of different clinical conceptualizations to one another, and to the different points of view (and methods) described in Shevrin's paper.

Any version of psychoanalytic theory requires a kind of translation of its concepts if it is to be compared with any other version or utilized in a nonclinical setting. Since the reverse is also true, the transfer of information from one area to another alters to some extent both the concepts and their application. This consideration leads to a more general point relevant to theory formation: the interrelation among domains of thought and their rendition in different media and in action.

One important point is that all of the perspectives summarized by Shevrin represent the interests of people currently interested in psychoanalysis. To characterize the series narrowly is to take a position both on the relationship among these different kinds of interest and on their relative value.

To Professor di Sapienza, who represents the view from outside anything called psychoanalysis, "psychoanalysis" looks like any other enterprise in which "rational" people are trying to accomplish something while disagreeing on the facts, what to accomplish, and how to accomplish it. The discussions of the other participants, according to di Sapienza, provide the evidence for this rational (but unscientific) conclusion. Di Sapienza's rational argument is itself an example of the kind of reasoning and relationship to observation that this point of view ascribes to its narrow perspective on "psychoanalysis."

However, from the "outside," it is possible to say much the same thing about "science." In fact it *has* been said, and cogently argued. One view argues that the technological success of science has been mistaken as proof of its underlying and untested metaphysical assumptions—i.e., articles of faith. Only the narrowest definition of science as a series of decisive experimental proofs can overlook the degree to which other factors play a role in the development of theories and their acceptance by their adherents.

One of the implications of Shevrin's presentation is that, whatever we may think a scientific theory *should* be, "science" involves a process of expanding knowledge and understanding in which discovery and belief are rarely based on decisive experiments that prove theories. Science involves an evolution of knowledge and ideas, with various steps from unacknowledged assumptions through systematic testing of specific limited processes by experiment of whatever kind.

Knowledge, understanding, and the philosophy of science are continuously changing, often revealing the inadequacy of prior proofs and dogmatically asserted conclusions. In these developments, some of the vagaries of mental life, as described by analysts, play an important part. However, this merely means that the process is probably an endless human enterprise, at least but not only a "rational enterprise." Aside from the fact that it is difficult to know what Professor di Sapienza means by "psychoanalysis," the mere fact of mutual disagreements and criticism does not rule out the possibility that it, or *some of its aspects*, may be or become science, after all. The various psychoanalytic points of view related to hermeneutic, dialogic, and textual analysis orientations are not considered directly in this paper, although their contributions to a clearer account of the clinical situation are relevant to some of the discussion.

Where the status of psychoanalysis as science is concerned, the definition of science often becomes a search for the right analogy for psychoanalysis. This search for an analogy has a certain value, since it leads to more detailed description of the ways knowledge is established, and how it can be tested. Acknowledged sciences vary considerably with respect to these questions, as do various aspects of any science at any given time. At any particular time, in any science, there are many conjectures that organize knowledge but for which no strict proof can be found. Proofs such as those correctly specified in Shevrin's paper are perhaps an end stage on a long road of hypothesis refinement and testing.

The theory of evolution by natural selection provides the best scientific analogue for psychoanalysis. It was used by Freud as a model for psychoanalysis, and it is similar to psychoanalysis with respect to the roles played by observation, history, and reconstruction in establishing knowledge in the two fields. In both, the recognition of the interplay of adaptation, chance, and history is a central organizing conception. Equally interesting are the vicissitudes of the social acceptance of Darwin's theory as "science" and the long road to its recent complex experimental demonstration. Darwin is said to have doubted that direct observation of natural selection would be possible. However, more than a hundred years of work with reconstructive methods, piecing together the results of careful observation of many different kinds, coupled with a variety of conceptions at different levels of complexity, has apparently been verified recently by prospective observation for twenty years of evolution of finches' beaks and other traits under changing environmental conditions (Grand and Grant, 1989; Weiner, 1994). More recently, experimental observations demonstrated the operation of natural selection in fish and bacteria (see Weiner, 1995).

This does not mean that the acknowledged limitations, and the many possibilities for error in the reconstruction of the past can be dismissed. It means that it is nonetheless useful to work with unprovable assumptions and hypotheses until it is possible to demonstrate the operation of complex processes in prospective studies. The research cited above employed methods that could not have been imagined when the first reconstructions of evolution were presented and hotly contested. At the same time, we are reminded that this is possible because of the use of methods of reconstruction based on the amassing of information based on various kinds of observations and organized according to *meaningful* schemata.

The parallel to the problem of psychoanalysis lies in the need for observing unfolding events in relation to issues of classification with many variables. The activities of observation involve simultaneous observation of phenomena whose interrelation cannot be examined until each phenomenon has been observed according to the methods appropriate to it. The end points of these observations can be combined, correlated, and integrated to provide a system based on these observations.

A specific hypothesis with a specific proof is the end point of a series of contributory investigations. These investigations themselves depend on methods which may have no relation to the methods employed in the other investigations. This may be thought of as a kind of parallel processing in the development of knowledge.

Shevrin's work and other research described in his paper are, like the observations of psychoanalysts conducting analysis, contributions to the parallel processing. While I regard this as a worthwhile undertaking, many respected colleagues do not share this interest or find it useful in their work. However, I believe this is what commonly takes place *as one step* in the development of any science in which a chain of inferences draws on many sources of information that are presumed to be relevant to the issue in question. Shevrin's own research is an example in which the idea that semiotics has relevance to the difference between conscious and unconscious thinking leads to experiments using different kinds of categories derived from a different area of knowledge. In his discussion of the relationship between the concept of the unconscious as an empirical generalization and then as a fundamental assumption of theory, he points to the idea that "science" refers not to a thing but to processes (see also Hull, 1988; Waelder, 1970).

If Professor di Sapienza presents one extreme from outside analysis, at the other extreme, from way inside the "psychoanalytic situation," nothing but that situation is regarded as *really* psychoanalysis. For Dr. Case, there is no other way to study psychoanalysis because its essence resides in particular kinds of "inner experiences" within a particular setting. Within the clinical setting, some phenomena can be observed repeatedly in ways not possible in other situations. Varying the parameters of the setting alters the ways in which the mental processes of the analysand can be *recognized* by both analyst and analysand. Other methods of studying the mind may come to conclusions similar to those reached via the psychoanalytic method, but this is not required and, I suspect, may not even necessarily be of interest. ·

Dr. Case's position, while in one sense claiming a great deal for clinical psychoanalysis, in fact understates the real value of the psychoanalytic situation as a source of information that can both draw on and enrich areas of knowledge outside of clinical psychoanalysis. Analysts necessarily use ideas drawn from many sources, wittingly or unwittingly, in their daily work. While it may be true that there are phenomena that are unique to the analytic situation, it ought to be possible to describe such phenomena with increasing precision. If the uniqueness of the setting is required to produce the phenomenon, we should not exclude the possibility that it can be rationally constructed from observations of component features obtained by other methods.

Dr. Sample accepts the idea that the psychoanalytic situation is what needs to be studied, because it *is* "psychoanalysis." He believes, however, that the psychoanalytic situation cannot be studied using public data and does not permit hypothesis testing that meets the requirements of "eliminative inductionism." Instead, he thinks concepts, exemplified by Luborsky's Core Conflictual Relationship Theme (an idea derived from the concept of transference), can be studied in other psychotherapy settings. In this way, some essential features of the psychoanalytic concept can be studied more rigorously. Everything depends on whether what is being studied *is* transference as the clinician understands it, or at least an important aspect of it. If not, what is being measured and how it is related to the analytic situation remains unclear. From Case's point of view, this is not psychoanalysis but an interest related to it.

The analyst-at-work takes for granted the flexibility and ambiguity of concepts like transference because the analyzing analyst is sorting out observations with his/her concepts in the background. The multilayering of clinical concepts becomes a problem when reflection on the concepts intrudes and definitions are attempted. At this point, the orientations of different points of view about clinical formulation diverge because they wish to limit the concept for purposes of differentiation from other phenomena. Proponents of different points of view want to emphasize different aspects of a concept like transference. The use of a clinical concept for research purposes faces the problem of an uncertainty principle of observation and definition: the phenomenon is best observed where it can be least defined in a precise operational way, while each effort to define the concept precisely so it may be tested in some other situation departs even further from the original concept. The same process accounts for the different ways concepts are used by the various psychoanalytic "schools." However, this is the way concepts and their applications evolve.

Of course, *any* fractionation of the complex situation of analysis for purposes of study creates a new area of interest, with its own goals and methods (see Kaplan, 1988). These new areas must then be reconstructed for a new view of the clinical situation. The points of view outlined in Shevrin's paper are such areas of interest. Although presented as competing, they are really supplementary with respect to a general or comprehensive theory of psychoanalysis.

Like Dr. Sample, Dr. Link believes that the *working ideas* of the psychoanalytic practitioner can be studied by research exploring their concepts. His approach is to prove underlying assumptions of psychoanalytic concepts. He believes that the properties of unconscious mental activities can be studied and the different characteristics of unconscious and conscious mental processes described. Using methods of subliminal stimulus presentation and neurophysiological measurements, Shevrin has demonstrated differences between conscious and unconscious perception, and differences between responses to conflict-related and conflict-unrelated words. At present, he has begun to demonstrate differences between conscious and unconscious categorization. Accordingly, he has begun to show the fine structure of the basis for the clinician's judgments from the combined viewpoints of semiotics, neuropsychology, and neurophysiology.

Shevrin addresses some fundamental processes underlying the concepts taken for granted by the practicing psychoanalyst in the consulting room. Since the practicing analyst uses fundamental presuppositions every day and does not investigate them, interdisciplinary proofs of basic processes are far from his immediate concerns. However, in my view, such questions as how unconscious processes can be recognized in clinical material by the way categories are organized are relevant to daily work, even if their systematic demonstration is not. Just how relevant Shevrin's observations can be for the practicing clinician remains to be explored. It is not difficult to show that analysts use assumptions about such matters all the time. When relevant aspects of the working analyst's concepts can be studied experimentally, the clinical analyst has a new basis on which to reexamine his assumptions. The repeated reexamination of some aspects of the analyst's own assumptions and thought processes is an essential part of any psychoanalysis.

Combined with other psychoanalytic interests, the arguments sketched in Shevrin's paper indicate that different kinds of psychoanalytic ideas taken together constitute a heterogeneous area of interest and knowledge. The problem for people interested in psychoanalysis *as a field of knowledge* is to understand how such different ways of using psychoanalytic ideas, findings, and assumptions can be usefully integrated, or at least, rendered mutually enriching. The discussion in the paper is to some extent about the ways any point of view looks from the other points of view.

Commentaries

The problems involved are formidable and can hardly even be articulated adequately in a brief discussion. The reason for this is that none of the interests outlined in Shevrin's paper, or in this commentary, is homogeneous. The experimental studies mentioned can be called "scientific," but they all involve methods, concepts, and interests that are not in themselves psychoanalytic, and that are not necessarily uncontroversial. On the other hand, the psychoanalytic situation is not homogeneous in its activities, some of which are not exclusively psychoanalytic. In both cases, it is a question of whether we are speaking of methods or rationales for activities, or of ways of inferring and drawing conclusions. The meanings and methods of verification and proof remain difficult problems in each area.

Finally, Shevrin's paper subtly brings out still another issue. The various points of view in dialogue demonstrate the problem of communication among people who share an interest in psychoanalysis as a system of related ideas but do not share the same observational contexts. This is a problem even when there is more of an overlap, and even if the overlap is that they all do analysis in addition to their particular investigations. In fact, this problem of psychoanalytic communication is one way of looking at the problem of comparing different clinical approaches to analysis. Much of what is said about the existence or nonexistence of common ground is questionable because people do not generally approach the problem as one requiring sufficient familiarity to do translations from one system to the other. Shevrin has presented cogent arguments for integration and greater attention to the problems of communication of ideas in our field.

REFERENCES

BERNARDI, R.E. (1989). The role of paradigmatic determinants in psychoanalytic understanding. *Int. J. Psychoanal.*, 70:341–357.

FREUD, S. (1912). Recommendations to physicians practising psycho-analysis. *S.E.*, 12:109–120.

GRANT, B.R. & GRANT, P.R. (1989). *Evolutionary Dynamics of a Natural Population: The Large Cactus Finch of the Galápagos.* Chicago: Univ. Chicago Press.

HULL, D.L. (1988). *Science as a Process: An Evolutionary Account of the Social and Conceptual Development of Science.* Chicago: Univ. Chicago Press.

KAPLAN, D.M. (1988). The psychoanalysis of art: some ends, some means. *J. Amer. Psychoanal. Assn.*, 36:259–293.

WAELDER, R. (1970). Observation, historical reconstruction, and experiment: an epistemological study. In *Psychoanalysis: Observation, Theory, Application*, ed. S.A. Guttman. New York: Int. Univ. Press, 1976, pp. 635–675.

WEINER, J. (1994). *The Beak of the Finch: A Story of Evolution in Our Time.* New York: Knopf.

——— (1995). Evolution made visible. *Science*, 267:30–33.

45 Oak Avenue
Tenafly, NJ 07670

Paul E. Meehl

A proper response to this clear, fair, forceful presentation of the three positions would require fifteen thousand rather than fifteen hundred words, so I apologize if the requirement of brevity makes my remarks sound dogmatic. The trialogue participants zero in on the big question—whether psychoanalysis is a science—as well as I can imagine anyone doing it. Nevertheless, it is useful to inquire, Why do we care? *We care because science has the best-attested knowledge claims.* Even laymen know that disciplines indisputably scientific (e.g., chemistry, physics, genetics) can lay better deserved claims to genuine, well-credentialed, objective knowledge than can other purported "cognitive" enterprises, such as theology, metaphysics, epistemology, aesthetics, ethics, politics, literary criticism, and journalism. Why do we regard the indisputable science so highly? It is because of the "scientific method" (consisting more of guidelines than strict rules, as philosophers of science now know). Its components include a general attitude of skepticism ("prove it"), the use of reliable observational procedures, and powerful modes of data analysis, especially mathematics and statistics. The third component is sometimes unnecessary (although never inappropriate); the first two are not. These characteristics achieve (ultimately) consensus among all competent persons who inquire. Does psychoanalysis have methods of observation and inference with these properties? The answer is clearly no.

The proof may be seen in the simple social fact that a century after Freud's interpretation of his dream of Irma's injection and publication of the Breuer-Freud *Studies on Hysteria* (1893–1895), it is possible for fair-minded, rational, but skeptical persons, trained in medicine or psychology, to deny some, much, or almost all of the Freudian corpus of beliefs. The conversation resulting in the rupture of the Fliess-Freud friendship concerned the *subjectivity* of the psychoanalytic method (Meehl, 1983). Further, the method itself is far from standard among presumed experts in it. The only systematic investigation of techniques (whether rules or merely guidelines) employed in the psychoanalytic hour is Glover's classic questionnaire study of British psychoanalysts in 1933 (Glover, 1940). Those analysts were probably more homogeneous, with regard to their training analyses and as a result of their high density of face-to-face discussions, than any group since. Yet one sees, already at that time, wide disagreement about important interview tactics, and subsequent conversations resulting in a supplementary questionnaire still did not lead to high consensus. (Discouragingly, one of the few principles commanding near-perfect assent, to emphasize transference interpretations, is not supported by quantitative research; see Silberschatz et al., 1986.) Since that second generation of analysts were either not analyzed or were analyzed by those of Freud's original group who themselves had not had analysis with Freud or with anyone else, it would be suprising if the results had been otherwise.

While we have no contemporary data comparable to the Glover study, anyone even slightly acquainted with psychoanalysis, whether conducted by physicians or by psychologists, would confidently predict that the diversity today would be far greater than in 1933. The notion that there exists a "standard (classical) analytic technique of investigation" is plainly false. I can personally attest, as can anybody who has had couch time with more than one analyst, to striking differences. The application of the "method" has not resulted in convergence, either in the sense of convincing outsiders or of preventing multiple splits within the broadly defined psychoanalytic group. A philosopher or historian of science, however sympathetic to analysis, would be forced to say that psychoanalysis at this time shows the major symptoms of a Lakatosian degenerating program (Barron et al., 1992; Eagle, 1984; Edelson, 1988; Lakatos, 1978; Meehl, 1993). Consider a few names that come readily to mind of analyzed therapists who deviated—on the basis of their clinical experience—in varying degrees, from making revisions in theory or technique to totally ceasing psychoanalytic practice: Franz Alexander,

Psychoanalysis as Science

Aaron T. Beck, Kenneth Mark Colby, Albert Ellis, Sandor Ferenczi, Daniel X. Friedman, Erich Fromm, Karen Horney, Melanie Klein, Heinz Kohut, Sandor Rado, Otto Rank, Wilhelm Reich, Roy Schafer, Melitta Schmideberg, Harry Stack Sullivan, Thomas Szasz, D.W. Winnicott, a fraction of those one could find by a literature search, not to mention the many who deviate silently. What scientific status would we accord physics, genetics, microbiology, or classical psychometrics if a comparable list of "big names," educated and experienced in their respective traditions, came to fundamental disagreement about the photoelectric effect, the structure of DNA, the germ theory of disease, or the high factor loadings of subtests vocabulary and block design on the g (general intelligence) factor? While Lakatos admits it is sometimes rational to stick to a degenerating program, what is forbidden is to falsify the track record, to deny the social fact of degeneration. But this is what Dr. Case, unwittingly, urges us to do.

The main reason for this unsatisfactory epistemological state is a fundamental error in Dr. Case's approach. Dr. Case believes that the informal, nonquantitative case study method suffices to produce a science. It certainly does not. We should honestly face the fact that the "case study method" and "clinical experience" are simply honorific labels for what in the field of comparative psychology has long been denigrated as "the anecdotal method." *'Clinical experience' is a phrase applied to the discredited anecdotal method when it is practiced by persons with Ph.D.s or M.D.s.* Historians of medicine tell us that prior to around 1880 or 1890 almost everything that physicians did was either irrelevant or counterproductive. Of the three standard treatment procedures—bleeding, purging, and blistering—the latter was perhaps merely irksome to the patient, whereas bleeding and purging were actively harmful. George Washington was probably killed by his physician, Dr. Benjamin Rush, the founder of American psychiatry and one of the signers of the Declaration of Independence. There are people now in their fifties who are totally blind due to the epidemic of an infantile disease new in the 1940s, retrolental fibroplasia, caused by excessive oxygen tension in the treatment of premature infants. Both those who thought it was caused by not enough oxygen and those who thought it was caused by too much invoked their clinical experience; the argument was settled by combining *statistical study* of premature babies delivered in homes by midwives, who could not use the oxygen intervention, and *experimental study* producing identical pathology in the eyeballs of kittens.

Military surgeons disagreed about the efficacy of wound debridement for four generations of clinical experience, a controversy finally settled by outcome statistics and experimental research on animals (Wangensteen and Wangensteen, 1978). The anecdotal method was inadequate to ascertain the relation between an objectively describable surgical procedure and the patients' survival or death a few hours or days later. How then can we argue that a variable, vague, personalized interview strategy (e.g., "interpret from the surface down") can be reliably correlated with alteration several *months* later (e.g., "decreased superego harshness")? While physicians may appropriately object to the slowness of federal bureaucracies (e.g., FDA, NIH, CDC), I am not aware of any practitioners or researchers who think there should be *no* requirements of statistical evidence on the admissibility of a new drug or treatment. While I myself have gained more conviction from my experiences on the couch and behind it than from reading a mostly irrelevant research literature, I realize this is a William James "over-belief." One need not apologize for having over-beliefs, since we cannot get along in daily life or even in science without them; but one should be crystal clear that they are over-beliefs rather than scientifically defensible positions.

Do we dismiss "ordinary, nonquantified" reports of clinical experience as valueless? Of course not. They can be a source of conjectured generalizations and (sometimes) refutations of them. They are usually indispensable for developing skills in applying confirmed conjectures. This practitioner shaping is not peculiar to psychoanalysis or to the healing arts generally, inasmuch as *using* theoretical (verbal) knowledge always requires perceptual and instrumental skills of noticing, classifying, distinguishing, and acting that are psychological functions discrete from formal conceptual knowledge. For example, I have known experimental psychologists who "knew" operant behavior theory, but who—not having been trained by a Skinnerian mentor—could not effectively shape a white rat's behavior into a simple response chain. There is nothing mysterious about this—it is merely the ordinary language philosopher's difference between "knowing that" and "knowing how." But what ordinary, informal clinical experience cannot do is to strongly corroborate complex generalizations. The psychological reasons for this inability have long been known (see, e.g., Francis Bacon's idols). They are inherent in the fallible operations of the human intellect, and the notion that acquiring a Ph.D. or M.D. (or having a training analysis!) eliminates them is a narcissistic illusion. Scientific research, from the study of the astronomer's "personal equation" to contemporary research on judgment and problem solving, suffices to deflate such a grandiose idea (see Arkes and Hammond, 1986; Dawes, 1988, 1994; Faust, 1984; Meehl, 1992, 1993; Nisbett and Ross, 1980; Plous, 1993).

"But surely we can learn about facts and their relations without conducting controlled experiments or computing statistics! We know that thunder occurs after lightning, that a wineglass shatters if dropped on a tile floor, that if you regularly say cruel things to people they will dislike you." Yes, of course. But humankind has also "learned" a large number of erroneous relations, about black cats and witches and petroleum dowsers. We label these superstitions—the ones *we* disbelieve in. The clear message of history is that the anecdotal method delivers both wheat and chaff, but it does not enable us to tell which is which. For a list of properties of relations that render this crucial discernment difficult, see Meehl (1983, pp. 18–21). For a long list of error sources (shared by clinicians *and* scientists), see Meehl (1992, pp. 353–354).

As to ignoring Dr. Link's research, there is a simple logician's answer to that dismissive proposal: the Total Evidence Rule. This does not depend on one's philosophy of science or one's ideology; it is learned in a freshman logic course. You cannot by fiat exclude evidence that has a logical bearing upon a conjecture any more than you can make irrelevant evidence germane by fiat. Thus, I would hold that research showing that non-Freudian therapists' ratings on patients' preferences among the major defense mechanisms predict the patients' similarities on a variety of descriptive trait characteristics far better than other theoretical concepts do (Meehl, 1960) tends to support the reality of the defense mechanisms and their importance in mental functioning. On the other side, studies in child development showing no relationship between toilet training and adult anal character traits cannot be dismissed as irrelevant; they speak against Freud's (1908) article on anal eroticism (Fisher and Greenberg, 1977).

Commentaries

My conclusion is that Dr. Sample has the best of the argument, but Dr. Link cannot be dismissed. Dr. Case is simply mistaken about the history of human knowledge. Given the beautiful formulation of the problem by the three discussants, I find Professor di Sapienza's "resolution" disappointing. Her choice of analogies is unfortunate. (Was it suggested by Freud's famous remark about the three impossible occupations?) As for governing, since I hold with the Swedish statesman Oxenstierna that we little know how badly we are governed, and I believe with Machiavelli that man is ruled by force and fraud, analogizing psychoanalysis to governing does not help me one bit. The analogy to education is simply incorrect as a matter of fact. Beginning shortly after World War I and extending to the present time, educational psychologists have published thousands of experimental and statistical studies of educational method. It is true that some of these are trivial, and there are always some studies that are not well done, but there is a solid body of knowledge about the educational process that has come from those investigations. Any competent psychologist knows that massed practice is inferior to distributed, that almost all learning curves are decelerated, that there are interaction effects between modes of instruction and the intelligence and other characteristics of the learners, that active recitation is superior to passive reception of material and the superiority is greater for relatively meaningless rote material, that class size influences achievement but the graph is markedly decelerated, and the like (see Gage, 1978; Hedges, 1987). Fred Keller's Personalized System of Instruction, based on Skinner's operant behavior theory, has consistently outperformed the traditional lecture as an instructional form. That the psychoanalytic process is one aimed at something practical, valued by two cooperating participants, does not provide a good reason for abandoning the rules of evidence as we find them in the scientific laboratory, courts of law, or the rational conduct of our ordinary affairs.

Nor will di Sapienza's seductive covering phrase, "rational human enterprise," do the trick. One must distinguish between *intending* to do something rational (i.e., using abstract categories, terms of art, formal definitions, purported relations, empirical findings) and *actually proceeding* in a manner that is effectively rational (i.e., conduces to the epistemic aim of truth). Kraemer and Sprenger, the scholarly authors of *Malleus Maleficarum* (1487), believed themselves to be pursuing a rational enterprise in detailing symptoms that diagnose witchcraft. Despite their scholarly efforts, we know today there are no persons who have made a solemn pact with Satan and thereby gained preternatural powers. If asked to support their theoretical system and the technical procedures warranted by it, Kraemer and Sprenger would doubtless have invoked the medieval equivalent of "clinical experience."

The yield of such studies as Shevrin's and those of Luborsky (1988) and Mahl (1987) may as yet be rather small for the ingenuity and assiduousness displayed, but it is the best we have and the best place to look. Had I space, I would try to answer Adolf Grünbaum's critique (1993) of that view, held by me and by others. His core objection, the epistemological difficulty of inferring a causal influence from the existence of a theme (assuming the latter can be statistically demonstrated), is the biggest single methodological problem that we face. If that problem cannot be solved, we will have another century in which psychoanalysis can be accepted or rejected, mostly as a matter of personal taste. Should that happen, I predict it will be slowly but surely abandoned, both as a mode of helping and as a theory of the mind.[1]

REFERENCES

Arkes, H.R. & Hammond, K.R. (1986). *Judgment and Decision Making: An Interdisciplinary Reader.* New York: Cambridge Univ. Press.

[1]This commentary reads more "antipsychoanalytic" than I personally think or feel (cf. Meehl, 1983). I came to psychology by reading Karl Menninger's *The Human Mind*; I found my personal analysis therapeutic, intellectually fascinating, and professionally invaluable; and for forty years I earned part of my living practicing psychoanalytic therapy. I believe I was helpful to many patients. But given limitations of space, I am forced to focus on the core error of Dr. Case, who in his naive trust of the unquantified case method lulls us into a false security in the face of grave problems and powerful criticisms. Psychoanalysis originated with the idea that warding off painful truths rather than confronting them squarely is bad for us. The psychoanalytic movement, like the individual neurotic, is sure to suffer from the return of the repressed. Recent attacks (e.g., Esterson, 1993; Grünbaum, 1993; Kerr, 1993; Macmillan, 1991) cannot be dismissed by saying they mostly revive the kinds of objections made in the 1920s, because *those old criticisms have never adequately been answered.* Dr. Case is like a physician who assures a patient with malignant melanoma that he is well, and Professor di Sapienza applies a poultice. It just won't do.

Commentaries

BARRON, J.W., EAGLE, M.N. & WOLITZKY, D.L. (1992). *Interface of Psychoanalysis and Psychology*. Washington: American Psychological Association.

BREUER, J. & FREUD, S. (1893–1895). Studies on hysteria. *S.E.*, 2.

DAWES, R.M. (1988). *Rational Choice in an Uncertain World*. Chicago: Harcourt Brace Jovanovich.

―――― (1994). *House of Cards: Psychology and Psychotherapy Built on Myth*. New York: Free Press.

EAGLE, M.N. (1984). *Recent Developments in Psychoanalysis*. New York: McGraw-Hill.

EDELSON, M. (1988). *Psychoanalysis: A Theory in Crisis*. Chicago: Univ. Chicago Press.

ESTERSON, A. (1993). *Seductive Mirage*. Chicago: Open Court.

FAUST, D. (1984). *The Limits of Scientific Reasoning*. Minneapolis: Univ. Minnesota Press.

FISHER, S. & GREENBERG, R.P. (1977). *The Scientific Credibility of Freud's Theories and Therapy*. New York: Basic Books.

FREUD, S. (1908). Character and anal erotism. *S.E.*, 9:167–175.

GAGE, N.L. (1978). *The Scientific Basis of the Art of Teaching*. New York: Teachers College Press.

GLOVER, E., ed. (1940). *The Technique of Psycho-analysis*. Baltimore: Williams & Wilkins.

GRÜNBAUM, A. (1993). *Validation in the Clinical Theory of Psychoanalysis*. Madison, CT: Int. Univ. Press.

HEDGES, L.V. (1987). How hard is hard science, how soft is soft science? *Amer. Psychologist*, 42:443–455.

KERR, J. (1993). *A Most Dangerous Method*. New York: Random House.

KRAEMER, H. & SPRENGER, J. (1487). *Malleus Maleficarum*. New York: Blom, 1970.

LAKATOS, I. (1978). *Philosophical Papers, Vol. I: The Methodology of Scientific Research Programmes*, ed. J. Worrall & G. Currie. New York: Cambridge Univ. Press.

LUBORSKY, L. (1988). Recurrent momentary forgetting: its content and its context. In *Psychodynamics and Cognition*, ed. M.J. Horowitz. Chicago: Univ. Chicago Press.

MACMILLAN, M. (1991). *Freud Evaluated*. New York: Elsevier Science.

MAHL, G.F. (1987). *Explorations in Nonverbal and Vocal Behavior*. Hillsdale, NJ: Lawrence Erlbaum.

MEEHL, P.E. (1960). The cognitive activity of the clinician. *Amer. Psychologist*, 15:19–27. Reprinted in P.E. Meehl, *Psychodiagnosis: Selected Papers*. Minneapolis: Univ. Minnesota Press, 1973, pp. 117–134.

―――― (1983). Subjectivity in psychoanalytic inference: the nagging persistence of Wilhelm Fliess's Achensee question. In *Minnesota Studies in the Philosophy of Science: Vol. 10. Testing Scientific Theories*, ed. J. Earman. Reprinted in *Psychoanal. & Contemp. Thought*, 17:3–82.

―――― (1992). Cliometric metatheory: the actuarial approach to empirical, history-based philosophy of science. *Psychol. Reports*, 71:339–467.

―――― (1993). If Freud could define psychoanalysis, why can't ABPP? *Psychoanal. & Contemp. Thought*, 16:299–326.

MENNINGER, K.A. (1930). *The Human Mind.* Garden City, NY: Garden City Publishing.

NISBETT, R.E. & ROSS, L. (1980). *Human Inference: Strategies and Shortcomings of Human Judgment.* Englewood Cliffs, NJ: Prentice-Hall.

PLOUS, S. (1993). *The Psychology of Judgment and Decision Making.* New York: McGraw-Hill.

SILBERSCHATZ, G., FRETTER, P.B. & CURTIS, J.T. (1986). How do interpretations influence the process of psychotherapy? *J. Consult. & Clin. Psychol.*, 54:646–652.

WANGENSTEEN, O.H. & WANGENSTEEN, S.D. (1978). *The Rise of Surgery.* Minneapolis: Univ. Minnesota Press.

Psychology Department
University of Minnesota
N218 Elliott Hall
75 East River Road
Minneapolis, MN 55455–0344

Robert Michels

Psychoanalysts have paid relatively little attention to the recent flurry of interest in psychiatric diagnostic categories. The reason for this is easy to understand. Unlike descriptive psychiatrists, psychoanalysts are interested in the meaning of the individual patient's experience, how it stems from his earlier life and will go on to shape his future, and how it is reflected in, and can be modified by, the analytic process, rather than the description and labeling of its surface manifestations.

When psychoanalysts shift their attention from their patients, where they are expert, to the world of scholarly dialogue, where they are amateurs, they often shift strategies as well. Now they are intensely interested in categories—for example, whether or not psychoanalysis is a science. This question may interest some philosophers of science, at least those who are concerned with demarcating the boundaries of their discipline rather than exploring fascinating phenomena wherever their method may prove fruitful. However, I don't understand why psychoanalysts should care, and I suspect that, other than for reasons of pride, most of them don't. How to learn more about people, about mental life, about the analytic process, about the efficacy of psychoanalysis as a therapy—which methods might lead to new knowledge, which are useless, which may be premature but deserving of future reappraisal—*these* are interesting questions. How to catalog these enterprises and whether they fall within, astride, or outside the boundaries of science is a question best left for future historians of science. The American Association for the Advancement of Science accepts our dues, and there doesn't seem to be any other arena in which the answer really makes any difference.

However, this is the question that Howard Shevrin, in the role of Professor di Sapienza, uses to frame the dialogue. He (she) points out that "to some this is an old chestnut, to others it is a boring question, and to still others it matters not at all." However, neither the professor nor any of her guests seems to belong to the last group (which includes most other psychoanalysts), so this fundamental issue is never addressed. Had I been invited, I would have suggested that it would be more fun to hear Dr. Case describe a patient, Dr. Sample review his survey data, or Dr. Link discuss his experimental strategies. Professor di Sapienza, if she desired, might tape the proceedings and play them for her undergraduate seminar, a far more appropriate group to address the fundamental question of whether their enterprises should be labeled as science.

It seems that I would have been outvoted, however, and we would have spent two August afternoons in Amagansett engrossed in the unlikely activity of discussing psychoanalysis and science. Drs. Case, Sample, and Link all make cogent points, and don't actually seem to be disagreeing with each other to any great extent. However, they are solely in need of a philosopher to help them unearth their fundamental points of agreement. The imprecision of their language confuses them. For example, they all talk about psychoanalysis, but the word has a different meaning for each. For Dr. Case, psychoanalysis is the clinical method and process of the practicing analyst, from which some theoretical generalizations have been abstracted. For Drs. Sample and Link, it is a method of treatment which, in Dr. Link's words, "applies a body of knowledge and theory . . . to a given patient's emotional disorder." For Dr. Sample, however, its body of knowledge is mentalist psychology, while for Dr. Link it embraces the science of brains and synapses as well. Their strategies follow from these different definitions and therefore are not really in conflict. Philosophers may debate which are scientific strategies and which are not; for most of us the question is which are interesting, generative, and worth our time and effort. Professor di Sapienza herself is concerned with a different question, one of power, but she seems to have forgotten Bacon's dictum that knowledge is power when she argues that in her view research is irrelevant. How does she think the powerful tool of psychoanalysis was first developed?

Shevrin himself is each of these four protagonists, but most of all Dr. Link, who in fact presents Shevrin's research. He invites us to decide whether bridge building is premature by having us join with him in undertaking the task, and offers as examplars two bridges, one from psychoanalysis to neurophysiology and the other to cognitive science. He promises that his studies will take into account unconscious processes and transformed contents—which he considers "essential elements of the psychoanalytic model." (Dr. Case, and I, would agree—just as we would agree that the alphabet is essential to Shakespeare, though we might balk if asked to conclude that alphabetology is the essential basic science of English literature.)

Shevrin's first study is said to draw on "the essentials of the psychoanalytic clinical method." (He means an unstructured interview and psychodynamic formulation—perhaps "one of the essentials" would be more accurate.) The subject is exposed to emotionally charged and neutral control words. Shevrin demonstrates that the pattern of EEG responses to subliminal and supraliminal exposure varies with the emotional valence of the stimulus and suggests that this tests the "presupposition of a causative psychological unconscious" and supports its validity. It would be more cautious to say the experiment fails to disprove the presupposition, but then it isn't clear that any experimental results would lead one to question the notion of a dynamic unconscious. However, the real question is, Do such an experiment and such results constitute a bridge, or do they suggest that the effort is still premature, that we would do better to map the neurophysiology of simpler and more superficial mental phenomena (an area where great progress is being made) before trying to build a bridge over a river that is so wide?

Shevrin's second study is a purely psychological one. It demonstrates that subliminal exposure to a priming word facilitates superficial, but not more complex, categorization. (For example, *Freud* would speed up linking *analysis* and *therapy* but not *analysis* and *natural science*.) He concludes that this provides "independent support for the . . . presupposition of the psychoanalytic method, that unconscious causes are inferred from so-called displaced and substitute formations.'' Once again, although it certainly doesn't disprove the presupposition, it doesn't really provide much in the way of support. This is not a bridge that can bear much weight.

Shevrin points to Reiser's brilliant monograph (1984) as a foundation for his position. In a 1987 review of that book, I commented:

> At present, our very best neurobiology has relatively little to say about how we carry out the simplest of mental activities—recognizing a figure, identifying a word, connecting the two, or remembering the connection. We have only the vaguest of notions about the difference between sleep and wakefulness, and less about the varieties of arousal—anger, anxiety, attention, desire, etc. In short, we do not yet have much convergence between neurobiology and the most elementary of cognitive psychologies. It would seem reasonable to wait for that to develop before using neurobiology to tackle the much more complex, and less easily formulated, concepts of psychoanalysis [Michels, 1987, p. 535].

The question, then, isn't really whether psychoanalysis is a science, or even whether the methods of these experiments are valid, but which psychoanalytic inquiries are interesting and to whom. Practicing psychoanalysts are interested in clinically relevant studies—Dr. Case's histories and, to a limited extent, Dr. Sample's data. Those who train therapists, triage patients, develop programs, and allocate resources are interested in Dr. Sample's findings, but are often disappointed by them and find personal clinical wisdom to be a better guide. Scientists who once wanted to be psychoanalysts and psychoanalysts who once wanted to be scientists are fascinated by Dr. Link's approach, and look forward to the day when its promise can be realized.

REFERENCES

MICHELS, R. (1987). Review of *Mind, Brain, Body* by M.F. Reiser. *Psychoanal. Q.,* 56:532–536.

REISER, M.F. (1984). *Mind, Brain, Body: Toward a Convergence of Psychoanalysis and Neurobiology.* New York: Basic Books.

1300 York Avenue
New York, NY 10021

Psychoanalysis as Science

Richard C. Simons

How does one write a commentary on a tour de force? Howard Shevrin is a gifted psychoanalytic clinician, educator, and researcher who is also a novelist and a poet. His impressive literary talents make this presentation truly unique among all of the plenary addresses ever published in this journal. Readers who are clinicians (I count myself among them) will immediately identify with Dr. Case and his passionately held belief that psychoanalysis is a science sui generis. But I would hope that most clinicians will remember that we are celebrating this year the hundredth anniversary of the birth of psychoanalysis—the publication of *Studies on Hysteria* in 1895. Over the course of this century, I would also hope, generations of clinicians will have accumulated enough wisdom to appreciate the plea of Dr. Sample for more sophisticated outcome and process research devoted to the psychoanalytic situation, and enough humility to respect the position of Professor di Sapienza that psychoanalysis is not a science at all, but rather one of the great humanistic enterprises (like teaching and governing) whose goal is to bring about significant rational changes both in individuals and in society. What is stunning about his presentation is that Shevrin, through his persona, Dr. Link, then asks us to stretch our professional identities still further to consider the possibility that psychoanalysis is actually two separate but related sciences, an applied clinical science and a basic science of the mind. Are we really ready for this challenge after only one century? Shevrin would answer that even though the unconscious may be timeless, life—and the scientific necessity of forming bridges between psychoanalysis and other basic sciences of the mind and brain—is not.

Shevrin proceeds to summarize his thirty-five years of elegant research, in which he and his colleagues provide experimental, laboratory evidence for two fundamental presuppositions of psychoanalysis. The first presupposition is the existence of a causative (dynamic) unconscious, demonstrated through data derived from the basic science of neurophysiology. The second presupposition is the existence of various substitute transformations in consciousness (displacements, reversals, symbols, and superficial associations) that are brought about by this causative (dynamic) unconscious, demonstrated through data derived from the basic science of cognitive psychology. Shevrin is well aware that these are only beginning "links,"

Commentaries

"piers on either side of the great divide" separating the mind of psychoanalysis from the brain of the neurosciences. But still, what a beginning!

There is a third fundamental presupposition of psychoanalysis, explicitly stated and embraced by Dr. Case, and presumably supported by Dr. Sample and Professor di Sapienza as well, namely that the elicitation, elucidation, and interpretation of conflicts present in the causative (dynamic) unconscious (manifested by their derivative transformations in consciousness) can bring about intrapsychic and interpersonal change. Where does Dr. Link stand on that issue? Is it conceivable that Shevrin and his colleagues will someday be able to demonstrate such changes in their laboratory? If so, which of the neurosciences will provide the data? Will it be neurochemistry, through changes measured in brain neurotransmitters? Will it be neuroendocrinology, through changes measured in the hypothalamic-pituitary-adrenal axis? Will it be neuroanatomy, through changes measured by various brain-imaging techniques? I hope that "time's wingéd chariot" brings Shevrin back to us in another decade or so with the beginnings of his bridges for this third, and ultimately crucial, presupposition, crucial at least for psychoanalysis as an applied clinical science. And by then, what further challenges will he be presenting to us? Though we cannot (and must not) make the sun of psychoanalysis stand still, we must yet be thankful to Howard Shevrin for inspiring us to make it run.

9823 Crestline Avenue
Englewood, CO 80111

Mark Solms

Among the four viewpoints Howard Shevrin presents in order to dramatize contemporary debates on the scientific standing of psychoanalysis, he situates his own research within the tradition championed by the fictional Dr. Link. I shall therefore focus my commentary on this aspect of his wide-ranging presentation.

Shevrin's conception of psychoanalysis rests on a basic postulate regarding its scientific foundations, namely, that "psychoanalysts practice a method based on certain presuppositions for which the . . . method itself cannot provide proof." The presuppositions he refers to are (1) that *conscious phenomena have unconscious psychological causes,* and (2) that *unconscious causes are represented indirectly in consciousness, due to the effects of various transformations.* Shevrin points out that "these presuppositions may turn out to be true or false, with fateful consequences for the science." This conception of the scientific foundations of psychoanalysis is attributed to both Dr. Sample and Dr. Link, but only the latter bases his entire argument on it. Whereas Dr. Sample calls for a "more rigorous" clinical research methodology, Dr. Link asserts that only "a science basic to psychoanalysis" can provide independent evidence for its presuppositions, for "if the research intends to address these two basic presuppositions, it must demonstrate how it can do so independently of the clinical method based on those presuppositions." He concludes that "research of this nature, to succeed, must either discover *new consequences* of these presuppositions independently arrived at, or provide evidence of what *underlying factors or preconditions* cause them" (emphasis added). He then summarizes two examples of Shevrin's research, to demonstrate how these criteria can be met.

In order to evaluate these arguments we need to determine, first, whether the basic postulate on which they are based is valid and, second, whether Shevrin's research satisfies his own criteria for "a science basic to psychoanalysis." I shall address these two questions separately.

Psychoanalysis is indeed based on a fundamental presupposition. Freud stated that presupposition repeatedly throughout his scientific writings, but nowhere did he do so more clearly than in the following passage:

> The psycho-analytic assumption of unconscious mental activity appears to us . . . as an extension of the corrections undertaken by Kant of our views of external perception. Just as Kant warned us not to overlook the fact that our [external] perceptions are subjectively conditioned and must not be regarded as identical with what is perceived though unknowable, so psycho-analysis warns us not to equate [internal] perceptions by means of consciousness with the unconscious mental processes which are their object. Like the physical, the psychical is not necessarily in reality what it appears to be [Freud, 1915, p. 171].

The fundamental presupposition of psychoanalysis is therefore the notion that *conscious perceptions represent an unconscious reality, which can never be known directly.* A subsidiary premise is that *there are two such classes of conscious perception*: (a) *physical* perceptions (of things which exist in the world around us), and (b) *psychical* perceptions (of things which exist inside of our own selves). These two classes of perception are presumed to arise from "two sensory surfaces" of consciousness (Freud, 1900, p. 574), which represent the "two terminal points of our knowledge" of the reality that lies beyond perception (Freud, 1940a, pp. 144, 196). Psychoanalysts study reality from the viewpoint of the *internal* surface of consciousness. Freud's detailed justification for describing this aspect of reality in *psychical* terms (1915, pp. 166–171; 1940b, pp. 282–286) need not be repeated here.[1] The essential point is that a psychical conception of the internal sources of consciousness "enabled psychology to take its place as a natural science like any other" (Freud, 1940a, p. 158), for it inserted our private thoughts and feelings into a natural causal framework. The alternative view, which held that subjective states of consciousness occurred inexplicably, in parallel with certain physical processes, "had the unwelcome result of divorcing psychical processes from the general context of events in the universe and of setting them in complete contrast to all others" (Freud, 1940b, p. 283). Insofar as psychoanalysis aims to provide a psychological account of the field of psychical processes and "to establish the laws which they obey and to follow the mutual relations and interdependences unbroken over long stretches" (Freud, 1940a, p. 159) it is a *basic* science of what Freud described as "psychical reality." In this respect it is analogous to physics in relation to material reality.

It is evident that the fundamental presupposition of psychoanalysis coincides with a limiting parameter of human knowledge. The domain of scientific inquiry lies entirely within the bounds of conscious perception; the "ultimate reality" that lies beyond is unknowable. The presupposition that conscious phenomena have

---

[1]Freud always acknowledged that internal reality can *also* be represented physically, via our *external* sensory organs, for "the mental apparatus . . . is also known to us in the form of an anatomical preparation" (Freud, 1900, p. 536). Thus, the object of study of psychoanalysis can be described either psychically (from the viewpoint of internal perception) or physically (from the viewpoint of external perception). Psychoanalysis describes it psychically; neuroscience describes it physically.

unconscious psychical causes is therefore no more open to *proof* than is the presupposition that external sensory perceptions are caused by real things existing independently of our knowledge of them. For that reason, as numerous philosophers have pointed out in recent years, all scientific knowledge is ultimately hypothetical, and every observational datum is also a theoretical inference. It is also within this context that we have been able to understand the fact—problematic both in physics and in psychoanalysis—that acts of observation determine the nature of the object perceived. Indeed it could be said that the more "basic" the science, the more this problematic indeterminacy of the perceptual object will be encountered.

Similar considerations apply to what Shevrin describes as the second presupposition of psychoanalysis. The presupposition that the unconscious determinants of psychical events are represented *indirectly* in consciousness, due to the effects of various transformations, is equivalent to the presupposition that the ultimate properties of physical matter are represented indirectly in perception, due to the effects of our external sensory apparatus. This is a fundamental presupposition, but nobody has called for a science basic to physics on those grounds. (I hope it is clear that I am not suggesting that psychoanalysis is a non-scientific enterprise; I am saying only that the presuppositions of psychoanalysis to which Shevrin refers are no different from the presuppositions of every other natural science. It is only when presuppositions of this sort are *questioned* that we engage in philosophical speculation.)

> In our science as in the others the problem is the same: behind the attributes (qualities) of the object under examination which are presented directly to our perception, we have to discover something else which is more independent of the particular receptive capacity of our sense organs and which approximates more closely to what may be supposed to be the real state of affairs. We have no hope of being able to reach the latter itself, since it is evident that everything new that we have inferred must nevertheless be translated back into the language of our perceptions, from which it is simply impossible to free ourselves. But herein lies the very nature and limitation of our science. It is as though we were to say in physics: 'If we could see clearly enough we should find that what appears to be a solid body is made up of particles of such and such shape and size occupying such and such relative positions.' In the meantime we try to increase the efficiency of our sense organs to the

furthest possible extent by artificial aids; but it may be expected that all such efforts will fail to affect the ultimate outcome. Reality in itself will always remain 'unknowable' [Freud, 1940a, p. 196].

The clinical method is therefore as incapable as any other scientific method of *proving* the existence of unconscious events, or of *directly* comparing them with their conscious transformations. In psychoanalysis, as in other sciences, we are charged with the task of developing "artificial aids" to probe the unknowable object of our study. Our estimation of the relative value of a psychoanalytic method should therefore be based on the extent to which it reliably translates "unknowable" unconscious processes into the language of our perceptions, so that we can construct a serviceable *model* of the unconscious processes themselves.

It would be unfair to ask whether Shevrin's methods achieve this goal better than the clinical method; clearly they do not. But his methods serve different aims. Shevrin aims to discover *new consequences* of the unconscious, and to reveal the *underlying causes* (or preconditions) of its modes of transformation in consciousness.

Do his methods achieve these goals? I believe that they do not; *stripped of the presuppositions they purport to examine*, Shevrin's methods reveal almost nothing about the unconscious and its modes of transformation. The first study that Dr. Link cites (Shevrin et al., 1992) demonstrates only that some indeterminate features of categories of words, when they are presented to the (external) perceptual apparatus in a particular way, correlate systematically with some gross feature of neural activity when it is measured in a particular way. The observed correlation between categories of words and patterns of cortical activity is a valid empirical finding, but the substantives in this correlation are wide open to *interpretation*. For example, the relationship between the so-called "unconscious conflict words" and the actual unconscious situation (assuming that such things exist) is highly debatable, especially in view of the small amount of clinical evidence on which the hypothesized conflicts are based. The unconscious consequences of the subsequent subliminal presentation of these words is equally debatable. Word-presentations that are exposed to the mind via the external surface of the perceptual apparatus (however briefly) cannot be considered "unconscious" in the dynamic sense, unless it can be demonstrated that they have been *repressed*. Shevrin seems to concede this when he states that the subliminal presentations are only *descriptively* unconscious. However, he immediately goes on to claim that the distinctive patterns of cortical activation these words evoke are manifestations of a "causative psychological unconscious." This crucial claim is unsubstantiated. The finding that slow or rapid presentations of words (which therefore attract more or less attentional cathexis) evoke different patterns of cortical activation, and the finding that these patterns covary with the different categories of words, will surprise no one. These findings demonstrate only that psychological content can be processed preconsciously; but nobody seriously disputes that.[2] This has nothing to do with the dynamic unconscious. Shevrin *presupposes* that the different patterns of cortical activation he evoked reflect the operation of a "causative psychological unconscious." However, many other interpretations are possible. For example, it could be argued that words which evoke an intense and immediate feeling of unpleasure (i.e., the "conscious symptom words") are correlated with patterns of cortical activation different from those correlated with words less intensely or directly evocative of unpleasure (i.e., the so-called "unconscious conflict words"), and that patterns of cortical activation vary in relation to the duration of the presentation of these words (i.e., in relation to the degree of attention they attract). These interpretations do not require the presupposition of a causative unconscious. The evoked responses therefore cannot be assumed to be "new consequences" of the unconscious.[3]

[2]The same facts were demonstrated long ago by Pötzl (1917) in his experimental manipulations of the manifest content of dreams. More recently, preconscious mental processing was rediscovered by Pöppel et al. (1973) and Weiskrantz et al. (1974), in relation to the curious phenomenon of "blindsight" (Weiskrantz, 1986). Similar phenomena are described by the general concept of "implicit memory" in contemporary cognitive science (Jacoby, 1984). It is also important to note in this regard that the (descriptive) dimension of consciousness/unconsciousness admits of *degrees*; consciousness is not an all-or-nothing phenomenon.

[3]Although physiological methods are incapable of *proving the existence* of the unconscious, they do enable us to study the *external perceptual realization* of the unconscious (see footnote 1 above). The value of physical methods should therefore not be underestimated. However, it is questionable whether the evoked-response method is adequate for correlating the two "terminal points of our knowledge"; it unduly constrains and distorts the psychical phenomena and provides only gross and nonspecific information about their physical correlates.

Commentaries

The results of the second study Shevrin cites (Snodgrass et al., 1995) are similarly open to interpretation. It could be argued, for example, that if two word-presentations are categorized on the basis of a brief exposure to the (external) perceptual apparatus (i.e., on the basis of minimal attentional cathexis and therefore minimal perceptual information), they will more readily be categorized according to simple attributes than complex ones. Increased duration of exposure (i.e., more attention and therefore more information redundancy) will alter the rate and complexity of categorization. This is because categorical decisions are made faster, but less securely, on the basis of minimal perceptual information. These interpretations have no bearing on the presupposition of indirect representation. The principle of categorization in question therefore cannot be described as an "underlying cause" of this process.

I trust that these brief remarks suffice to demonstrate that Shevrin's research is no less dependent on the presuppositions of psychoanalysis than is our classical (clinical) methodology, and that his observations are no less open to interpretation than are the free associations of our patients. Our estimation of the value of these methods for psychoanalysis should therefore be judged by the same criteria as the clinical method.

REFERENCES

FREUD, S. (1900). The interpretation of dreams. *S.E.*, 4/5.
——— (1915). The unconscious. *S.E.*, 14:166–215.
——— (1940a). An outline of psycho-analysis. *S.E.* 23:139–207.
——— (1940b). Some elementary lessons in psycho-analysis. *S.E.*, 23:279–286.
JACOBY, L. (1984). Incidental vs. intentional retrieval: remembering and awareness as separate issues. In *The Neuropsychology of Memory*, ed. L. Squire & N. Butters. New York: Guilford Press, pp. 145–156.
PÖPPEL, E., HELD, R. & FROST, D. (1973). Residual visual function after brain wounds involving the central visual pathways in man. *Nature*, 243:295–296.
PÖTZL, O. (1917). Experimentell erregte Traumbilder in ihren Beziehungen zum indirekten Sehen. *Z. ges. Neurol. Psychiat.*, 37:278.
SHEVRIN, H., WILLIAMS, W.J., MARSHALL, R.E., HERTEL, R.K., BOND, J.A. & BRAKEL, L. (1992). Event-related positive indicators of the dynamic unconscious. *Consciousness & Cognition*, 1:340–366.
SNODGRASS, M., SHEVRIN, H., BRAKEL, L. & MEDIN, D. (1995). Qualitative differences in the principles of organization in conscious and unconscious categorization. Presented to American Psychological Society, New York, July 1, 1995.

WEISKRANTZ, L. (1986). *Blindsight.* Oxford: Clarendon Press.

———— WARRINGTON, E., SANDERS, M. & MARSHALL, J. (1974). Visual capacity of the hemianopic field following a restricted occipital ablation. *Brain,* 97:709–728.

Academic Department of Neurosurgery
Alexandra Wing (4th floor)
The Royal London Hospital (Whitechapel)
London E1 1BB
England

Amagansett Revisited: Howard Shevrin

It is a rare opportunity and a special privilege to respond to the thoughtful commentaries of seven colleagues who have devoted time and effort to evaluating my contribution. When I was invited to give the plenary address printed in these pages I wanted most of all to portray how the *community* of psychoanalysts looked upon psychoanalysis as a science. It was for this reason that I chose to imagine an informal meeting of friends talking about their views of psychoanalysis as a science. And it is thus fitting for a group of psychoanalysts to comment on my effort and for me to respond. I was also careful to select participants in my Amagansett colloquy who would in my judgment represent the different points of view on the subject that characterize contemporary psychoanalysis. For this reason I was gratified by Meehl's referring to my effort as a "clear, fair, forceful presentation."

But I also had another objective, which very much depended on achieving a "clear, fair, forceful" presentation of these different points of view: to suggest a way in which these points of view, each representing an important conception of psychoanalysis as a science, can productively complement and strengthen one another. For this reason I was gratified that Grossman emphasized early in his commentary that I was calling for an "integration of approaches to gathering and collating information for the development of psychoanalytic theory" and "a scientific method of observation consisting of the therapeutic setting, experimental methods outside that setting, or some combination of methods." Grossman correctly depicts the initial positions of my Amagansett colleagues and where I wanted so much for them to end up:

> By presenting these issues in the form of a debate, he demonstrates that much of our discussion on these matters emphasizes critiques, limitations, and differences among approaches. Such critiques can be supplemented by developing ideas on the ways diverse approaches to the acquisition of knowledge can be integrated, and the information gained by each method can be used to construct a multifaceted picture of mental function.

As I consider myself in most matters to be a realist, my Amagansett colloquy did not end in an agreement to join hands in the effort to "construct a multifaceted picture of mental function." Nor have these seven commentaries. It seems we must continue still to "emphasize critiques, limitations, and differences among approaches." I will try to identify, by way of my colleagues' commentaries, the reasons for these continued disagreements and to respond as best I can to their arguments and concerns. I will also return to my own work, offered in the article as a contribution to constructing a "multifaceted picture of mental functioning," and in that context consider several criticisms of the research made by some of the commentators.

At the heart of my argument is the belief that the integration Grossman talks about could best be achieved by considering the clinical method championed by Dr. Case to be the backbone of a clinical science whose basic presuppositions would be supported by findings from other sciences such as psychology and neurophysiology. In retrospect, I made the mistake of referring to the clinical science as *applied* and to the other sciences as basic, which to judge from several of the commentaries (viz. those of Bucci, Goldberg, and Michels) was considered an invidious distinction; basic somehow came across as better than applied. Bucci, for example, in her playful dialogue, insists that psychotherapy research is also basic science. By distinguishing between basic and applied I did not mean that one is more important or more essential than the other. Quite otherwise. Each is important and essential, but in different and complementary ways. Psychology and neurophysiology are basic only in the sense that they can provide support for the *basic* presuppositions of the clinical science; the clinical science is applied only in the sense that it *applies* the knowledge and support thus gained. However, my argument does insist that the clinical science of psychoanalysis is not a science sui generis insofar as its basic presuppositions are in need of support from elsewhere. And on this point Meehl, Grossman, and Simons agree with me, Bucci agrees and disagrees, and Solms and Michels disagree. Goldberg would prefer the matter not be raised at all.

Meehl assails Dr. Case's belief that the "informal, nonquantitative case study method suffices to produce a science." He cites the example of retrolental fibroplasia demonstrating that relying on clinical experience alone resulted in contradictory conclusions, while a combination of a clinically based hypothesis, statistical study, and experiment established a cause and a cure. Meehl laments the fact that over the century of its existence psychoanalysis has been marked by increasing divergence rather than convergence among its practitioners. He believes that this is due mainly to the absence of a "general attitude of skepticism ('prove it')" and of reliable observational procedures. Although believing the yield is as yet small, he refers to Luborsky's momentary forgetting research, Mahl's investigations of nonverbal behavior, and my own research as the "best we have and the best place to look." Nevertheless, he reports that he has "gained more conviction from my experiences on the couch and behind it than from reading a mostly irrelevant research literature," a view Dr. Case would endorse enthusiastically, although Meehl is quick to add that this conviction is a belief rather than a scientifically defensible position.

Yet why does the analytic experience inspire belief? It does so because it draws on the most fundamental of human capacities, the capacity to test reality even in the most complex, demanding, and confusing circumstances. Remarkably, people down the ages have discovered curative drugs, selecting them from among thousands of potential candidates; our ancestors have nourished themselves on plants they have discovered in the wilds around them; they have built pyramids and irrigation systems before the formalizations of geometry and experimental physics; and they figured out how procreation works, no mean feat. Somehow they were able to "separate the wheat from the chaff," an operation Meehl does not believe the "anecdotal" clinical method allows. I do not mean to say that psychoanalysis is a primitive trial-and-error undertaking unguided by theory, but rather that Dr. Case has a point to make about the unique virtue of the clinical method as a dynamic generator of experience and discoveries drawing upon the full range of observations that only the clinician, confronted daily with the enormous complexity of human beings, can make. Or, as Grossman observes, "the use of a clinical concept for research purposes faces the problem of an uncertainty principle of observation and definition: the phenomenon is best observed where it can be least defined in a precise operational way. . . ."

For this reason and others that will appear further on in my discussion of Grossman's commentary, I argued behind my Dr. Link mask that the clinical method was essential, in Grossman's words, to "constructing a multifaceted picture of mental functioning." It was not simply to be put in the straitjacket of Dr. Sample's psychotherapy research methodological manipulations, or its blood drawn for the laboratory, but advantage taken of its unique naturalistic approach. How to do so remains a challenge worth taking up. Meehl, in my judgment, underestimates the special role that the clinical method must play in the systematic development of psychoanalytic science. He also does not give sufficient attention to the *interrelationships* among the approaches Dr. Link considers so important, or to how the different methods throw light on one another, thus clarifying and strengthening themselves.

In his commentary, Grossman devotes special attention to this issue of interrelationship among methods and succeeds in clarifying the matter, while pointing to several limitations in Link's position. To take up the limitations first, Grossman correctly notes that Link does not deal at all with developmental conceptions and their related observations in clinical work. This is a serious oversight insofar as the psychoanalytic method has built into it a fundamental genetic assumption and its causative explanations are cast in terms of individual history. This genetic assumption can best be supported by research in developmental psychology and neurophysiology. A good example of such relevant research is the burgeoning literature on early attachment and its relation to later parenting. There is also some interesting work on the physiology of nursing and its relation to early attachment supporting the anaclitic hypothesis. Grossman also points out that Link overlooks the problem of "validating particular interpretations in any ongoing analysis." I do not take him to be asking for psychotherapy-type research on the problem—for this Dr. Sample's approach is available—but to be addressing the limits of the psychoanalytic situation itself for this purpose. Again this constitutes an unmet challenge.

But it is in Grossman's extrapolation from Link's position that he makes his most interesting and useful points. Grossman cautions that there is a necessary evolution in the development of a science, in particular one as complex as psychoanalysis: "Science involves an evolution of knowledge and ideas, with various steps from unacknowledged assumptions through systematic testing of specific limited processes by experiment of whatever kind." He cites the theory of evolution, which itself evolved from painstaking observation in the field (akin to a clinical method) to startling prospective experiments on the evolutionary process itself in species whose evolution can be compressed into a remarkably brief time by manipulating their environment. But the experiments were possible only because of the preceding hundred-year history of systematic observation and theory development. He refers to a "parallel processing" of different methods, each with its own approach, but dealing with aspects of the same problem. In this respect my experimental research and that of others can contribute to this "parallel processing": "When relevant aspects of the working analyst's concepts can be studied experimentally, the clinical analyst has a new basis on which to reexamine his assumptions. . . . an essential part of any psychoanalysis."

Finally, Grossman underscores perhaps the most important point I wished to make by way of the dialogic form: "The various points of view in dialogue demonstrate the problem of communication among people who share an interest in psychoanalysis as a system of related ideas but do not share the same observational contexts." And yet these different observational contexts can be a source of strength and scientific excitement if we can only overcome our narrow methodological loyalties and prejudices.

The third commentator generally in agreement with my position is Simons. He calls attention correctly to the need to study the change process itself, including the role of interpretation stressed by Grossman. Simons wonders if laboratory methods might someday be able to demonstrate the existence of intrapsychic and interpersonal change brought about by psychoanalysis. We have been giving this matter some thought in the context of our experimental investigations of unconscious conflict. In principle, it is possible; but the study of the change process might be one of those areas in which much more theoretical clarity needs to be achieved before experimental work becomes feasible. Nevertheless, a good working hypothesis would assume that significant psychological change would involve significant neurophysiological and even neuroanatomical change. Consider the findings that an enriched milieu results in a proliferation of new synaptic connections in rats and in older humans. Does not successful psychoanalysis result in enriching the milieus of our patients, let alone in enriching their internal milieu?

I will now turn my attention to those commentators who had reservations about my methodological strategy for psychoanalysis.

Bucci appears to both agree and disagree. She sees psychoanalysis as one aspect of psychological science characterized by a nomological network that appears to provide a comprehensive, if abstract, conceptual framework; in this important respect she seems to agree that different approaches can be included. Unfortunately, in my judgment, she appears to consider this framework to be a sufficient basis for incorporating different methods. She does not devote attention to the way in which different methods can be integrated.

But her essential disagreement with Link's strategy is set forth in one crucial sentence put in the mouth of one of her protagonists, Emotion-Mind: "In contrast to Link's position, my claim is that the psychoanalytic situation provides a controlled, naturalistic research context ideally suited for testing the propositions of a general theory of emotion and mind." She ignores Link's argument that any use of the psychoanalytic situation must take for granted its two basic presuppositions about a causative unconscious manifested through various transformations. These two significant propositions of a "general theory of emotion and mind" cannot, as a result, be tested in the psychoanalytic situation, no matter how controlled and systematic the approach. For this task other independent methods are required. This point appears to be ignored by Bucci in her fervor for Dr. Sample's position.

Psychoanalysis as Science

Solms presents an entirely different argument against the Linkian strategy, one that is tendentiously philosophical in nature and, in my judgment, wide of the mark. Nevertheless, his is an attack at the heart of that strategy insofar as it denies that psychoanalytic presuppositions can be supported independently from elsewhere. His argument is based on a misapplication of Kant's epistemological position that we can never know reality for what it really is (*das Ding an sich*) and must settle for approximations limited by the intrinsic nature of our minds. He then applies this principle to psychoanalysis, claiming that the presupposition of an unconscious known only through its conscious transformations is a case in point; therefore, he argues, we must settle for what we can learn about the unconscious from the psychoanalytic situation, for we can do no better, but only run into other forms of the Kantian dilemma.

Kant's epistemology identifies those forms of knowledge that are assumed to be a priori and to be distinguished from knowledge that is derived empirically. Solms confounds these two kinds of knowledge. Let me give an example. Microbiologists employ microscopes based either on optical or atomic principles. When they look into their microscopes they know that what they are observing, no matter how magnified, are really minute and invisible. How can they be so sure? An untutored child or naive person might in fact believe otherwise. Microbiologists know they are right because the principles on which the microscopes are built have been well established in the sciences of optics and subatomic physics. What are for them necessary presuppositions are findings in these other sciences. Microbiologists *apply* this knowledge in their own field and are enabled to discover matters totally different from the subject matter of physics. The bacteria and viruses thus studied by microbiologists are known empirically, albeit on the basis of certain reasonable propositions themselves empirically derived. Yet it is also the case that both the microbiologists' and the physicists' observations are constrained, according to Kant, by certain a priori epistemological principles that place a shadow between themselves and *any* reality (*das Ding an sich*) that they observe; thus, none of them can lay claim to knowing what is really there, although they can find out an enormous amount about their own perceptions of that reality and check them out against each other.

Commentaries

According to Link, the psychoanalyst is in the same position as the microbiologist using a method based on certain presuppositions that cannot be proven within the provenance of its use. But, as with the microbiologist, other fields can provide independent evidence to support these presuppositions. My research and that of others is a contribution to that cause; it is not an exercise in circularity in which there is no escape from Kantian a priori categories.

The spirit of Michel's commentary can be captured in a phrase—"much ado about nothing." He professes to being wearied by essentially sophomoric discussions about whether or not psychoanalysis is a science, and would much prefer to listen to Dr. Case's histories. As for Dr. Link, "Scientists who once wanted to be psychoanalysts and psychoanalysts who once wanted to be scientists are fascinated by Dr. Link's approach, and look forward to the day when its promise can be realized." It is hard to say to which, if either, of these categories Michels himself belongs, although he leaves unstated the implication that psychoanalysts are not scientists at all despite the fact that some, having once been so, retain a certain sentimental attachment to those days. At present and presumably well into the future, according to Michels, psychology and neuophysiology have very little of value to address to psychoanalysis. As for the two basic presuppositions, they are no more essential than an alphabet is to "Shakespeare, though we might balk if asked to conclude that alphabetology is the essential basic science of English literature."

The alphabet analogy is worth a closer look because it contains implicitly a potentially serious critique of Link's position. Letters are the constituents of words, but they are not, like words, carriers of reference or meaning; in philosophical terms, they are not the vehicles of intentionality, or "aboutness." Is it the case that the assumptions of a causative unconscious manifested in conscious transformations are the "letters" of psychoanalytic "words"? Or is it rather that they constitute the assumed principles or rules by which meaning is constituted and conveyed? Thus, a relevant question would be, Does unconscious meaning exist—that is, unconscious "words," not just "letters"? And if so, "How do such meanings become known?" It would seem that a basic science of unconscious meaning and their manner of becoming known would be of relevance to psychoanalysis no matter how long it might take to achieve it.

Psychoanalysis as Science

In his references to the research itself, Michels misunderstands the nature of the research, which might account for his minimizing its import. He describes the crucial comparison in the study of unconscious conflict to be between "emotionally charged and neutral control words." The actual comparison is between unconscious conflict and conscious symptom words. The results thus do have immediate bearing on clinical aspects of psychoanalysis and are not simply promissory notes for the future. Similarly, he misconstrues the nature of the classification findings in the second experiment, as evidenced by his erroneous illustration. It is not that *Freud* presented subliminally would speed up responses to *therapy* rather than *natural science*, both are instances of category and not property classification. The illustration would be more pertinent if *Freud* would speed up responses to *beard* or *cigar*, each a property associated with Freud that might serve as displacements or substitute formations.

Goldberg is concerned that Link and his companions might be attempting to take out a patent on the definition of psychoanalysis as a science. He would prefer to leave the matter open because a "golden opportunity" now exists to "stake out a new definition of psychoanalysis as science." He advises us to "await a philosopher who will undertake that task while not chastising us for not being what someone else wants us to be." He laments that, "Alas, none of the people involved in the conversation was qualified to be that person." My aim was not to settle on a definition of psychoanalysis as a science, but rather through a discussion of scientific issues to arrive at a more comprehensive conception of the scientific tasks of psychoanalysis and how best to achieve them. As best as I can determine, Goldberg does not comment on these matters.

Critiques of the Shevrin research cited by Link. The research described by Dr. Link was intended as an illustration of the way in which different methods might be integrated, both methodologically and theoretically. No effort was made to present the research in the detail required for a full appreciation of the research itself. As a result, some of the commentators may have been misled by Dr. Link's presentation, for which I must apologize.

The research cited was intended to address the two fundamental presuppositions of the psychoanalytic method: (1) the existence of a causative psychological unconscious, and (2) the indirect (transformed) manifestation of these unconscious causes in consciousness. Aside from Solms's effort—in my judgment, misconceived—at a philosophically based dismissal of the empirical nature of these presuppositions, no other commentator disputed their centrality or the relevance of the research to them. Meehl felt the research went in the right direction, but still far from enough; Michels felt that its promise of fulfillment was far off in the future, if ever. Simons, without in any way challenging the research, would like to see it move in the direction of measuring change. But Bucci and Solms had serious reservations about the research itself, while Grossman saw promise in its implications for current theory and practice. Goldberg chose not to comment on the research.

I will first take up the Bucci and Solms criticisms, and then consider Grossman's evaluation.

Bucci raises two problems with respect to the research: (1) the use of words as stimuli to investigate unconscious conflict and categorization erroneously ascribes to the unconscious a linguistic character it does not have; (2) in the study of unconscious conflict the unconscious conflict words do seem to be distinguished supraliminally from the conscious symptom words and thus do seem to go together consciously, contrary to my claim that they do not.

The first criticism, according to Bucci, leads to a theoretical contradiction: on the one hand, the research appears to demonstrate that accessibility to awareness is a major determinant of cognitive processing, while the assumed linguistic organization of the unconscious is at variance with these topographic considerations. She concludes that the research as a result fits into no existing psychoanalytic theory. Although I may not fully appreciate Bucci's point on the nonverbal nature of the unconscious, I find myself surprised at the claim. From the earliest times Freud gave clinical example after clinical example of primary process unconscious reworking of language in symptoms, dreams, parapraxes, and psychosis. I believe Bucci confounds type of organization and the principles governing different organizations (primary vs. secondary, or combinations of them) with the content of those organizations (verbal or nonverbal). It is thus entirely possible for subliminal verbal stimuli to register preconsciously and then to be reworked by dynamically unconscious primary processes before they appear in consciousness in some transformed manner. Fisher has described many such instances in his pioneering subliminal research (Shevrin, in press). Evidence of this kind does require that topographic considerations be incorporated in neostructural theory, and in a monograph on the research (Shevrin et al., in press) my colleagues and I offer a way in which this can be accomplished drawing upon a model developed by Fisher.

Bucci's second criticism is understandable given the curtailed presentation of the research by Dr. Link. Our monograph on the research provides the answer. Briefly, it must first be borne in mind that the main finding was that the unconscious conflict words were better classified as going together subliminally than supraliminally, while the reverse was the case for the conscious symptom words. The electrophysiological time-frequency features that successfully categorized them subliminally failed to do so supraliminally. Moreover, a finding not mentioned in Link's presentation is that subjects failed to classify the unconscious words as going together when asked to do so, while they succeeded in doing so for the conscious symptom words. Both electrophysiologically and psychologically the unconscious conflict words simply did not go together when they were in consciousness, even though electrophysiologically they had done so when they were not in consciousness (subliminal). However, even though the time-frequency features failed to classify the unconscious conflict words as going together, they showed differences in latencies from the conscious symptom words, suggesting that the *individual* words, while bearing no relationship to each other (not in the same category), elicited a different brain response. In our monograph we hypothesized that it was the relationships among the words that suffered repression, rather than the individual words, a finding in accord with clinical experience in which elements of a repressed memory can appear in consciousness while their interrelationships remain repressed.

Solms attacks frontally both the substance and method of the research findings. He rejects the claim that they address the two presuppositions, on the grounds (already discussed) that no evidence is adduceable to support presuppositions that are in effect Kantian a prioris. And he also rejects any empirical claim they might have, disputing the interpretations offered. First, it needs to be stressed that no empirical finding is subject to only one interpretation. All findings, in whatever field, as the philosopher of mind Owen

Flanagan (1992) has pointed out, are indeterminate in that sense. However, some interpretations are reasonable, while others are arbitrary and merit little consideration. I will try to show that Solms's alternate interpretations are of the latter sort.

Solms states: "The finding that slow or rapid presentations of words (which therefore attract more or less attentional cathexis) evoke different patterns of cortical activation, and the finding that these patterns covary with the different categories of words, will surprise no one." In a footnote he states further that "the same facts were demonstrated long ago by Pötzl." These are remarkable statements in view of the fact that, to my knowledge, no one prior to our research, going back to our first publication in *Science* (Shevrin and Fritzler, 1968), and certainly not Pötzl has demonstrated "different patterns of cortical activation" associated with subliminal stimuli. Solms then offers his own interpretation of the findings as due to differences in immediate feelings of unpleasure, the conscious symptom words eliciting more such unpleasure than the unconscious symptom words when both are presented supraliminally. He also dismisses the clinicians' selection of these unconscious conflict words as based on too little clinical evidence. His interpretations, however, do not account for all of the findings.

First, no matter how slender the clinical data may be, the clinicians formulated hypotheses about unconscious conflict and selected words to accord with those hypotheses. This was done independently of the brain measures. They hypothesized in advance that there would be brain response differences between the unconscious conflict words and the conscious symptom words as a function of exposure duration. We found that the unconscious conflict words were better classified as going together subliminally than supraliminally, while the reverse was true for the conscious symptom words. No such differences were found for the nonconflictual, non–symptom-related unpleasant words. Now Solms would need to argue that it was because the unconscious conflict words were "less intensely or less directly evocative of unpleasure" than the conscious symptom words (and the control words) that accounts for these differences rather than the fact that these words were selected beforehand by trained psychoanalytic clinicians to be related to unconscious conflict. If less unpleasure resulted in the unconscious conflict words not being classified as belonging together supraliminally, why should the same factor work to classify them together subliminally, and the reverse be true for the conscious symptom words? There is no theory or body of evidence concerning unpleasure that would account for these findings. Solms's interpretation is at bottom arbitrary and obfuscating.

Solms does no better in his alternate interpretation of the categorization findings, although in this instance there are extenuating circumstances because Link did not describe all of the relevant findings. Essentially Solms argues that the brevity of the exposure accounts for the simpler categorization by attribute rather than by relationships among attributes, and that this has little to do with indirect representations of unconscious registrations. The finding Link did not mention is that unconscious categorization can *also* be based on complex relationships among attributes; thus, brief exposure does not simply result in simpler forms of categorization. Rather, both types of categorization occur unconsciously, while consciously only one (the more complex) is favored. Once we eliminate brevity of exposure as an explanatory factor, we can consider what the brief exposure makes possible: unconscious processing. It is the fact that the categorization goes on unconsciously that favors the attribution basis for categorization in addition to the more complex categorization. Unconsciously, cigars are categorized simultaneously as belonging in the category of smoking equipment *and* in the category of elongated objects such as smokestacks, snakes, and phalluses; consciously they are categorized only as smoking equipment. It is when the instigation (or "priming" in cognitive terms) for categorization is unconscious that these differences emerge and suggest that when these processes are unconscious that the capacity for indirect representation is more likely to occur. Interestingly, since our experiment used neutral rather than conflict-related stimuli, it appears that differences in unconscious categorization are a function of preconscious rather than dynamic unconscious factors. Dynamic influences use the forms of categorization already available preconsciously, findings already apparent in Fisher's original subliminal research (Shevrin, in press).

Commentaries

In his comments on the research, Grossman arrives at the heart of the matter in a quotation worth repeating: "When relevant aspects of the working analyst's concepts can be studied experimentally, the clinical analyst has a new basis on which to reexamine his assumptions." By beginning to demonstrate differences between conscious and unconscious categorization, according to Grossman, we have begun to "show the fine structure of the basis for the clinician's judgments from the combined viewpoints of semiotics, neuropsychology, and neurophysiology." It is the ability to show this "fine structure" that makes the integration of clinical and experimental methods so promising.

Final thoughts. There is much I have learned from my colleagues' commentaries, and I hope I have done right by them in my response. I would like to leave them and all my psychoanalytic colleagues with the following thoughts, which we might continue to discuss in an Amagansett of the mind.

As psychoanalysis begins its second century, it is my hope that it can mobilize its resources for a concerted effort toward developing a comprehensive science drawing on the strengths of its clinical method, psychotherapy research, and the experimental approaches now becoming available to investigate its fundamental propositions. It is my belief that once we can resolve to move in that direction a new excitement will be felt in the field. And then we will have the opportunity to attract new, imaginative minds for whom we must be ready to provide the opportunity to learn and conduct psychoanalytic research, within the psychoanalysis itself and bridging over to other disciplines. If this were to happen, our second century would be a fitting successor to the first.

REFERENCES

FLANAGAN, O. (1992). *Consciousness Reconsidered.* Cambridge, MA: MIT Press.

SHEVRIN, H., ed. (in press). *Subliminal Explorations of Perception, Dreams, and Fantasies: The Pioneering Contributions of Charles Fisher.* Psychological Issues Monographs. Madison, CT: Int. Univ. Press.

——— BOND, J.A., BRAKEL, L., HERTEL, R.K. & WILLIAMS, W.J. (in press). *Conscious and Unconscious Processes: An Experimental Investigation Based on Convergent*

Psychodynamic, Cognitive, and Neurophysiological Methods. New York: Guilford Press.

———— & FRITZLER, D. (1968). Visual evoked response correlates of unconscious mental processes. *Science,* 161:295–298.

A THIRD INDIVIDUATION: IMMIGRATION, IDENTITY, AND THE PSYCHOANALYTIC PROCESS

Immigration from one country to another is a complex psychosocial process with lasting effects on an individual's identity. The dynamic shifts, resulting from an admixture of "culture shock" and mourning over the losses inherent in migration, gradually give way to psychostructural change and the emergence of a hybrid identity. This paper delineates the factors affecting the psychological outcome of immigration and describes four interlinked strands in the fabric of identity change in immigrants. These involve the dimensions of drive and affects, interpersonal and psychic space, temporality, and social affiliation. Issues of idealization and devaluation, closeness and distance, hope and nostalgia, the transitional area of the mind, superego modification, mutuality, and linguistic transformation are highlighted. Implications of these ideas for the psychoanalytic process and technique in instances where the analysand, the analyst, or both are immigrants are briefly touched upon, as are caveats and limitations with regard to the proposed conceptualizations.

Thirty-two thousand years ago, hunters from north central Asia migrated across land bridging the tip of Siberia and the tip of Alaska. Of their path, long since submerged, only the Bering Strait is left. By the era of European exploration, in the late fifteenth century, descendants of these Asian nomads had migrated down through the Americas, forming distinctive tribes and evolving a cultural and linguistic heterogeneity comparable to that of the Europeans who mislabelled native tribesmen and their families "Indians" [Kraut, 1990, pp. 17–18].

Professor of Psychiatry, Jefferson Medical College; Training and Supervising Analyst, Philadelphia Psychoanalytic Institute.

Invited Keynote Address to the Division 39 Spring Meeting of the American Psychological Association, Washington, DC, April 13–17, 1994. The author thanks Drs. Anni Bergman, Alexis Burland, Philip Escoll, Daniel Freeman, Dorothy Holmes, Selma Kramer, and Eric Lager for their helpful suggestions on earlier versions of this paper. Submitted for publication August 1, 1994.

Salman Akhtar

Immigration from one country to another is a complex and multi-faceted psychosocial process with significant and lasting effects on an individual's identity. Leaving one's country involves profound losses. Often one has to give up familiar food, native music, unquestioned social customs, and even one's language. The new country offers strange-tasting food, new songs, different political concerns, unfamiliar language, pale festivals, unknown heroes, psychically unearned history, and a visually unfamiliar landscape. However, alongside the various losses is a renewed opportunity for psychic growth and alteration. New channels of self-expression become available. There are new identification models, different superego dictates, and different ideals. One thing is clear: immigration results in a sudden change from an "average expectable environment" (Hartmann, 1950) to a strange and unpredictable one.

The anxiety consequent upon this "culture shock" (Ticho, 1971; Handlin, 1973; Garza-Guerrero, 1974) challenges the stability of the newcomer's psychic organization. Another threat to it is posed by the mourning over the losses inherent in immigration. This coexistence of culture shock and mourning causes a serious shake-up of the individual's identity. A state of psychic flux, reminiscent of the "second individuation process of adolescence" (Blos, 1967), ensues. Reaching ontogenetically backward, one can also discern psychodynamic echoes of the childhood separation-individuation phase (Mahler et al., 1975)—the first stepping-stone for identity formation—in the immigrant's turmoil. The similarities between the two earlier individuations and the immigrant's identity transformation explain the phrase "a third individuation" in the title of this paper.[1] However, it must be emphasized that phenomenological resemblance does not mean genetic equation. In describing individuals migrating at significantly later stages of development, I am referring to characterological processes that are certainly more subtle and complex than those of early childhood or even adolescence. Much psychic structuralization has already ensued in these individuals; drives have

[1]That the phrase had been used earlier by Colarusso (1990) in describing the effects of biological parenthood on the separation-individuation process in adulthood was brought to my attention by Dr. Dorothy Holmes after I had decided the title of my paper. Having thought of it on my own, and for use in a considerably different context, I decided to retain the phrase in the title of my paper. However, I remain grateful to Dr. Holmes for informing me of this earlier use of the phrase.

attained fusion and genital primacy, the ego is better organized, and a postadolescent superego is in place. Their moral, aesthetic, social, temporal, and linguistic transformation as a result of immigration is more a matter of adult adaptation than of a replicated childhood scenario, though the two cannot entirely be separated. The term *third individuation* should therefore be seen as denoting an adult life reorganization of identity, a potential reworking of earlier consolidations in this regard, and a semiplayful extension of a useful psychoanalytic metaphor.

With this as a backdrop, let me outline the scope of my contribution. In this paper, I will describe the psychic processes involved in the identity change consequent upon immigration. Although I will refer to the contributions of others, my views on the impact of immigration on identity will be based largely on the work of Mahler (Mahler, 1958a, 1958b; Mahler and Furer, 1968; Mahler et al., 1975; Mahler and McDevitt, 1980). Its combined interactive and intrapsychic emphasis lends itself especially well, both as a conceptual tool and a metaphorical counterpart, to elucidating the vicissitudes of identity in immigrants. I will begin by delineating the factors that affect the psychological outcome of immigration. Then I will describe four interconnected strands in the fabric of identity change in immigrants. Finally, I will comment on the implications of these ideas for the psychoanalytic process and technique.

FACTORS AFFECTING THE OUTCOME OF IMMIGRATION

Clearly, the immigrant must give up part of his individuality, at least temporarily, in order to become integrated in the new environment. The greater the difference between the new community and the one to which he once belonged, the more he will have to give up [Grinberg and Grinberg, 1989, p. 90].

Since moving from one location to another involves loss—loss of country, loss of friends, and loss of previous identity—all dislocation experiences may be examined in terms of the immigrant's or the refugee's ability to mourn and/or resist the mouning process. The extent to which the individual is able intrapsychically to accept his or her loss will determine the degree to which an adjustment is made to the new life [Volkan, 1993, p. 65].

The psychological outcome of immigration is determined by a multitude of factors (Park, 1928; Brody, 1973; Favazza, 1980; Grinberg and Grinberg, 1989; Waters, 1990; Hertz, 1993; Ritsner et al., 1993; Volkan, 1993). *First*—and foremost—is whether the immigration is temporary or permanent. The situation of a diplomat assigned for a predetermined length of time to a foreign country differs from the migrant who has left home in the hope of settling down in a new land. *Second*, the degree of choice in leaving one's country also affects the subsequent adaptation. In this context, the following observation of Grinberg and Grinberg (1989) is highly significant: "Parents may be voluntary or involuntary emigrants, but children are always 'exiled': they are not the ones who decide to leave and they cannot decide to return at will" (p. 125). Also pertinent here is the time available for preparing oneself to leave a place. A sudden departure precludes anticipatory mourning and might complicate subsequent adaptation. *Third*, the possibility of revisiting the home country has its own effects on the outcome of the migratory process. Those who can easily and frequently visit their countries of origin suffer less than those who are barred from such "emotional refueling"; herein lies the main difference between the immigrant and the exile. *Fourth*, the effects of immigration on identity might differ in intensity with the age at which immigration occurs.[2] Children, for instance, being more open to learning and having emigrated in the company of the people in their immediate environment, might be less traumatized. At the same time, their dependence on caretaking adults who themselves are psychologically stressed might render

[2]Freud's three immigrations occurred during early childhood (at age three from Freiberg to Leipzig, and at age four from Leipzig to Vienna) and old age (at age eighty-two from Vienna to London). They did not therefore significantly affect his identity, which remained ethnically Jewish and culturally Viennese. At the same time, they were not devoid of psychic impact. Freud "never forgot the forests around Freiberg" and his "vocal, often reiterated detestation of Vienna" (Gay, 1988, pp. 9, 10) reflected not only the hardship, solitude, and anti-Semitism he faced there but also the fact that Vienna was not Freiberg. At the same time, when toward the end of his life he had to leave Vienna for London, Freud expressed much grief. "The feeling of triumph at liberation is mingled too strongly with mourning, for one had still very much loved the prison from which one has been released" (letter to Max Eitingon; Freud, June 6, 1938, quoted in Gay, 1988, p. 9).

them more vulnerable. A role is also played by phase-specific unconscious fantasies at the time of immigration. In infants and toddlers, the impact is largely through the mother's psychic reality. However, in oedipal-age children more specific fantasies, related to the fact that the decision to immigrate is a parental prerogative, might be mobilized. Similar differential effects on adolescents, young adults, the middle-aged, and the elderly are not difficult to imagine. *Fifth,* the reasons for leaving one's country also play a role in determining success or failure in adapting to the new environment. As regards external reality, was one "escaping from" financial hardship, political persecution, or ethnic strife, or was one "heading toward" new opportunities, wider horizons? Psychologically, was immigration an anxious or angry repudiation of primary objects or a manifestation of the ego's healthy alloplastic capacity? To be sure, such dichotomies are artificial, but the outcome of immigration might indeed vary with the economic balance of reality vs. intrapsychic and adaptive vs. neurotic components. *Sixth,* the extent to which an individual has achieved the intrapsychic capacity for separateness prior to immigration will also influence the effects of the actual separations involved in immigration. *Seventh,* the emotions with which the host culture receives the migrant also play a role in the latter's assimilation and associated identity change. A particular era in the history of a nation might be more receptive than another era to receiving immigrants. In an ironic twist to Freud's "anatomy is destiny" remark (1924, p. 178), skin color and the thickness of epicanthic folds acquire significance in this context. In other words, race might also play a role here. The forced immigration of Black slaves,[3] the desperate refuge-seeking of East European Jews, the influx of ambitious (if a

---

[3]The situation of Black slaves brought to this country was devastating not only because their immigration was forced and they lacked "emotional refueling," but also because they were psychophysically manhandled by the "host" population. They were used as targets of projection and, in an act of collective "soul murder" (Shengold, 1989), brainwashed to believe in their inherent racial inferiority. Effects of the intergenerational transmission of this trauma (Apprey, 1993) are still evident. However, the civil rights movement of the 1960s, the subsequent "Black is beautiful" and similar esteem-building social voices, the search for heritage and legacy (memorialized in Alex Haley's 1976 *Roots*), and the emergence (as well as belated recognition) of national and international heroes from within the group—are all signs of a reversal of the situation. Remembering Abraham's (1911) paper on the "determining power of names," the transition, in this context, from "Negro" to "Black" to "African-American" seems rich with psychosocial connotations.

bit colonially gaslighted) Indians and Pakistanis—the "midnight's children" of Salman Rushdie (1980)—and the recent spate of refugees from Cuba, Haiti, Laos, Cambodia, and Vietnam might indeed have elicited varying emotional responses from the American culture at large. *Eighth*, the magnitude of cultural differences between the adopted and the home country is an important variable. A move into the United States from Canada or England is clearly not the same as one from Korea or Yemen.[4] Settlage's observation (1992) that marked actual difference in parental personalities puts self- and object constancy to the test is pertinent here. It echoes Freud's earlier warning (1923) that if the ego's identifications "become too numerous, unduly powerful and incompatible with each other, a pathological outcome will not be far off" (p. 30). However, linguistic and skin-color similarities do not preclude the mourning of immigration. Such "invisible immigrants" (Stephen Shanfield, personal communication) also experience the losses and anxieties of immigration. *Finally*, the extent to which one's original role (especially one's vocation) can be resumed upon immigration also effects the assimilation process; maintaining one's professional identity assures an "inner continuity in change" (Lichtenstein, 1963). This hints at the fact that there are vocations and skills that are less transportable than others across cultures. To wit, this might involve psychoanalysis itself,[5] though one is readily tempted to think of more esoteric examples.

This long list of variables might give the impression that no two immigrations are the same and that even the use of the singular

---

[4]In the emphasis on the immigration from one country to another, it should not be overlooked that similar issues can be faced by individuals moving to culturally diverse regions within the same country. A poignant example of such "interior migrations" (Grinberg and Grinberg, 1989, p. 17) is the character played by Jon Voight in the popular 1969 movie *Midnight Cowboy*. See also the sociological observations of Coles (1967) on south-to-north migration in this country and of Brody (1973) on interior migrations within Brazil. The New Zealand poet James Baxter (1958) has rendered his experience of moving from one to another region of his country in a beautiful poem entitled "The Return."

[5]Babcock and Caudill (1958) report the situation of a Western analyst who, working for many years in Japan, had given up psychoanalysis. He found that whenever he attempted to analyze the hostile dependency on parental figures in Japanese patients, they reacted with severe depression. Noting that such depression necessitated many supportive measures, the analyst gradually began restricting his work to psychotherapy.

form *immigration* is questionable. While this might be the case, a core migratory process, resembling separation-individuation, does seem to unfold in most adult immigrants.[6] In tandem with the developmental tasks of the rapprochement subphase and the beginning of self- and object constancy (Mahler et al., 1975), this process can be seen as comprising of four interlinked journeys involving the dimensions of drives and affects, space, time, and social affiliation. Alternatively, these can be seen as involving psychic travel (1) from love or hate to ambivalence, (2) from near or far to optimal distance, (3) from "yesterday" or "tomorrow" to "today," and (4) from mine or yours to ours.

FROM LOVE OR HATE TO AMBIVALENCE

Idealized, "all good" object images have to be integrated with "all bad" object images, and the same holds true for good and bad self images. In this process of synthesis, partial images of the self and of the objects are integrated into total object and self representations, and thus self and object representations become . . . more realistic [Kernberg, 1975, p. 27].

[6]I have arrived at these ideas from six convergent routes: (1) my own experience of two immigrations (the first an "interior migration" of considerable significance within India, the second from India to the United States, where I have lived for the past twenty-one years, been analyzed, and practiced analysis and psychotherapy, with both "native" and immigrant patients); (2) ethnographic observations made in intermingling with a large number of fellow immigrants from India; (3) regular, almost yearly reunions, spanning over two decades, with immigrant physicians who entered the U.S. at about the time I did and with whom in 1973–74 I completed my first year of residency in psychiatry—Drs. Getulio Tovar (Brazil), Aarno Vuotila (Finland), Harish Malhotra, Maya Malhotra, Kanan Patrawala, and Lila Rao (India), Danilo Campos (Philippines), and Young Ho Kim (South Korea); (4) a study of psychoanalytic and psychiatric writings on migration; (5) perusal of certain literary contributions dealing with the topic; and (6) formal and informal conversations with a number of immigrant colleagues within the profession about their experiences with migration—Drs. Nora Kramer (Argentina), James Hamilton and Stephen Shanfield (Canada), Mladan Stivic (Croatia), Vamik Volkan (Cyprus), Wilfred Abse (England), Maurice Apprey (Ghana), Subhash Bhatia, Shashi Bhatia, and Dilip Ramchandani (India), Roknedin Safavi and Hossein Etezady (Iran), Shimon Waldfogel (Israel), Rita Rogers (Romania), and Dragan Svrakic (Yugoslavia). My conversations with Dr. Purnima Mehta, who emigrated from Idi Amin's Uganda to (successively) India, England, and the U.S., and my correspondence with Drs. Lilka Croydon and Julian Stern (who have immigrated from Poland to Canada and from South Africa to England, respectively) has also furthered my knowledge of immigration-related experiences.

It is possible that we move beyond splitting by flickering back and forth fast enough to begin to see new pictures, much as the illusion of motion in motion pictures depends upon a succession of still pictures rapid enough to enlist persistence of vision to produce the subjective experience of continuity [Lewin and Schulz, 1992, p. 51].

Like the rapprochement subphase toddler (Mahler et al., 1975) and the transiently regressed adolescent (Blos, 1967; Kramer, 1980), the immigrant is vulnerable to splitting of the self- and object representations (Kernberg, 1967) along libidinal and aggressive lines. The drastic change in external environment taxes the ego's adaptive capacities, and changed societal dictates on acceptable behavior cause drive disregulation. A male immigrant from a sexually repressive culture, such as Saudi Arabia or Iraq, might find the casual friendliness of Western women uncomfortably stimulating. A female of similar background might unconsciously equate the Western woman with the oedipal rival and be stirred in her aggressive and competitive strivings; alternatively, the day-to-day intermingling with men might stimulate her repressed erotic longings. By contrast, a Western immigrant to a culture such as Japan, which prizes group affiliation over individuation, might suddenly be faced with repudiated symbiotic longings and wishes for masochistic submission to a dissociated harsh superego. Regardless of the specific form it takes, the cultural change consequent upon immigration is bound to test ego resilience, both from outside and from the forces unleashed within.

A frequent consequence, once the initial "disorienting anxieties" (Grinberg and Grinberg, 1989, p. 2) are overcome[7] and before more adaptive ego defenses can be put into place, is regression. Splitting becomes predominant and colors the immigrant's feelings about his two lands and his two self-representations. The country of origin is idealized, the new culture devalued. For an East-to-West immigrant, this often gives rise to the idea that Western culture is characterized by greed, sexual promiscuity, violence, and disregard

[7]A practicing subphase–like hypomania, with both defensive and adaptive functions, is also characteristic of this early period of entry into a new culture. However, unlike the early anxieties, this hypomania is never fully renounced. It resurfaces again and again throughout the life cycle whenever the need for mastering new cultural tasks arises (Anni Bergman, personal communication).

of generational boundaries; the Eastern, by contentment, instinctual restraint, love, humility, and respect for both young and old. For a West-to-East immigrant, a similar splitting of object representations yields a view of the East as riddled with indolence, filth, superstition, subservience, and a pathetic withering of instincts; the West as industrious, conscientious, orderly, instinctually gratifying, and encouraging of self-actualization.

Three points need to be added. First, these split views are subject to convincing shifts. One day the country of origin is idealized and the country of adoption devalued. The next day, it is the reverse. Second, such contradictory attitudes, while phenomenologically akin to the splitting seen during the rapprochement subphase, contain the projective repudiation of developmentally higher level conflicts as well. Falk (1974), for instance, has noted that countries or territories on the two sides of a border often unconsciously symbolize early parental figures. One country (usually that of origin) might come to represent the mother, and the other country the father, thus setting up a fertile ground for oedipal fantasy and enactment on the immigrant's part. Third, splitting, in no wise restricted to the object world, also afflicts the immigrant's self-representation. Being Belgian, Brazilian, Chinese, German, Indian, Iranian, Korean, or Filipino tends to be libidinized and to become a source of pride. The newly emergent self-representation, say American, is devalued and seems shameful. Indeed, such one-sided instinctual investment often reverses itself; what was once idealized becomes devalued and vice versa. Here also, the phenomenological similarity with childhood libidinal-aggressive splitting should not lead one to overlook other issues (e.g., bisexual or oedipal) that might be involved. For instance, one self-representation might become imbued with male and the other female attributes,[8] one with the oedipally accepting and the other with oedipally defiant qualities in the unconscious. Guilt at success in the new country, "separation guilt" (Modell, 1965) vis-à-vis the old country, and "survivor's guilt" (Niederland, 1968) might also play a role here.

---

[8]Silber (1993) has recently argued that around the end of Civil War the North constructed a feminized interpretation of the South that validated the former's superiority. In emphasizing Southern helplessness, the Northerners even couched descriptions of Southern landscapes in feminine terms.

Gradually, a synthesis of two self-representations sets in. For this to take place, however, ample sustenance of "growth needs" (Casement, 1991, p. 274), enough "efficacy experiences" (Wolff, 1994, p. 73), and a positive balance of libido over aggression are necessary. Settlage's succinct remark (1992), made in connection with the initial achievement of self-constancy, is no less pertinent here: "The predominance of love is the glue of a unified self-representation" (p. 352). As a result of this synthesis, a capacity for good-humored ambivalence toward both the country of origin and that of adoption develops. A hyphenated identity now emerges. Such an identity, though perhaps lacking a deep anchoring in either historical-identification system, might yet possess a greater than usual breadth of experience, a sense of relativity, knowledge, and, at times, wisdom. An external manifestation of this psychostructural achievement is the immigrant's increasing comfort in simultaneously associating with individuals from both of his two cultures. A "mixed" guest list for a dinner at the immigrant's house is a telltale sign of such advance in identity consolidation.

FROM NEAR OR FAR TO OPTIMAL DISTANCE

> . . . going away leads to different consequences for a man's human and non-human experience. He can reproduce the old life with people in the new place, because people do not differ greatly from one to the other. He eventually finds new friends. But places can differ so profoundly that it is no longer possible to have certain sorts of experiences of place at all. Such deprivations and losses inevitably increase awareness of the non-human world, both the old and the new [Denford, 1981, p. 325].

> It was not simply owing to the stressful circumstances attending the emigration that I became newly creative. It was rather that, with the stress came new vistas, new curiosity, new opportunities, and vital new sources of collegiate support. It was only in America, and only owing to the tremendous professional encouragement I received in America, that I no longer felt I was laboring under the shadow of titans [Mahler in Stepansky, 1988, p. 121].

Elsewhere (Akhtar, 1992a) I have reviewed in detail the conceptual ambiguities, developmental origins, cultural vicissitudes, and technical implications of optimal distance. Here I will mention only that it is a hybrid concept (Bouvet, 1958; Balint, 1959; Escoll, 1992) that can be viewed from either the interpersonal or the intrapsychic perspective. Mahler herself describes it both as a position "between mother and child that best allows the infant to develop those faculties which he needs in order to grow, that is, to individuate" (Mahler et al., 1975, p. 291) and as a later ego capacity for establishing an optimal distance from the internal representation of the mother (and, subsequently, of others). Mahler notes that during the symbiotic phase there is no outside world for the infant and hence no distance. Gradually there develops "the space between mother and child" (Bergman, 1980, p. 201). Created by both the mother's comings and goings and a decrease in the baby's bodily dependence on her, this space[9] permits the child to look "beyond the symbiotic orbit" (Mahler, 1966, p. 155). The infant attempts to break away from passive lap-babyhood. During the practicing subphase, the child shows even greater ability to move away from the mother, at first by crawling and later by upright locomotion. The child makes pleasurable forays into the external world and seems oblivious to the mother's presence. Yet, revealing his continued need for a "home base," he periodically returns to the mother. In the rapprochement subphase, no distance from the mother appears satisfactory, but if the mother remains emotionally available despite the child's oscillations, the capacity for optimal distance gradually develops.

Reverberations of these themes can be found in the immigrant's interpersonal and intrapsychic life. At the external level, the immigrant has to rediscover the acceptable limits of interpersonal space (for a sociological perspective on interpersonal distance, see Hall, 1973; Zerubavel, 1991). The extent of physical contact, spatial proximity and psychological intimacy becomes a matter of renewed psychosocial negotiation and practice. More important, the immigrant finds himself "too far" from his country of origin, a distance that he, like the practicing phase toddler, might greatly enjoy for some time. Sooner or later, however, the anxiety of having exceeded the symbiotic orbit surfaces. The immigrant's ego loses the support it

---

[9]Winnicott (1971) is also interested in this space. However, his focus is not on the child's ambivalent efforts to minimize it but on its persistence and varying psychic uses throughout life.

had drawn from the familiar environment, climate, and land-scape—all unconsciously perceived as extensions of the mother (Krystal and Petty, 1963). "Attempts at restoration of such ego support may lead the immigrant to seek a climate and ethnic surrounding much like his original, and may become involved in a life-long attempt at symbolic restitution of his motherland" (Krystal, 1966, p. 217).[10] A fantasy of return to the home country also emerges. The wish, like the rapprochement subphase child's regressive search for symbiosis, is, however, not free of ambivalence. In myriad rationalized ways, acting on it is postponed. Conditions (e.g., saving money, earning a diploma) are set for one's return but their fulfillment eludes the immigrant like a mirage. A frequent stopgap measure is actual travel back to the country of origin. Carrying back gifts to relatives left behind, and bringing cultural artifacts and mementos back to his new home, the immigrant reminds one of a toddler crisscrossing the space between himself and his mother. Bergman's comment (1980), though made in the latter connection, seems equally applicable to the immigrant.

> As . . . he is able to move away farther, his world begins to widen, there is more to see, more to hear, more to touch, and each time he returns to mother he brings with him some of the new experience. In other words, each time he returns he is ever so slightly changed. The mother is the center of his universe to whom he returns as the circles of his exploration widen [p. 203].

The distance between two lands (two mothers, the "mother of symbiosis" and the "mother of separation") is also bridged by homoethnic ties in the new country, international phone calls, and listening to one's native music. These serve as "transitional objects" (Winnicott, 1953) and help bring what has become externally "too far" a bit nearer.[11]

---

[10]According to Krystal (1966), the artist Giorgio de Chirico's preoccupation with Italian landscapes is a conspicuous example of such a need.

[11]The situation is more complex for exiles (i.e., involuntary migrants who cannot return to their homelands). This blocks access to refueling. The child within is orphaned and must reclaim inch by inch the psychic territory lost. This is achieved with the aid of new transferences, introspection, and creativity, as well as old photographs, music, books, relics, etc.; under such circumstances physical possessions acquire the status of "linking objects" (Volkan, 1981). Such a mourning process may last a lifetime and still remain incomplete (see Pollock, 1989). The availability of a

On an internal level too, the immigrant fluctuates between extremes of distance from his native self-representation and his newly emerging self-representation as a resident of the adopted country. Failure to negotiate the distance between these self-representations results in two problematic outcomes of identity (Teja and Akhtar, 1981): ethnocentric withdrawal and counterphobic assimilation. The first involves clinging to an idealized view of one's earlier culture. Individuals so withdrawn eat only the food of their native land and associate only with homoethnic groups. Their residences, replete with artifacts from "back home," take on a shrinelike quality. Such persons become more nationalistic vis-à-vis their country of origin than they were while still living there. To buttress such secondary nationalism, they often forge unlikely alliances and develop new prejudices. In contrast to this ethnocentric withdrawal, counterphobic assimilation is a caricature of the practicing subphase toddler. Intoxicated by the widening horizon of their experiential world, these individuals totally renounce their original culture. In an "as if" fashion (Deutsch, 1942) and through "magic identification" (Jacobson, 1964), they rapidly incorporate the host culture. Clearly, both ethnocentric withdrawal and counterphobic assimilation are multiply determined (Waelder, 1930), though difficulty with aggression perhaps plays a large role here. More common are solutions that appear to be compromise formations but nonetheless emanate from a splitting of the self and the object world. These include (1) pragmatic assimilation masking nonassimilation, the relationship between the two structures being akin to the "false" and "true" selves of Winnicott (1960), and (2) temporally alternating phases of closeness and distance from one or the other culture. An individual caught up in the latter solution ends up having "native phases" and "assimilated phases" in a "life lived in pieces" (Pfeiffer, 1974).

A deeper mending of being "too close" or "too far" from one or the other culture begins if the "holding environment" (Winnicott, 1960), within both the family[12] and the culture at large, provides

---

proxy base for "emotional refueling" (e.g., the state of Israel for East European Jewish migrants to, say, the United States) might prevent such frozen grief.

[12]In a study of 385 Soviet immigrant physicians to Israel, Ritsner et al. (1993) found the prevalence of depression to be strongly correlated with disturbed intrafamilial relations.

ample libidinal sustenance and containment of aggression. Manifestations of such mending include (1) increased comfort with one's ethnic/national origins in the workplace, along with greater use of one's new self-representation at home. This results in an enhanced "continuity of personal character" (Erikson, 1956, p. 102), a hallmark of solid identity; (2) establishment of a predictable and reality-governed rhythm of refueling through international phone calls and visits; and (3), in the case of those who become parents in the adopted country, deeper acceptance of their offspring's mixed but predominantly local loyalties.

FROM YESTERDAY OR TOMORROW TO TODAY

> The failure of mourning leads to a continuing search for the idealized lost object, an inability to love new objects, a depreciation of objects in one's current life, and an endless pursuit of nostalgic memories for themselves at the expense of an inhibition in many areas of existence [Werman, 1977, p. 396].

> I would give all the landscapes of the world for that of my childhood. I must add, though, that if I make a paradise out of it, only the tricks or infirmity of memory can be held responsible [Cioran, 1982, p. 12; quoted in Amati-Mehler et al., 1993, p. 266].

The separation-individuation phase contains elements of mourning. With each progressive move toward autonomy and identity consolidation, there is an incremental loss of infantile omnipotence, symbiotic bliss, and ego simplification through splitting and projection. Compensation for this is found in the secondary narcissism of burgeoning ego capacities, autonomous functioning, a realistic self-concept, and deeper object relations. A similar sequence of loss and restoration is evident in the psychic journeys described so far. I will now focus on its impact on the immigrant's rootedness in the time experience.

Facing the "mental pain" (Freud, 1926, p. 169) of separation, the immigrant often resorts to a hypercathexis of the lost objects. Described originally by Freud (1917) in "Mourning and Melancholia," this mechanism results in an idealization of the immigrant's past. Often such idealization centers more upon memories of places than of people. This is not surprising. Throughout childhood and adolescence, the nonhuman environment presents itself as a relatively neutral alternative area in which all the vicissitudes of human interactions can be expressed, experienced, and worked through in relative psychic privacy (Searles, 1960). The inherent repudiation of aggression and the screen functions of nostalgia for lost places (Sterba, 1940; Freedman, 1956; Werman, 1977) notwithstanding, the immigrant employing this mechanism comes to live in the past. His most powerful affects are reserved for his recall of the houses, streetcorners, cafés, hills, and countryside of his homeland. Like an emotionally deprived child with but one toy, he clings to their memories. Ever wistful, the immigrant convinces himself that "if only" (Akhtar, 1991, 1994) he had not left these places, his life would have been wonderful or, more frequently, that when he was there he had no problems. The sharp retort of the great Urdu poet Ghalib (1797–1869) finds no resonance in him:

"Karte kis munh sey ho ghurbat ki shikayat Ghalib?
Tum ko bemehriye—yaaran—e—watan yaad nahin?"
[O Ghalib, with what audacity do you complain of being in a strange land?
Have you forgotten the callousness of friends at home?]
(Ghalib, 1841, p. 84)

The fantasy of a lost paradise expresses a position whereby primary objects are neither given up through the work of grieving nor assimilated into the ego through identification. The result is a temporal fracture of the psyche. This can at times manifest itself in the immigrant's fervent plans to "someday" (Akhtar, 1991, 1994) return to his homeland; fantasies of retirement or burial in one's country of origin are versions of this wish temporally displaced even further. With such a dynamic shift, the future comes to be idealized, robbing the present of full commitment. Often these "if only" and "someday" fantasies coexist, with nostalgia providing the fuel for the hope of return.[13]

[13]In discussing Freud's love of England, Ivan Ward (1993), educational director of the Freud Museum in London, touches on many factors, one of which echoes the "if only"–"someday" connection mentioned here: "It appears, then, that Freiberg was an encapsulated ideal in the past, and that England was an ideal 'other place' in the future. . . . Freud's Journey to England, therefore, may also have been a return to something; a return to some idyllic fantasy of childhood" (p. 38).

The temporal direction of the "if only" and "someday" fantasies differs, but their message is essentially the same. Also, while their conscious focus is on immigration, both fantasies clearly contain ontogenetically earlier issues. At bottom, the "if only" fantasy says, "I wish the day had not come when I lost the blissful symbiotic dual unity with my mother, or the day when I became aware of sexual differences and oedipal boundaries." The "someday" fantasy says, "A day will come when I will recapture the lost mother of symbiosis and overcome the sexual and oedipal barriers." The former attitude fixates the immigrant in the past, the latter in the future. Both cause a temporal discontinuity in the self-experience (Akhtar, 1984, 1992b). The revered Chilean poet Gabriela Mistral (1889–1957) has captured the essence of such psychic fracturing in the following lines of her poem "The Immigrant Jew": [14]

> I am two. One looks back,
> the other turns to the sea.
> The nape of my neck seethes with good-byes
> and my breast with yearning.

With progressive deidealization of lost objects, however, meaningful living in the present becomes possible. This does not imply a total renunciation of past objects, only of their hypercathexis. Indeed, continued updating and an ongoing psychic dialogue with the past (Erikson, 1950a; Lichtenstein, 1963) are not only inevitable but necessary for healthy psychic functioning. However, in such instance, past and future do not replace today. They enrich it.

FROM YOURS OR MINE TO OURS

The Japanese person would feel uncomfortable in thinking of his "self" as something separable from his role. To actualize oneself is to fulfill one's family and social group role expectations. In a traditionally oriented Japanese mind, to be "individualistic" in a Western moral sense would almost be equal to being "selfish" in the worst sense of the term. Japanese tend

---

[14]I am indebted to Dr. Peter Olsson for bringing this poem to my attention.

to equate "individualism" (kojinshugi) with "selfishness" (rko-shugi) [Yamamoto and Wagatsuma, 1980, p. 123].

Shortly after my landing in the United States I received a rejection to an application for an internship from a southern hospital worded as follows: "we have found that persons not of our denomination do not feel comfortable working here." A similar letter was sent to my wife and me from an Adirondack mountain resort. Still later, when we purchased a vacation home in Connecticut, we were quickly informed that the nearby country club (to which we had no intentions of applying) would not admit Jews [Wangh, 1992, p. 16].

In an extension of Mahler's observations regarding the symbiotic dual unity gradually yielding to self- and object differentiation, Bergman (1980) suggests that the sense of "mine" and "yours" develops out of an earlier sense of "ours." She adds that the feeling of "we" is "psychically experienced as the 'me' of primary narcissism which still dominates the symbiosis. Only gradually does this archaic 'we' experience develop to include differentiated 'me' and 'we' experience" (p. 205). While I understand this formulation, my notions about the development of mutuality follow the opposite trajectory. Or perhaps I am simply referring to Bergman's "differentiated 'we' " experience. True mutuality, codified through "we" and "ours," while containing symbiotic roots, has additional developmental origins. Klein's views (1937) about the child's dawning sense of gratitude toward the mother are pertinent in this regard, as are Winnicott's notions (1963) about the development of the capacity for concern. The experience of sharing the parents (and even aspects of one's own personality) with siblings also contributes to the capacity for mutuality. More important, a successful resolution of the oedipal phase consolidates the capacity for mutuality ("my father is also your husband; my mother is also your wife; we share him/her"). This sketchy ontogenesis of mutuality demonstrates that a differentiated "we" follows "mine" and "yours" and lays the groundwork for elucidating the immigrant's struggles in this regard.

For a considerable time after his arrival in the new land, the immigrant resorts to a "mine" and "yours" split. It is only by resolving this split that he can experience "ours." Until then, customs, food, language, games, and moral values are seen as either "mine" or "yours." An important vehicle in the move toward "we-ness" and the associated identity change is the filling-in of the "transitional area" (Winnicott, 1953) by local culture. The immigrant's starting to enjoy the movies, literature, and games of his new country heralds such a move. They provide him a ready-made zone of mutual interest with the "foreigners" of his new country. A second medium that facilitates cultural mutuality is the progressive alteration of the immigrant's superego in an encounter with externally changed prohibitions and sanctions. The situation is akin to adolescence (Erikson, 1950b; Blos, 1967), though clearly the drive upsurge is only relative and is mobilized by altered realities. An instinctually more permissive society, which presents a threat to ego stability, might at first cause anxiety in the immigrant. Then a liquid phase might set in during which experimentations with new id freedoms fluctuates with retribution from the "imported" superego. Gradually these dynamic shifts give way to structural alteration with the deployment of new ego defenses and a softening of the superego. The immigrant's notions about right and wrong shift and come into greater accordance with the culture at large.[15]

The most important vehicle for the emergence of "we-ness" is, however, the acquisition of (or, increased idiomatic fluency in) a new language. The journey from speaking only one's "mother tongue," through an introject-like use (Kernberg, 1976) of a new language, to true bilingualism, is as difficult as it is salutary.[16] Early in this journey, the native language can become an object of idealization and create the narcissistic illusion that only it can express things well (Stengel, 1939; Grinberg and Grinberg, 1989). Its "sonorous

[15]In an application of the Russian thinker Bakhtin's theory of "dialogism" to cross-cultural hermeneutics (1986, 1990), Harris (1993) notes that the encounter between the immigrant and his adopted culture is not one-sided. Though the impact on the immigrant is clearer, the culture itself is affected and inherently altered by the newcomer's interpretation of it.

[16]The paucity of psychoanalytic literature on polylingualism and polyglottism is striking, especially since (1) many early analysts were analyzed in languages other than their mother tongue; (2) most analysts read Freud's writings in translation; (3) many analysts have experience with being analyzed or conducting analysis in a language that is not their mother tongue or with analyzing patients whose mother tongue is one other than their own; and (4) most important, words form such an important medium of communication in the analytic enterprise. The early contributions of Ferenczi (1911) and Stengel (1939), the later work of Buxbaum (1949) and Greenson (1950, 1954), a more recent essay by Flegenheimer (1989), and a most outstanding monograph by Amati-Mehler et al. (1993) on this topic are exceptions in this regard.

wrapping" (Anzieu, 1976) is tenaciously clung to; after all, the "mother tongue" is a link to the earliest maternal imago. The new language, accordingly, is devalued as being weak and ridiculous. Consequently, the immigrant lives in two linguistic worlds, pronouncing his own name in two different ways, and switching with relief to his mother tongue once the workday is over. However, such aching polyglottism[17] adds to the splitting of self-representations. Francois Cheng (1985), a Chinese emigré to France, who did not know a word of French until he was twenty, eloquently describes such a linguistic cleavage of the self.[18] The same pain is reflected by Julia Kristeva (1988):

> Not to speak your own mother tongue. To live with sounds, logics, that are separated from the nocturnal memory of the body, from the sweet-sour sleep of childhood. To carry within yourself like a secret crypt or like a handicapped child—loved and useless—that language of once-upon-a-time that fades and won't make up its mind to leave you ever. You learn to use another instrument, like expressing yourself in algebra or on the violin. You can become a virtuoso in this new artifice that provides you with a new body, just as false, sublimated—some would say sublime. You have the impression that the new language is your resurrection: a new skin, a new sex. But the illusion is torn apart when you listen to yourself—on a recorded tape, for example—and the melody of your own voice comes back to you in a bizarre way, from nowhere, closer to the grumble of the past than to the [linguistic] code of today. . . . Thus, between two languages, your element is silence [p. 20; quoted in Amati-Mehler et al., 1993, pp. 264–265].

A more optimistic note is struck by the writer Eva Hoffman (1989), who describes her inner translations from her native Polish

---

[17]Amati-Mehler et al. (1993) distinguish polylingualism from polyglottism. The former refers to the acquisition of various languages, often simultaneously, throughout childhood. The latter refers to the learning of a new language later in life, based predominantly on translation, and with many fewer emotional connotations than accompany the early natural acquisition of a language.

[18]In a less dramatic vein, Freud also expressed a similar emotion. Soon after his arrival in England, he wrote to Raymond de Saussure, the Swiss psychoanalyst who had congratulated him on his escape: "Perhaps, you have omitted the one point that the emigrant feels so particularly painfully. It is—one can only say—the loss of the language in which one had lived and thought, and which one will never be able to replace with another for all one's efforts at empathy" (Freud, June 11, 1938; quoted in Gay, 1988, p. 632).

into English, which she had to learn when she immigrated to the anglophone world:

> [In] my translation therapy, I keep back and forth over the rifts, not to heal them but to see that—one person, first person singular—have been on both sides. Patiently, I use English as a conduit to go back and down, all the way down to childhood, almost to the beginning. When I learn to say those smallest, first things in the language that has served for detachment and irony and abstraction, I begin to see where the languages I've spoken have their correspondences—how I can move between them without being split by the difference [p. 273].

Perhaps the degree to which a linguistically lacerated self can be healed is variable.[19] However, mending is in evidence with an increasing dominance of the acquired language, which begins to appear in spontaneous humor, dreams, and in talking in one's sleep. Another indicator of linguistic identity change is seen when the immigrant begins to treat the obscenities, terms for genitals, and curses of his new language with an instinctual and moral valence comparable to that invested in similar words of his mother tongue. For a long time, the immigrant's unblinking use of obscenities in his acquired language neither provides him a gratifying id discharge nor causes him a noticeable superego admonishment. ("When you say 'fuck' it doesn't sound dirty, but when I say 'fuck' it sounds dirty," said a perceptive medical student to me some twelve years ago!) For "real" cursing, the immigrant uses his native language only. Gradually, however, as the associative networks of both languages begin to interdigitate, the more recently acquired obscenities too gather affective valence, though perhaps never of truly equal degree to the obscene words in the mother tongue (see Ferenczi, 1911).

Two more points need to be considered. First, different self-representations might remain under the influence of different languages and express different (developmentally earlier and later?)

---

[19]Nabokov, Beckett, and Rushdie are three immigrant writers who show three completely different attitudes in this regard. Nabokov moved in succession from a mastery of Russian, French, and German to English, in which he wrote his best-known works. Beckett "migrated" to French and after many years returned to writing in his native English (for Beckett's relationship with his mother tongue, see Casement, 1982). Rushdie freely sprinkles his English text with Urdu/Hindi colloquialisms from India and thus creates a hybrid language of his own.

conflicts and aspirations.[20] Second, adopting a new language might at times represent the acquisition of a developed identity for the first time. Amati-Mehler et al. (1993), who have authored the most searching psychoanalytic investigation of language so far, conclude that

> a multilingual dimension certainly does allow for an internal enrichment not only at the cognitive level. However, it is also true that the actual mental organization of the multilingual subject lends itself in particular to the enacting of defenses, splittings, and repressions. Occasionally a new language represents a life-saving anchor which allows for "rebirth." At other times it can be a justification for the mutilation of the internal world of the self [p. 108].

TECHNICAL IMPLICATIONS

> One must distinguish the acquisition of knowledge, which comes about as a result of modification of pain (then the knowledge obtained will be used for new discoveries), from possession of knowledge, which is used to avoid painful experiences [Grinberg and Grinberg, 1989, pp. 65–66].

> polylingual patients . . . will have at their disposal a defense that allows them to avoid areas in their psychic life that are problematic. By changing language, they will be able to avoid not only the subset, but the whole language of infantile sexuality, thus denying themselves and us access to an area so intimately linked to specific verbal sounds and special names [Amati-Mehler et al., 1993, p. 34].

Having myself been both an immigrant analysand and an immigrant analyst, I can attest that both facts do impact on the technical aspects of psychoanalysis. In this section, I will comment on some of the vicissitudes of the analytic process from both perspectives. I am not recommending specific strategies, only a background[21] for the

[20]Could this partly explain the fact that unlike great prose, great poetry, which draws heavily on the prosodic qualities of a language, has never been written in a later-acquired language?

[21]"A background," said the eminent British photographer Lord Snowdon, "has to be just this side of being something, and just the other side of being nothing" (*Time*, August 27, 1984).

"evenly suspended attention" (Freud, 1912, p. 111) mandatory for our work. My recommendations should therefore not be construed as rigid, or as necessary in all instances. At the same time I believe that in working with immigrant patients the following eight guidelines need to be kept in mind.

1. Certain matters regarding the analytic framework, especially the issue of punctuality for sessions, may be affected by cultural differences. The analyst must keep in mind that there might exist discrepancies in the experience of time[22] and in the conventions used to manage time between his and the patient's society of origin. What constitutes punctuality varies cross-culturally and even within subcultures (Pande, 1968; Lager and Zwerling, 1980; Antokoletz, 1993). Such awareness will enhance the analyst's empathic ability to distinguish between a culturally determined trivial lateness for sessions from a meaningful "attack on the analytic process" (Limentani, 1989, p. 252). Similar considerations might apply to the analysand's degree of deference and his ease or difficulty in negotiating a fee.

2. In a related vein, the analyst must help the patient disengage cultural from intrapsychic conflicts, however much the two might overlap. Analysands might seek to distance themselves from their own inner psychic lives, as well from the emerging wishes in the transference, by invoking cultural issues. Such use of "reality" as a defense must be vigilantly observed and interpretively handled, although the rapidity and depth of such uncovering must be guided by tact (Poland, 1975) and by regard for optimal distance (Bouvet, 1958; Akhtar, 1992a).

3. The analyst must watch for ways in which cultural differences affect transference and countertransference. In this context, the literature on biracial (black/white) analyses suggests that racial difference contributes not only to stereotyped transferences, resistance, and countertransference difficulty in maintaining an analytic stance (Fischer, 1971; Goldberg et al., 1974) but also to facilitating individual specific transference developments (Holmes, 1992).

---

[22]"For the East, relatively speaking, past, present, and future merge into one another; for the West they are discrete entities. For the East, experience in time is like water collected in a pool (stagnant perhaps); for the West, time is more like water flowing in a stream, and one is acutely aware that what flows away, flows away forever" (Pande, 1968, pp. 428–429).

4. The analyst might at times validate the immigrant's feeling dislocated in the mainstream culture before handling the material interpretively or for reconstruction. In cases where the analysand is the subject of significant prejudice, the use of such "mirroring" (Kohut, 1977) and affirming interventions can have healing effects of their own without compromising the analytic approach. Crucial here is the analyst's capacity to oscillate between a credulous and a skeptical listening attitude (Strenger, 1989) with the former yielding "affirmative interventions" (Killingmo, 1989) and the latter, interpretive interventions.

5. The analyst must recognize that mourninglike elements, integral to all analyses, carry greater significance in the treatment of immigrants. He must empathize with the immigrant analysand's loss of historical continuity and the need for its restoration. Patients' lapses into nostalgia must find respect and empathic counterresonance in the analyst, though clearly not at the cost of his overlooking the "screen" functions of such nostalgia (Sterba, 1940; Werman, 1977). Similarly, the analyst must permit the patient ample psychic space to dwell on his lost culture, while all the time keeping an eye on the covert resistance functions and transference messages in the material. A Peruvian woman in analysis, for instance, began talking about her beloved grandmother's funeral some years ago, soon after I had told her of my unavailability for a few days. The connection was obvious. I waited. Gradually, intricate details of Peruvian funeral rituals began to occupy her associations. Her sadness of a few minutes ago was replaced by a vigorous tone, as I found myself raptly absorbed in the material and felt enriched. Returning to a self-observing stance, I noted that she not only had defensively thwarted her pain but had also given me a parting gift. Interpretive intervention along this line deepened the material and facilitated the analytic work.

6. With patients who come from cultures in which a "familial self" (Yamamoto and Wagatsuma, 1980; Kakar, 1985; Roland, 1988) is the modal psychic structure, the analyst must be tolerant not only of seemingly inoptimal individuation (both in character and as a result of analytic work), but also of multiple transferences (with figures other than parental) and a profusion of close and distant relatives in the associative material. Taketomo's observations (1989)

regarding the Japanese analysand's "teacher transference" are significant in this context.

7. The analyst must squarely face the challenge posed by the patient's polyglottism to the task of analysis. On the one hand, the analyst must remain aware of the defensive and resistance aspects of the patient's use of a second language.[23] "This certainly allows for an emotional separation from the words of the birth language which retains the whole load of emotional, sensory, and perceptual vicissitudes linked to corporal experiences within the primary relationship" (Amati-Mehler et al., 1993, p. 71). Following Ferenczi's terse reminder (1911) of the difference in the use of obscene words in one's original language, as opposed to their use in an acquired language, many analysts (Buxbaum, 1949; Greenson, 1950) require that the patient speak, or at least utter some significant words, in his mother tongue. Others differ, including Lagache (1956); Benani (1985), who conducts analyses in both Arabic and French; and Amati-Mehler et al. (1993). They recommend that the analyst be more interested in the defensive uses of the second language, the forces underlying the emergence of a wish to speak in one's mother tongue, the rigid and apprehensive avoidance of the mother tongue, the meaning of wanting an analyst who does or does not speak one's mother tongue, and, in essence, the dynamic "moment when the analytic relationship reconfronts the themes linked to the mother tongue" (Amati-Mehler et al., 1993, p. 80). Viewed in this fashion, technical choices regarding language must derive not from rigid formulas but from the specific ebb and flow of the analytic material and the emotional ambience both of the relationship and of the particular session.

8. The analyst must bear in mind his relatively greater role as a new object in the treatment of immigrant patients. The similarities between the developmental process and the analytic process (Loewald, 1960; Blum, 1971; Fleming, 1972; Greenacre, 1975; Robbins, in Escoll, 1977; Schlessinger and Robbins, 1983; Burland, 1986; Settlage, 1992, 1993) may be more marked in such analyses. At the

---

[23]Freud's lapsing into Latin, *matrem nudam,* while describing at age forty-one the childhood memory of having seen his mother naked is a striking example of such defensive use of a second language (letter to Fliess, October 3, 1897, in Masson, 1985, p. 268).

same time, this should propel the analysis neither into unneeded supportive measures nor into manipulative attempts at superego alteration, however adaptive the latter might seem from the analyst's own cultural vantage point.

Now let me add a few words about conducting analysis as an immigrant analyst.[24] Important here is the analyst's own "third individuation" and continuing self-analysis. His ability to maintain cultural neutrality and optimal distance between his own hybrid identity and his native patient's relatively monolithic one is of course crucial. The analyst should be unobtrusively curious about the analysand's choice of analyst. However, the resulting skepticism should be tempered by the recognition that at times such choices may not have "deep" significance. (Only a third of my analytic patients have revealed significant conscious or unconscious motivations involving my being an immigrant in their choice of me as an analyst.) Similarly, he should scan the associative material for disguised and displaced references to his ethnicity/race, but not without an interest in their deeper psychic meanings for the patient or at the cost of considering every such reference as transferentially significant. His occasional wishes to intervene in his mother tongue have usually to be met with ego restraint and, more important, with further grief work and self-analytic inquiry into the specific dyadic transaction triggering such a wish. Finally, his deep conviction of the universality of fundamental psychic configurations and the ubiquitousness of human conflicts will help him hear and understand (both within himself and in his patients) "voices that are not necessarily unified and not always unifiable" (Amati-Mehler et al., 1993, p. 283), while continuing his analytic work. A tricky situation might appear when an immigrant (especially one from the analyst's native country) presents for analysis. On the one hand, the potential for "shared ethnic scotoma" (Shapiro and Pinsker, 1973) is heightened under such circumstances. On the other, the situation brings an immigrant analyst one

---

[24]In light of the fact that a large number of early British and American analysts were immigrants (and there still are many), the lack of literature in this area is surprising. Perhaps this omission can best be explained by the reluctance of mainstream psychoanalysis to deal with sociological, historical, and cultural factors in adult life in favor of an exclusive focus on the intrapsychic residues of early childhood.

step closer to his native-born colleagues who are exposed daily to such clinical pitfalls.

CONCLUDING REMARKS

A new identity will reflect the final consolidation into a remodeled ego identity of those selective identifications with the new culture which were harmoniously integrated or fitted in with the past cultural heritage. What actually ensues from the crisis of culture shock, if adequately solved, is a fecund growth of the self. What began as a threat to identity, mourning, and low self-esteem ends in a confirmation of both ego identity and self-esteem [Garza-Guerrero, 1974, p. 425].

Instead of positing unified, discrete cultures and nations to which we can all someday claim to belong, recent works suggest that we are bound to have fragmented allegiances, and dissonant voices within ourselves that name our world. This is not, I believe, some new version of the melting pot, for that assumes a synthesis which seems not only overly idealistic, but in fact undesirable. Instead of synthesis, there is the frightening but also exciting potential of multiplicity. Instead of completion or closure, there is the anxiety of partial identities as well as the challenge of ongoing process [Copelman, 1993, p. 79].

Throughout this paper my emphasis has been on the resolution of splitting of self and object world that tends to result from immigration. I have proposed that mending of such splits in four dimensions—drives and affects, space, time, and social affiliation—is what leads to a psychic rebirth, the emergence of a new and hybrid identity. Now I wish to offer some caveats in order to "soften" the proposed model and render it more realistic. (1) The four dynamic progressions described earlier are neither independent of each other nor exhaustive. There might be dimensions that I have failed to include or even recognize. (2) These developmental tracks do not have clear end points. The identity change of immigration continues to evolve throughout the life span. (3) The progression outlined here is characteristic only of uncomplicated cases where the capacity for intrapsychic separateness existed before immigration, where there was at least some choice in leaving one's country, and where the host country was more or less welcoming. However, in instances where the preimmigration character structure is problematic, where migration is forced and the possibility of revisiting the country does not exist, and where a good-enough holding environment is not found in the new land, the mourning necessary for such psychological advance might not be feasible. (4) Even the hybrid identity that emerges as a consequence of advance along these four lines is not a rocklike structure. Indeed, in certain psychosocial realms one or the other self-representation might continue to predominate. Searles' (1968) reminder that a healthy identity does not possess a monolithic solidity is pertinent here. Eisnitz's (1980) view of a well-functioning self as comprising of subsets of self-representations with variable proximity to affect, action, and fantasy also speaks to this point. (5) It is the intrapsychic meaning that various self- and object representations come to acquire—the resistance purposes (including defensive functions against drive derivatives) served by shifts in them, their adaptive aspects, and their vivid or concealed unfolding in the transference-countertransference axis—that is of technical significance of our work as analysts.

I will conclude with a poem and a final comment. The poem is entitled "A World without Seasons."

In the greedy flim-flam
For two worlds, we have lost the one in hand.
And now,
Like the fish who chose to live on a tree,
We writhe in foolish agony.
Our gods reduced to grotesque exhibits.
Our poets mute, pace in the empty halls of our conversation.
The silk of our mother tongue banned from the fabric
Of our dreams.
And now,
We hum the national anthem but our
Pockets do not jingle with the coins of patriotism.
Barred from weddings and funerals,
We wear good clothes to no avail.
Proudly we mispronounce our own names,
And those of our monuments and our children.
Forsaking the grey abodes and sunken graves of
Our ancestors, we have come to live in
A world without seasons.

Salman Akhtar

I wrote this poem of loss, linguistic cleavage, wistfulness, temporal dislocation, and cultural unbelonging in 1982, nine years after my immigration to the United States. Now, twelve years further down the road, I have authored this paper. While even the most cursory look at the two would readily reveal the advance in my own mourning process, there do remain unanswered questions. What does including this poem in the paper indicate? Continued pain or its mastery or some combination of both? More important, why is it that I expressed my pain of loss in poetry and my pride over mastery of this loss in prose? Is poetry the "language of the id" (Karpf, 1935) and prose that of the ego? If so, is my move from poetry to prose, in this context, a reflection of what Freud (1933) declared the goal of psychoanalysis to be: "Where id was there ego shall be"?

REFERENCES

ABRAHAM, K. (1911). On the determining power of names. In *Clinical Papers and Essays on Psychoanalysis*. New York: Brunner/Mazel, 1955, pp. 31–32.

AKHTAR, S. (1984). The syndrome of identity diffusion. *Amer. J. Psychiat.*, 141:1381–1385.

——— (1991). Three fantasies related to unresolved separation-individuation: a less recognized aspect of severe character pathology. In *Beyond the Symbiotic Orbit: Advances in Separation-Individuation Theory—Essays in Honor of Selma Kramer, M.D.*, ed. S. Akhtar & H. Parens. Hillsdale, NJ: Analytic Press, 1991, pp. 261–284.

——— (1992a). Tethers, orbits and invisible fences: clinical, developmental, sociocultural, and technical aspects of optimal distance. In *When the Body Speaks: Psychological Meanings in Kinetic Clues*, ed. S. Kramer & S. Akhtar. Northvale, NJ: Aronson, 1992, pp. 21–57.

——— (1992b). *Broken Structures: Severe Personality Disorders and Their Treatment.* Northvale, NJ: Aronson.

——— (1994). Object constancy and adult psychopathology. *Int. J. Psychoanal.*, 75:441–455.

AMATI-MEHLER, J., ARGENTIERI, S., & CANESTRI, J. (1993). *The Babel of the Unconscious: Mother Tongue and Foreign Languages in the Psychoanalytic Dimension*, trans. J. Whitelaw-Cucco. Madison, CT: Int. Univ. Press.

ANTOKOLETZ, J. C. (1993). A psychoanalytic view of cross-cultural passages. *Amer. J. Psychoanal.*, 53:35–54.

ANZIEU, D. (1976). L'enveloppe sonore du soi. *Nouvelle Rev. Psychanal.*, 13:161–179.

APPREY, M. (1993). The African-American experience: forced immigration and the transgenerational trauma. *Mind and Human Interaction*, 4:70–75.

BABCOCK, C. & CAUDILL, W. (1958). Personal and cultural factors in treating a Nisei Man. In *Clinical Studies in Culture Conflict,* ed. G. Seward. New York: Ronald Press.

BAKHTIN, M. M. (1986). *Speech Genres and Other Late Essays,* trans. V. W. McGee. Austin, TX: Univ. Texas Press.

—— (1990). *Art and Answerability,* trans. V. Liapunov. Austin, TX: Univ. Texas Press.

BALINT, M. (1959). *Thrills and Regressions.* London: Hogarth Press.

BAXTER, J. K. (1958). *In Fires of No Return.* London: Oxford Univ. Press.

BENANI, J. (1985). *Bilinguisme.* Paris: Denoel.

BERGMAN, A. (1980). Ours, yours, mine. In *Rapprochement: The Critical Subphase of Separation-Individuation,* ed. R. F. Lax, S. Bach, & J. A. Burland. New York: Aronson, 1980, pp. 199–216.

BLOS, P. (1967). The second individuation process of adolescence. *Psychoanal. Study Child,* 22:162–186.

BLUM, H. P. (1971). Transference and structure. In *The Unconscious Today,* ed. M. Kanzer. New York: Int. Univ. Press, 1971, pp. 177–195.

BOUVET, M. (1958). Technical variations and the concept of distance. *Int. J. Psychoanal.,* 39:211–221.

BRODY, E. B. (1973). *The Lost Ones: Social Forces and Mental Illness in Rio de Janeiro.* New York: Int. Univ. Press.

BURLAND, J. A. (1986). Illusion, reality, and fantasy. In *Self and Object Constancy,* ed. R. F. Lax, S. Bach, & J. A. Burland. New York: Guilford Press, 1986, pp. 291–303.

BUXBAUM, E. (1949). The role of a second language in the formation of ego and superego. *Psychoanal. Q.,* 18:279–289.

CASEMENT, P. J. (1982). Samuel Beckett's relationship to his mother-tongue. *Int. Rev. Psychoanal.,* 9:35–44.

—— (1991). *Learning from the Patient.* New York: Guilford Press.

CHENG, F. (1985). Le cas dre chinois. In *Du Bilinguisme.* Paris: Denoel.

CIORAN, E. M. (1982). *Storia e utopia.* Milan: Adelphi.

COLARUSSO, C. A. (1990). The third individuation: the effect of biological parenthood on separation-individuation processes in adulthood. *Psychoanal. Study Child,* 45:179–194.

COLES, R. (1967). *Children of Crisis: Vol. 3. The South Goes North.* Boston, MA: Little, Brown.

COPELMAN, D. (1993). The immigrant experience: margin notes. *Mind and Human Interaction,* 4:76–82.

DENFORD, S. (1981). Going away. *Int. Rev. Psychoanal.,* 8:325–332.

DEUTSCH, H. (1942). Some forms of emotional disturbance and their relationship to schizophrenia. *Psychoanal. Q.,* 11:301–321.

EISNITZ, A. (1980). The organization of the self-representation and its influence on pathology. *Psychoanal. Q.,* 49:361–392.

ERIKSON, E. H. (1950a). Growth and crises of the healthy personality. In *Identity and the Life Cycle.* New York: Int. Univ. Press, 1959, pp. 50–100.

—— (1950b). *Childhood and Society.* New York: Norton.

—— (1956). The problem of ego identity. *J. Amer. Psychoanal. Assn.*, 4:56–121.

—— (1958). *Young Man Luther: A Study in Psychoanalysis and History.* New York: Norton.

Escoll, P. J. (1977). Panel report: the contribution of psychoanalytic developmental concepts to adult analysis. *J. Amer. Psychoanal. Assn.*, 25:219–234.

—— (1992). Vicissitudes of optimal distance through the lifecycle. In *When the Body Speaks: Psychological Meanings in Kinetic Clues*, ed. S. Kramer & S. Akhtar. Northvale, NJ: Aronson, 1992, pp. 59–87.

Falk, A. (1974). Border symbolism. *Psychoanal. Q.*, 43:650–660.

Favazza, A. R. (1980). Culture change and mental health. *J. Operational Psychiat.*, 11:101–119.

Ferenczi, S. (1911). On obscene words. In *Final Contributions to the Problems and Methods of Psycho-Analysis.* London: Hogarth Press.

Fischer, N. (1971). An interracial analysis: transference and countertransference significance. *J. Amer. Psychoanal. Assn.*, 19:736–745.

Flegenheimer, F. (1989). Languages and psychoanalysis: the polyglot patient and the polyglot analyst. *Int. Rev. Psychoanal.*, 16:377–383.

Fleming, J. (1972). Early object deprivation and transference phenomena: the working alliance. *Psychoanal. Q.*, 21:23–49.

Freedman, A. (1956). The feeling of nostalgia and its relationship to phobia. *Bull. Phila. Assn. Psychoanal.*, 6:84–92.

Freud, S. (1912). Recommendations to physicians practising psycho-analysis. *S.E.*, 22:111–120.

—— (1917). Mourning and melancholia. *S.E.*, 14:237–258.

—— (1923). The ego and the id. *S.E.*, 19:1–66.

—— (1924). The dissolution of the Oedipus complex. *S.E.*, 19:173–179.

—— (1926). Inhibitions, symptoms and anxiety. *S.E.*, 20:87–174.

—— (1933). New introductory lectures on psycho-analysis. *S.E.*, 22:5–182.

Garza-Guerrero, A. C. (1974). Culture shock: its mourning and the vicissitudes of identity. *J. Amer. Psychoanal. Assn.*, 22:408–429.

Gay, P. (1988). *Freud: A Life for Our Time.* New York: Norton.

Ghalib, A. U. K. (1841). *Diwan-e-Ghalib.* New Delhi: Maktaba Jamia, 1969.

Goldberg, E. et al. (1974). Some observations on three interracial analyses. *Int. J. Psychoanal.*, 55:495–500.

Greenacre P. (1975). On reconstruction. *J. Amer. Psychoanal. Assn.*, 23:693–712.

Greenson, R. R. (1950). The mother tongue and the mother. *Int. J. Psychoanal.*, 31:18–23.

—— (1954). About the sound 'mm . . .'. *Psychoanal. Q.*, 22:234–239.

Grinberg. L. & Grinberg, R. (1989). *Psychoanalytic Perspectives on Migration and Exile*, trans. N. Festinger. New Haven, CT: Yale Univ. Press.

Haley, A. (1976). *Roots.* New York: Doubleday.

Hall, E. (1973). *The Silent Language.* New York: Doubleday.

Handlin, O. (1973). *The Uprooted: The Epic Story of the Great Migration That Made the American People.* Boston: Little, Brown.

HARRIS, M. (1993). Performing the other's text: Bakhtin and the art of cross-cultural hermeneutics. *Mind and Human Interaction*, 4:92–97.

HARTMANN, H. (1950). Comments on the psychoanalytic theory of the ego. In *Essays on Ego Psychology*. New York: Int. Univ. Press, 1964, pp. 113–141.

HERTZ, D. G. (1993). Bio-psycho-social consequences of migration: a multidimensional approach. *Israel J. Psychiat.*, 30:204–212.

HOFFMAN, E. (1989). *Lost in Translation: A Life in a New Language*. New York: Dutton.

HOLMES, D. E. (1992). Race and transference in psychoanalysis and psychotherapy. *Int. J. Psychoanal.*, 73:1–11.

JACOBSON, E. (1964). *The Self and the Object World*. New York: Int. Univ. Press.

KAKAR, S. (1985). Psychoanalysis and non-Western cultures. *Int. Rev. Psychoanal.*, 12:441–448.

KARPF, E. (1935). The choice of language in polyglot psychoanalysis. *Psychoanal. Q.*, 24:343–357.

KERNBERG, O. F. (1967). Borderline personality organization. *J. Amer. Psychoanal. Assn.*, 15:641–685.

——— (1975). *Borderline Conditions and Pathological Narcissism*. New York: Aronson.

——— (1976). *Object Relations Theory and Clinical Psychoanalysis*. New York: Aronson.

KILLINGMO, B. (1989). Conflict and deficit: implications for technique. *Int. J. Psychoanal.*, 70:65–79.

KLEIN, M. (1937). Love, guilt and reparation. In *Love, Guilt and Reparation and Other Works, 1921–1945*. New York: Macmillan, 1975.

KOHUT, H. (1977). *Restoration of the Self*. New York: Int. Univ. Press.

KRAMER, S. (1980). Residues of split-object and split-self dichotomies in adolescence. In *Rapprochement: The Critical Subphase of Separation-Individuation*, ed. R. F. Lax, S. Bach, & J. A. Burland. New York: Aronson, 1980, pp. 417–437.

KRAUT, A. M. (1990). Historical perspectives on refugee movements to North America. In *Mental Health of Immigrants and Refugees*, ed. W. H. Holtzman & T. H. Bornemann. Austin, TX: Univ. Texas Press.

KRISTEVA, J. (1988). *Etranges a nous memes*. Paris: Fayard.

KRYSTAL, H. (1966). Giorgio de Chirico: Ego states and artistic production. *Amer. Imago*, 23:210–226.

——— & PETTY, T. A. (1963). Dynamics of adjustment to migration. Proceedings III World Congress of Psychiatry. *Psychiat. Q. Suppl.*, 37:118–133.

LAGACHE, D. (1956). Sur le polyglottisme dans l'analyse. *La Psychoanalyse*, 1:167–178.

LAGER, E. & ZWERLING, I. (1980). Time orientation and psychotherapy in the ghetto. *Amer. J. Psychiat.*, 137:306–309.

LEWIN, R. A. & SCHULZ, C. (1992). *Losing and Fusing: Borderline Transitional Object and Self Relations*. Northvale, NJ: Aronson.

LICHTENSTEIN, H. (1961). Identity and sexuality: a study of their interrelationship in man. *J. Amer. Psychoanal. Assn.*, 9:179–260.

———— (1963). The dilemma of human identity: notes on self-transformation, self-objectivation and metamorphosis. *J. Amer. Psychoanal. Assn.*, 11:173–223.

LIMENTANI, A. (1989). *Between Freud and Klein: The Psychoanalytic Quest for Knowledge and Truth*. London: Free Association Books.

LOEWALD, H. W. (1960). On the therapeutic action of psychoanalysis. *Int. J. Psychoanal.*, 41:16–33.

MAHLER, M. S. (1958a). Autism and symbiosis: two extreme disturbances of identity. *Int. J. Psychoanal.*, 39:77–83.

———— (1958b). On two crucial phases of integration of the sense of identity: separation-individuation and bisexual identity. *J. Amer. Psychoanal. Assn.*, 6:136–139.

———— (1966). Notes on the development of basic moods: the depressive affect. In *Psychoanalysis: A General Psychology*, ed. R. Loewenstein, L. M. Newman, M. Schur, & A. J. Solnit. New York: Int. Univ. Press, 1974, pp. 152–168.

———— (1971). A study of the separation-individuation process. *Psychoanal. Study Child*, 26:403–424.

———— & FURER, M. (1968). *On Human Symbiosis and the Vicissitudes of Individuation*. New York: Int. Univ. Press.

———— & McDEVITT, J. B. (1980). The separation-individuation process and identity formation. In *The Course of Life*, ed. S. I. Greenspan & G. H. Pollack. Bethesda, MD: NIMH, 1980, pp. 395–406.

———— PINE, F. & BERGMAN, A. (1975). *The Psychological Birth of the Human Infant*. New York: Basic Books.

MASSON, J. M. (1985). *The Complete Letters of Sigmund Freud to Wilhelm Fliess.* Cambridge, MA: Harvard Univ. Press.

MISTRAL, G. (1971). *Selected Poems of Gabriela Mistral*, trans. D. Dana. Baltimore, MD: Johns Hopkins Univ. Press.

MODELL, A. (1965). On aspects of the superego's development. *Int. J. Psychoanal.*, 46:323–331.

NIEDERLAND, W. (1968). Clinical observations on the "survivor syndrome." *Int. J. Psychoanal.*, 49:313–315.

PANDE, S. K. (1968). The mystique of "Western" psychotherapy: an Eastern interpretation. *J. Nerv. & Ment. Dis.*, 146:425–432.

PARK, R. E. (1928). Human migration and the marginal man. *Amer. J. Sociol.*, 36:881–893.

PFEIFFER, E. (1974). Borderline states. *Dis. Nerv. System*, 35:212–219.

POLAND, W. (1975). Tact as a psychoanalytic function. *Int. J. Psychoanal.*, 56:155–163.

POLLACK, G. (1989). On migration—voluntary and coerced. *Ann. Psychoanal.*, 17:145–619.

RITSNER, M., MIRSKY, J., FACTOUROVICH, A. et al. (1993). Psychological adjustment and distress among Soviet immigrant physicians: demographic and background variables. *Israel J. Psychiat.*, 30:244–254.

ROLAND, A. (1988). *In Search of Self in India and Japan: Toward a Cross-Cultural Psychology*. Princeton, NJ: Princeton Univ. Press.

RUSHDIE, S. (1980). *Midnight's Children.* New York: Knopf.

SCHLESSINGER, N. & ROBBINS, F. P. (1983). *A Developmental View of the Psychoanalytic Process.* New York: Int. Univ. Press.

SEARLES, H. F. (1960). *The Nonhuman Environment in Normal Development and in Schizophrenia.* New York: Int. Univ. Press.

——— (1968). *My Work with Borderline Patients.* Northvale, NJ: Aronson.

SETTLAGE, C. (1992). On the treatment of preoedipal pathology. In *Beyond the Symbiotic Orbit: Advances in Separation-Individuation Theory—Essays in Honor of Selma Kramer, M.D.*, ed. S. Akhtar, & H. Parens. Hillsdale, NJ: Analytic Press, 1992, p. 351–367.

——— (1993). Therapeutic process in the restructuring of object and self constancy. *J. Amer. Psychoanal. Assn.*, 41:473–492.

SHAPIRO, E. T. & PINSKER, H. (1973). Shared ethnic scotoma. *Amer. J. Psychiat.*, 130:1338–1341.

SHENGOLD, L. (1989). *Soul Murder: The Effects of Childhood Abuse and Deprivation.* New Haven, CT: Yale Univ. Press.

SILBER, N. (1993). *The Romance of Reunion: Northerners and the South, 1865–1900.* Chapel Hill, NC: Univ. North Carolina Press.

STENGEL, E. (1939). On learning a new language. *Int. J. Psychoanal.*, 20:471–479.

STEPANSKY, P. E. (1988). *The Memoirs of Margaret S. Mahler.* New York: Free Press.

STERBA, E. (1940). Homesickness and the mother's breast. *Psychiat. Q.*, 14:701–707.

STRENGER, C. (1989). The classic and romantic visions in psychoanalysis. *Int. J. Psychoanal.*, 70:595–610.

TAKETOMO, Y. (1989). An American-Japanese transcultural psychoanalysis and the issue of teacher transference. *J. Amer. Acad. Psychoanal.*, 17:427–450.

TEJA, J. S. & AKHTAR, S. (1981). The psycho-social problems of FMG's with special references to those in psychiatry. In *Foreign Medical Graduates in Psychiatry: Issues and Problems*, ed. R. S. Chen. New York: Human Sciences Press, 1981, pp. 321–338.

TICHO, G. (1971). Cultural aspects of transference and countertransference. *Bull. Menn. Clin.*, 35:313–326.

VOLKAN, V. D. (1981). *Linking Objects and Linking Phenomena: A Study of the Form, Symptoms, Metapsychology and Therapy of Complicated Mourning.* New York: Int. Univ. Press.

——— (1993). Immigrants and refugees: a psychodynamic perspective. *Mind and Human Interaction*, 4:63–69.

WAELDER, R. (1930). The principle of multiple function: observations on multiple determination. *Psychoanal. Q.*, 5:45–62.

WANGH, M. (1992). Being a refugee and being an immigrant. *Int. Psychoanal.*, 1:15–17.

WARD, I. (1993). Examining Freud's "phantasy" about England. *Psychiatric Times*, 10:38.

WATERS, M. C. (1990). *Ethnic Options: Choosing Identities in America.* Berkeley: Univ. Calif. Press.

WERMAN, D. S. (1977). Normal and pathological nostalgia. *J. Amer. Psychoanal. Assn.*, 25:387–398.

WINNICOTT, D. W. (1953). Transitional objects and transitional phenomena: a study of the first not-me possession. *Int. J. Psychoanal.*, 34:89–97.

——— (1960). Ego distortion in terms of true and false self. In *The Maturational Processes and the Facilitating Environment.* New York: Int. Univ. Press, 1965, pp. 140–152.

——— (1963). The development of the capacity for concern. In *The Maturational Processes and the Facilitating Environment.* New York: Int. Univ. Press, 1965, pp. 71–82.

——— (1971). *Playing and Reality.* London: Tavistock.

WOLFF, E. (1994). Selfobject experiences: development, psychopathology, treatment. In *Mahler and Kohut: Perspectives on Development, Psychopathology and Treatment,* ed. S. Kramer & S. Akhtar. Northvale, NJ: Aronson, 1994, pp. 65–96.

YAMAMOTO, J. & WAGATSUMA, H. (1980). The Japanese and Japanese American. *J. Operational Psychiat.*, 11:120–135.

ZERUBAVEL, E. (1991). *The Fine Line: Making Distinctions in Everyday Life.* New York: Free Press.

1201 Chestnut Street, Suite #1503
Philadelphia, PA 19107

PSYCHOANALYSIS AND DYNAMICAL SYSTEMS THEORY: PREDICTION AND SELF SIMILARITY

The theory of dynamical systems (sometimes called chaos theory) has emerged in the past two decades as a powerful tool for understanding the evolution of complex systems. Attempts to develop psychoanalysis along the lines of nineteenth century physical science have proven unsatisfactory. The theory of dynamical systems provides another route for development. It suggests that prediction should aim at describing the overall evolution of systems and that the possibilities for such evolution are broader than classical theory suggested. It also shows that complex systems often involve structures that repeat basic features on several different levels of observation. This suggests a method for systematically exploring the overly rich data of psychoanalysis.

Two central problems for psychoanalysis as a systematic discipline are prediction and data collection. It has been argued that psychoanalysis should not attempt to emulate nineteenth century physical sciences. It should not attempt to predict the course of psychological events in the way physical scientists traditionally have tried to predict the evolution of physical systems (Galatzer-Levy and Cohler, 1990). However, insofar as psychoanalysis wishes to be a science in a traditional sense, the problem of prediction must be addressed (Waelder, 1963; Wallerstein, 1964; Sargent, Horwitz, Wallerstein, and Appelbaum, 1968).[1] Collection of meaningful, publicly communicable data is of central importance to systematic investigations.

Training and supervising analyst, child and adolescent supervising analyst on the faculties of the Chicago Institute for Psychoanalysis and the University of Chicago.

Submitted for publication September 12, 1994.

[1]The notion that prediction is a uniquely appropriate measure of scientific status is faulty. It ignores the historical background of the prestige inherent in the capacity of astrologers and astronomers to predict (Schaffer, 1993). It also ignores accepted scientific disciplines, such as plate tectonics in geophysics and meteorology, the study of which do not lead to satisfactory predic-

Dynamical Systems Theory

But the collection and communication of psychoanalytic data presents many challenging problems for psychoanalysts (Klumpner and Frank, 1991). In this paper I show how chaos theory, a new branch of mathematics, with profound implications for scientific investigation of many kinds, can help us address these problems.

Psychoanalysts, when functioning as investigators (as opposed to therapists), have often wanted to be physicists of the mind. But forced by the lack of success of Freud's original theoretical program of reducing psychology to physics, psychoanalysts have moved on to other goals (Galatzer-Levy and Cohler, 1990). The most valuable psychoanalytic contributions have been to clinical theory, the exploration of human meanings and motives (Klein, 1976), which has progressed over the course of nearly a century. Both systematic and clinical studies have enriched our picture of development. Today developmental descriptions usefully organize our discussions of motives and meanings. But, despite valiant efforts, theoretical work that does more than clarify psychoanalytic concepts is rare. Papers in which theoretical explorations lead to testable hypotheses are the rarest in the psychoanalytic literature (Edelson, 1983).

Many reasons have been suggested for this situation. Beginning with Freud (1920), analysts have pointed to the insufficiency of quantitative data and inadequate means of measurement of psychological forces and energies as the source of difficulty. Even precise mathematical formulations cannot predict outcomes without accurate measures of pertinent quantities. No one has found ways to quantitatively measure the forces and energies posited in metapsychology. For this reason alone we would not expect quantitative prediction to be possible in psychoanalysis.

Robert Waelder (1963) understood that something even more fundamental was amiss. His insight that prediction in complex systems was *intrinsically* difficult or impossible anticipates some of the findings of chaos theory. In the mid- 1970s many analysts repudiated traditional metapsychology and its underlying project of reducing

---

tion. Conversely, prediction and understanding are not necessarily linked. Many statistically excellent but meaningless correlations are found in economic data. The most highly predictive science, quantum electrodynamics, is said by its inventor to provide no understanding of the matters it so satisfactorily predicts (Feynman, 1985).

psychological phenomena to quantitative equations (Gill and Holtzman, 1976; Klein, 1976). Some analysts sought other forms of reduction than to energy and force, including the study of brain
mechanisms, ethology, developmental description, information processing and computer models, and revamping of older theories (e.g.
Peterfreund and Schwartz, 1971; Basch, 1976, 1985; Rosenblatt and
Thicksten, 1977; Bowlby, 1982; Galatzer-Levy, 1983, 1984, 1988,
1991; Reiser, 1984, 1985). Other analysts believed that reductionism
was an inappropriate tack altogether. Observing that the significant
contributions of psychoanalysis are its clinical theories, its understanding of people in terms of meanings and motives, they suggested
that attempts to replace metapsychology within a better reductionist
framework only diverted psychoanalysts' attention from areas to
which they might make real contributions (Ricoeur, 1970, 1977;
Schaefer, 1976, 1980, 1992; Klein, 1976; Spence, 1982, 1987, 1989).
The hermeneutic trend in psychoanalysis embraces this abandonment of the reductionist program (Ricoeur, 1970; Goldberg, 1988;
Galatzer-Levy and Cohler, 1990).

Chaos theory and related developments in mathematics suggest
that the received version of mathematical understanding in the physical sciences is unduly narrow. Some psychoanalysts have proposed
that the new mathematics of chaos theory may provide an alternate
route for psychoanalytic theory (Moran, 1991; Spruiell, 1993) based
on an emerging, richer version of theory. The theory has been applied to clinical material, and it has been used erroneously to attempt
to support the concept of free will (Pragier and Faure-Pragier, 1991),
based on the mistake of equating unpredictability with freedom.
Chaos theory concepts have been employed metaphorically to describe psychological functions (Grotstein, 1991). There have even
been discussions of the dangers of analysts adopting in chaos theory
another, inappropriate physicalistic model of human psychological
function. In this paper I explore two specific applications of chaos
theory to psychoanalysis.

CLASSICAL PREDICTION

Part of the pessimism about the reduction of psychological to physical phenomena originates in the received picture of the physical

sciences. The working paradigm of modern physical science is the work of Newton. This is not to say that the content of Newton's theories continues to be accepted, but his model for doing science was almost universally agreed upon in our society, by all but a handful of philosophers, until the last decade (Toulmin, 1990). In the Newtonian paradigm the scientist proposes theories which, ideally, can be encompassed in mathematical equations. Quantitative predictions based on solutions of these equations are compared to experimental findings to confirm or disconfirm the hypothesis. For example, based on his theory of universal gravitation, Newton predicted the moon's position in the heavens. The satisfactory comparison of his predictions with his (slightly fudged) observations were taken as confirmation of the underlying theory. Three centuries later, Feynman (1985), using essentially the same paradigm of scientific investigation, characterized his theory of quantum eletrodynamics as successful because it predicts atomic spectra correctly to seven decimal points.

Newton also introduced the main tool of theoretical physics, the differential equation, a mathematical statement that relates the rates of change of various aspects of a system to other aspects of a system. Saying the downward acceleration of a baseball is a constant is equivalent to writing a differential equation. The acceleration is the rate of change of velocity, which, in turn, is the rate of change of position. So if we call the height of the ball e, and indicate the rate of change by a dot above the variable (so that two dots indicate the rate of change of the rate of change), the equation for a falling baseball is

$$\ddot{e} = G$$

where G is the gravitational constant.

This is a "nice" equation in the sense that we can write down its solution explicitly:

$$e = {}^1\!/_2 G t^2 + kt + h$$

where k is the initial downward velocity and h the height from which the ball was thrown.

Thus given the time, initial position, and initial velocity we can explicitly compute the height of the ball from the ground. Fortunately for baseball fans, this is a very incomplete description of the motion of a baseball, which is influenced by complex frictional forces as well as the force of gravity. But it remains a good first approximation of the motion of a falling object.

Much of the physical world can be modeled using differential equations. Most of physical science consists in the search for appropriate differential equations to describe systems. This approach was so successful, and so dominated physical science, that by the 1950s, authors like Eugene Wigner (1960) began to puzzle about the "unreasonable effectiveness of mathematics" in describing the physical world. Wigner wondered how such simple ideas were so effective in clarifying a wide range of phenomena. The power of simple mathematical ideas in describing and predicting physical events is such that thinkers ranging from Descartes to Einstein believed it suggested an intelligence behind the manifest universe.

Retrospectively, the "unreasonable effectiveness" resulted, in part, because theoreticians systematically ignored phenomena that could not be encompassed using the mathematical methods of the time (Thom, 1975), and because scientists chose problems that are mathematically tractable (Gribbin, 1994). If one ignores those matters that are not well described by differential equations it is not surprising that these equations appear to describe all phenomena. For example, since surf and the physics of breaking water waves could not be satisfactorily treated using differential equations, "comprehensive" theories of water waves simply omitted these obvious physical events (Stoker, 1957). Researchers could maintain the illusion of the universal effectiveness of differential equations by ignoring phenomena for which they were ineffective.

PROBLEMS WITH THE CLASSICAL MODEL AND THE EMERGENCE OF NEW MODELS

Mathematicians, and occasionally physicists, struggled with what at first seemed to be technical problems in the theory of differential equations. By the middle of the last century, a type of differential equation called linear differential equations was very well understood. In mathematics the word *linear* means that the equation involves adding together derivatives that are multiplied by constants. None of the terms of a linear differential equation involve multiplying variables or their derivatives by one another. Mathematicians do not mean by linear that the solution is a line, is simple, proceeds step by step, or is easy to conceptualize. Nor do they mean by "nonlinear" anything mysterious, mystical, or related to "new age" thinking.[2] So that the equation for a spring

$$\ddot{e} - ke = 0$$

is linear because the position of the spring (e) and its derivatives do not appear as multiples of each other. In this case the solution is a sine curve. If we add a term for friction that is proportional to the square of the velocity the equation becomes,

$$\ddot{e} + k_1\dot{e}^2 - k_2e = 0$$

which is no longer linear because the velocity term appears multiplied by itself.

Linear equations are "nice" equations, that is, there are very well-developed methods for solving them and for describing their solutions. But they are "nice" in a much more fundamental way. Insofar as phenomena are governed by such equations the world is very predictable. If you change the initial conditions of a situation governed by a linear equation a little bit the change in the resulting behavior of the system is small. The idea that small changes in initial conditions cause small changes in outcome *seems* to correspond to our intuition. If I throw a ball slightly harder I expect it will go slightly further. When I press the accelerator of my car down a bit harder, I expect that the car will go a little faster.

---

[2]Only confusion results when analysts and others borrow technical terms from other disciplines and use them in ways suggested by their common rather than their technical usage. The term *nonlinear* has a particularly unfortunate history in this regard, having been taken up as part of psychobabble to refer to nonpropositional thinking. Chaos theory is in the process of suffering a similar fate. Confusion of technical terms and common usage leads to attributions to the mathematical theory that are not supported by its actual content.

This seeming intuition derives from systematically excluding data from experience. The fate of the pitched baseball may be very different depending on miniscule differences in its velocity (a strike vs. a home run) and the additional gasoline flowing to the engine may make the difference between the car moving or stalling. The more we look at the idea that our experience of the physical world corresponds to the behavior of linear differential equations, the more it becomes apparent that this belief is achieved by systematically excluding the data of daily experience (Thom, 1975). Many of our experiences with machines that suggest the linearity of the physical world result from the careful design of those machines to behave in a linear fashion within the range of intended function. Imagine if automobile brakes always "grabbed" (i.e., the braking force was not smoothly related to the pressure applied to the foot pedal).

Equations that are not linear are usually not "nice." Their solutions usually cannot be written down explicitly. In fact they tend to be intractable. For many years mathematicians did a bit of fudging to deal with this problem. They approximated the nonlinear equations by linear equations. Texts and teachers of elementary physics usually derive the equation for a pendulum's motion by first observing that the forces acting on the pendulum lead to the equation

$$\ddot{e} - k sine = 0$$

Then the instructor observes that for small

$$e \approx sin\ e$$

where $\approx$ means "is approximately equal to" so the equation becomes

$$\ddot{e} - ke \approx 0$$

This is useful because the instructor does not know how to solve the first equation and he does know how to solve the second. The only trouble is that the approximation is only good for small e and the difference between e and $sin\ e$ really becomes quite important without e getting very big at all (Figure 1).

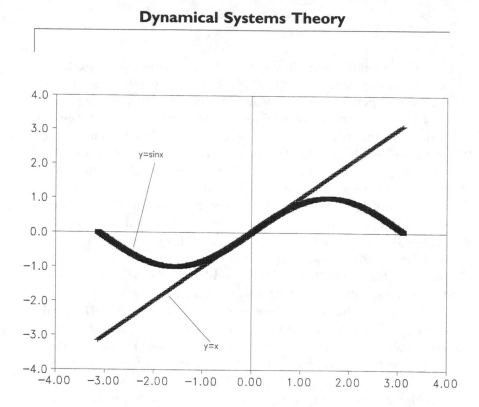

Figure 1. Comparison of $y = \sin x$ to $y = x$. Note the approximation $x \approx \sin x$ is only valid for small x.

The trend toward using linear approximation was so powerful that most physicists simply ignored phenomena that could not be approximated using these methods. At best they regarded the non-linear realm as unusual or representing "pathological" variations. As mentioned before, major texts about water waves simply did not refer to breaking surf (Stoker, 1957). This was because there was no satisfactory mathematical method to deal with surf, so the phenomenon was ignored. René Thom (1975) observed the wide areas of physical phenomena that were ignored for this reason. This tendency was reinforced because technologists tried to design equipment governed by linear equations because, of course, when you build something you want to be quite certain what it will do. This supports the impression that the world is governed by linear differential equations.

Robert M. Galatzer-Levy

Starting around 1970 computers became sophisticated enough that the properties of previously intractable equations could be explored through direct computation. It had been clear for many years that some of the linear approximations were simply inadequate, but until new methods became available to examine the actual properties of nonlinear equations these inadequacies tended to be treated as esoteric technical problems. With the development of the computer it became possible to study the world of differential equations, or dynamic systems as they came to be called, in an entirely different way. At first this required very sophisticated machines, but now the computers many of us have in our homes are quite adequate for some of these explorations. With the new computer technology it became possible to experiment with differential equations and to produce pictures of the phenomena associated with them. A new world opened in these studies, a world much closer to our complex everyday reality.

At the turn of the century the great French mathematician Henri Poincaré (see Kline, 1972) realized that the most important features of differential equations were not their solutions in numbers but the qualitative properties of their solution. Typical questions in this context were, Would the system go on forever repeating the same states? Would it gradually damp down? Would it go into ever larger oscillation? What form would these changes take? In the early 1960s another French mathematician, René Thom, systematically explored the qualitative features of an important class of differential equations. He discovered two important facts: first, contrary to expectations quite simple differential equations could lead to a variety of not only discontinuous solutions but solutions in which, for example, the final state of the system depends on its history. In addition, Thom was able to characterize all the types of abrupt changes that the kinds of differential equations he was studying could undergo. This new branch of mathematics was humorously labeled *catastrophe theory* because the abrupt changes can be thought of as catastrophes.

In this study of the simplest of these differential equations, Thom's model predicts that the system will be characterized by two distinct regimens with abrupt transitions between them (Figure 2). Unlike the situation that is described in older models, in which the current forces acting on the system completely determine its current

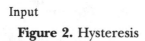

Figure 2. Hysteresis

status, the models of catastrophe theory predict that the immediate past history of the system will shape the system's further evolution. If the system is in one state it will tend to remain in that state until it abruptly shifts to the other. This property, called hysteresis, is actually observed in a number of physical systems. We can observe it easily when trying to push an object over a rough surface. If the object is not yet moving, considerable force may be necessary to get it going. But once in motion the same amount of force will cause considerably more change in position. This corresponds rather nicely to observations of psychological situations of ambivalence, in which we see sharp, abrupt transitions from one state to another, and at any given moment, we do not feel confident that the sum of the current forces determines the person's position but rather that we are dealing with a phenomenon, like the snapping of a twig, as a person moves from one position to another (Galatzer-Levy, 1976).

Catastrophe theory models lead to specific predictions about how quantitative changes in intensity result in qualitative changes in a system's activity. At a minimum, the ideas of catastrophe theory lead us to recognize that apparently abrupt and discontinuous changes in a system are real phenomena and that qualitative changes in systems can arise from quantitative change.

Jerome Sashin (1985; Sashin and Callahan, 1990) began to explore the systematic application of catastrophe theory to psychoanalysis. His work went beyond generalized theorizing. On the basis of the study of a catastrophe theory model he predicted a previously unobserved phenomenon. The prediction has not been verified because there has been no attempt to do so. But Sashin's contribution is unique in the specific prediction of a qualitatively new psychological phenomenon on the basis of the study of dynamical systems.

Despite its many promising features, catastrophe theory focused both on too narrow a range of systems and too specific qualitative features about systems to bring out the full fruit of the exploration of the qualitative features of differential equations. The extreme claims about the power of catastrophe theory by some of its students led to its being held in some ill repute. In recent years a broader group of ideas about dynamical systems has come to prominence.

In the 1970s, mathematicians started experiments of a kind they had never done before. Massive computational power made it possible to sit at a computer terminal and "fool around" with the graphic solution of differential equations. The resulting graphical displays are not only mathematically interesting, they are aesthetically pleasing. The result was an empirically richer picture of the possibilities for dynamical systems. With this richer picture came a change in the "intuition" of students about the possibilities of these systems.

Greater computational power also made it possible to actually test the accuracy of predictions by using classical models from physics. These models often did not work well, particularly in predicting real world phenomena. Practical long-term weather forecasting, for example, was a complete bust. This failure occurred despite certainty that basic physical principles on which the forecast were made were correct. Study showed that the problem was not in the underlying physical concepts but in striking computational features of the equations generated from the physical theory. Very small changes in the initial conditions of the system resulted in dramatic changes in predictions.

Dynamical Systems Theory

An important repercussion of the idea that small changes should result in small consequences is that minor errors of measurement should not greatly affect the predictions derived from the equations. It we put another straw on the camel's back, we expect the animal to bend very slightly further. The straw that breaks the camel's back, takes us out of the world of linear differential equations. The result is a seeming paradox. A system may be entirely deterministic in the sense that its future evolution is completely set by its features at a certain time, there are no random or probabilistic effects, the rules governing its evolution are entirely known, and still it remains impossible to predict its development (Kilert, 1993). This situation arises whenever small changes in initial conditions result in large changes in the final state of the system and hence any prediction about the system.

The problem is not resolved by making more precise initial measurements. The nature of the divergence of the predictions that results from the small differences in initial condition is such that it grows very rapidly no matter how small the initial deviation, so that while more precise specifications of initial condition does result in better predictions, the investment in precision required to improve the predictions slightly becomes ever larger.[3] This phenomenon came to be known as the "butterfly effect" because it can be shown in studies of long-term weather forecasting that a butterfly flapping (or not flapping its wings) in Sumatra, could result in a 5 degree change in the temperature in Atlanta 8 days later. In the late 1970s, a British research group used equations of atmospheric dynamics that were known to be correct to make long-term weather forecasts. The results were appalling. They predicted five inches of snow in London in mid-July. Close inspection of the equations they used showed that their solutions were highly unstable in response to initial conditions. Even though the weather was completely determined and there was no thought of supernatural forces affecting it, it would be theoretically impossible to predict weather in detail over the long range. Thus chaos theory was born out of the recognition of what

---

[3]In this context the phrase *growing very rapidly* has the specific meaning that the effect of a change in initial values on later conditions can be described as greater than some mathematical function of this change and the elapsed time. These findings often demonstrate that the difference in effect is exponentially related to the initial difference.

could not be done. Any reasonably complex system is not predictable in its details over a long period of time. Certainly the human mind is at such a level of complexity.[4]

CHAOS LEADS TO A NEW VISION OF PREDICTION

But our knowledge that the prediction of five inches of snow in London in midsummer is wrong, points to the statistical or probabilistic prediction that we *can* make about system. Though we cannot predict the weather in London at any moment, we can predict temperatures by time of year and time of day with a fair degree of confidence since their average values and the variation likely to occur around those average values are well known. In some sense, complex systems seem to often "average out." Such statistical prediction is also possible for matters involving people, including their psychological function. While such a prediction may be of more value to psychoanalysts than is generally believed, it remains distant from the type of statement we would like to be able to make about people.

At the same time that students of dynamic systems were discovering that certain kinds of predictions were not possible, explorations of dynamical systems showed that a different and surprising kind of prediction was possible. In complex systems researchers were often able to discern well-defined tendencies within the system. The evolution of systems tended toward stable overall patterns with characteristic form, even though the precise position of the system was almost entirely unpredictable. Many of the phenomena that had previously been described as the results of probability and chance, that somehow mysteriously resulted in a reliable statistical distribution, could now be reinterpreted as samplings of deterministic phenomena of this new, and hitherto unappreciated, type. These stable configurations of system evolution, called attractors of dynamical systems, have been classified with increasing clarity and thoroughness (e.g., Ott, 1993). The description of an ever-widening range

---

[4]Given these results, the ideas of meaning and motive take on new predictive value for a complex system. Such systems can often, in some sense, be said to be "trying" to do something, including trying to remain stable. In this instance prediction becomes more possible.

of attractors has been the principal technical result of the study of chaos.

We are familiar with attractors where the particle follows a given path or at least asymptotically approaches a stable orbit. For example, if we observe the motion of a pendulum we see a regular progression of oscillations which either repeat, or if we wait long enough, are gradually damped to no oscillation by the air's friction. Similarly, oscillators into which additional energy is placed, say by a driving motor, evolve toward relatively easily described paths of motion.[5] One of the major findings of research into apparently chaotic systems is the existence of "strange" attractors. At first the motions in systems seem random and disorganized, but after many repetitions we can see they tend toward a particular pattern, not in the sense that they settle down, but rather that the apparently wild shifts in the motion represent tendencies to complex but representable patterns.

As discussed earlier, attempts at long-term weather prediction have proved impossible. Lorenz (1963) used the equations of fluid dynamics to try to attempt to make long-term weather predictions based on the flow of the atmosphere as warm air rises and cold air falls. His computations showed him a new kind of attractor, one in which the observer could not predict the immediate movements of the system and yet an overall pattern emerged (for an accurate, more detailed discussion, that demands little mathematical background, see Stewart [1989]).

The observation of these more complex forms of attractors, was the first step in which students of dynamical systems discovered order in chaos. For psychoanalysts these systems of attractors are important as possible models of the ways systems can evolve. Currently much work is being devoted to the question of how empirical data can be matched with a known catalog of attractors (Morrison, 1991). The description of analytic data in a fashion that allows comparison with

[5]The description of these paths of motion is often facilitated by representing them graphically or by other means than depicting position as a function of time. For example, one might more clearly depict important features of a planetary orbit by showing the relationship between velocity and position rather than position and time. Selection of appropriate graphic representation often results in deep insights into the nature of dynamical systems (Abraham and Shaw, 1992) and allows one to recognize regularities that would not be evident from direct observation or simple plotting of variables.

known descriptions of chaotic systems may result in the enrichment that comes when predictions can be made.

Let us look briefly at what behavior under the influence of a strange attractor might look like in the analytic situation:

A woman sought analysis for recurrent depressions accompanied with the desperate search for a man who would make things right. She believed that by associating with a handsome and brilliant man her own reputation would be enhanced. The man would give her ideas that would let her finish a doctoral dissertation. Sexual acts would magically give her his power. The analyst's every remark was, at best, useless and often made matters worse by reminding her of her problems. The patient seemed "set off" into inconsolable crying by the analyst's requests for clarification or the session's ending before the patient had come to a resolution of the topic she was discussing. All the people she discussed were petty, exploited her, and were the object of her angry contempt. The patient lived in a rageful world. Her major problem was to avoid being utterly plunged into its abyss. As had happened in previous psychotherapies the patient experienced dramatic improvement in her symptoms after a few months of treatment.

Now she appeared as a competent student. She had an ironic sense of humor and was compassionately interested in others. She sought men who liked and were interested in her. She thought of the men she had so desperately wanted as "narcissistic jerks." In the sessions she worked with the analyst's interpretations. She could step back from and examine transference phenomena. She no longed panicked when the analyst did not immediately understand her or when it was necessary to continue a topic into another session. Her major concerns were those of a moderately inhibited student, combined with a mild fear that her depression would return.

The analytic process centered on the movement between these two seemingly distinct states, which occurred in response to the analyst's availability. For example, the analyst's summer vacation regularly resulted in a panicked depression in the patient, and his sustained presence gradually relieved that depression. Early in the analysis it was as if the patient had two distinct, noninteracting modes of psychological function. The transition between these modes occurred abruptly and for reasons that were obscure to the patient. The *total* pattern of the patient's psychological functioning was like a strange attractor with two basins. When in either basin the behavior was consistent (if distressing). At least as interesting as these stable states was that there were two quite distinct major modes of functioning. The process of transition between the two required understanding.

The vision of prediction that derives from the modern study of dynamical systems is different from classical prediction, in which investigators attempt to predict the state of a system at a given later time from data about the system's earlier state. Haley's comet was predicted to appear in the heavens at a particular location and on a particular date based on previous observations of the comet and Newton's theory of gravitation. In the new vision of prediction the investigator predicts patterns of change and stability of systems, not their moment-to-moment status. This type of prediction corresponds better to what we are often interested in when conducting psychoanalytic investigations than the older predictive goals. For example, we care much less which side of a predicament an obsessional person adopts at a particular moment than that he is likely to oscillate between two opposing positions. We are not so interested in the momentary level of regression of a patient as in his or her capacity to move in and out of regressed states in the course of the analysis. Predicting the form of evolution of a system is thus closer to our clinical interests than classical prediction was.

SELF SIMILARITY

A second kind of order emerged through the study of chaotic systems. As we have seen, even in simple dynamical systems initial conditions can grossly modify the results in the evolution of the system. Minute changes in the initial state of a system can result in qualitatively different regimes. A group of mathematicians inquired about the form of the sets of initial conditions that resulted in various regimens. Although some progress was made on this problem early in the century, the findings were abstruse and seemed to be mathematical oddities. With the development of increased computational capacity, the explorations of these odd and fascinating structures became possible. Among them the Mandelbrot set has become the object of extensive study and fascination because of its aesthetic, as well as mathematical features. The set is constructed as follows: Starting with a point in the plane a simple rule is used to move to another point. The same rule is again applied at the new point and this process is repeated indefinitely. For some initial points this process results in a series of moves that makes an ever more distant path; starting from other points the path is bounded. The initial point is colored or not depending on whether the path generated from the point is bounded or not. This coloring resulted in a startling map (see Figure 3).

The resulting patterns are things of extraordinary beauty. They have many unusual mathematical properties, but in a sense their most remarkable property is how strikingly they resemble natural forms like the spray of surf, or coastlines (Barnsley, 1988).

For the purposes of this paper we will concentrate on just one feature of these structures, which are called fractals. Looking at a series of pictures of progressively enlarged segments of the Mandelbrot set we observe a remarkable property (see Figures, 4, 5, 6).

Using computers of only the power now common at home, we can zoom in on a small segment of the set—here is a picture of the small square outlined in the previous diagram (Figure 4).[6] At first it gives the appearance of a wholly different landscape, but look carefully, there appear to be little Mandelbrot sets in it, the overall landscape is quite different.

Let's zoom in on another edge from this picture, again, magnifying a thousand times, a new and distinct landscape but it too is populated by the Mandelbrotlike sets (see Figure 5).

This process can be continued indefinitely (see Figure 6) for we can compute the configuration of the Mandelbrot set to any magnification we wish. The result is always the same. At every level, new and distinctive landscapes appear but at every level of magnification we find yet more Mandelbrotlike sets.

When a set is magnified and reveals an image of itself again it is called "self similar." Self similarity may be precise, exactly the same set may reappear on each magnification, or it may be with modification, as is the case with the Mandelbrot set where the new images are similar but distinct from the original ones. Self similarity is not only an inordinately powerful mathematical concept but is at the core of much of what we think of as natural phenomena.

---

[6]The fractal graphics in the paper were easily created on a home computer using the shareware program Fractint, Version 15.0 (Tyler, Wegner, Peterson, and Branderhorst, 1990).

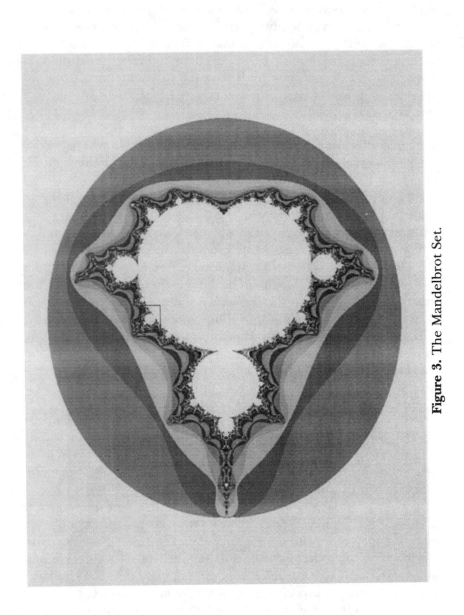

Figure 3. The Mandelbrot Set.

Figure 4. Magnified Area from Figure 3.

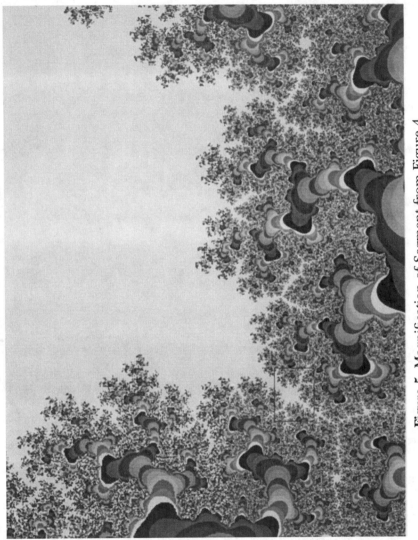

Figure 5. Magnification of Segment from Figure 4.

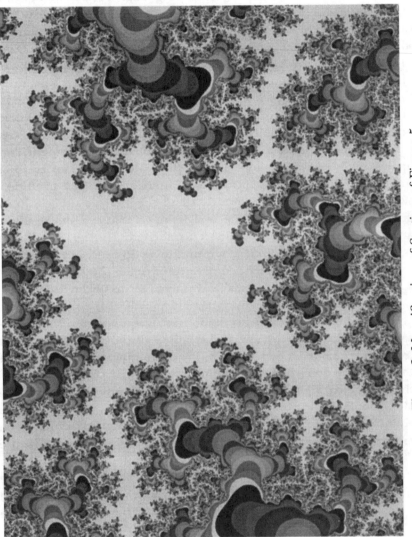

Figure 6. Magnification of Section of Figure 5.

How is the concept of self similarity of value to psychoanalysis? The central research problem for psychoanalysis is how to explore psychoanalytic work in an empirically rigorous but psychologically rich fashion. Any systematic investigation of psychoanalytic material quickly reveals that hours can be spent untangling a few minutes interchange between analyst and patient. Investigators like Dahl (1974, 1988; Dahl, Teller, Moss, and Trujillo, 1978; Dahl, Kachele, and Thomä, 1988) have found it useful to explore psychoanalytic material on the level of words and sentences. Others like Luborsky (Luborsky and Crits-Cristoph, 1990) and Gill (1982) examine single analytic hours in great detail. Yet, while we all agree that analysis can only go on in the details of the interaction between patient and analyst, most analysts believe that psychoanalytic processes are best understood in terms of much longer intervals, and that to understand an analysis we want to understand the analytic process in its entirety. Thus investigating the analytic process appears to result in an enormous practical difficulty. To understand material well one must study it in depth, but to capture analytic processes one must explore material over extended periods of time. The study of analyses would then appear intractable simply in terms of the time necessary to investigate an analysis thoroughly.

Self-similar structures are important to empirical research because one can study the essential qualities of those structures or at least some major aspects of them, by examining small portions of them microscopically. In an absolutely self-similar structure, such as the Sierpinski triangle,[7] looking at any subunit gives one essentially all the information that can be had about the system. For more complex systems, such as the Mandelbrot set, important qualitative elements can be found from arbitrarily small samples, but there are differences between the various levels of Mandelbrotlike set within the Mandelbrot set. In natural occurring phenomena, for example the growth of plants, obviously more significant samples are needed to be able to see the underlying structure. As Fibinacci realized three

---

[7]To make a Sierpinski triangle start with an equilateral triangle. Draw lines connecting the midpoint of each side. This produces four new triangles. Color the central triangle, the one with the down pointing apex and repeat the process for the remaining three triangles. Continue this process, ad infinitum. The result is the Sierpinski triangle. Note, except for size, each upward pointing triangle is identical to all the others.

centuries ago, basic patterns of a tree's growth can be inferred from very small amounts of data about the underlying pattern of growth, and indeed on the computer we can grow things like ferns and trees, not to mention realistic looking coastlines, on the basis of specifying very few elementary features of the system.

Psychoanalytic material commonly has strikingly self-similar aspects. Here is an example taken from the analysis of an obsessional patient, looked at on several levels of magnification:

Years Long Magnification

Mr. A. first exhibited obsessional symptoms at age 7 following his mother's remarriage. To others he seemed withdrawn, but in fact his time was spent fretfully counting objects in his room and worrying that something was missing. His symptoms were relieved by psychotherapy. Although he remained inhibited and rather meticulous he did fairly well until he was 11. Then, apparently in response to puberty and tension in his mother's marriage, he again became symptomatic. He worried that he had not completed homework assignments and was so concerned to eat properly that charting the nutritional values of food disrupted his life. There were other less prominent obsessional symptoms. The patient interrupted a second round of psychotherapy by a conscious decision to suppress obsessional symptoms, which he did until he left home to go to college. In the uncontrolled, sexually liberal atmosphere of the college dormitory Mr. A. became anxious and severely obsessional, worried that the cafeteria food might be bad for him, that he had prepared for his class inadequately, and that he was dressed improperly.

Months Long Magnification

Mr. A. wanted very much to "do it (the analysis) right." In part based on his past therapeutic experience, he approached analysis by expressing jarringly intense feelings. Both the patient and the analyst regarded these expressions as deeply authentic and representative of major analytic progress. Often, after several weeks of talking in this way, the affect intensified further. At these times the patient demanded the analyst's direct assistance in managing the affects and, partly because the analyst did not know how to help him, became increasingly anxious. He feared going mad. This sense lasted for at most a couple of days. Then the patient regularly first became angry at the analyst for failing to manage some aspect of the analysis correctly (such as billing for missed sessions), and subsequently became enmeshed in sorting out the failing (e.g., developing elaborate moral arguments for and against charging for missed sessions).

Analytic Hours

Mr. A. began most analytic sessions with some topic in mind about which he felt strongly. He developed it at some length. (For example, he would speak with rage about his father's departure.) After the topic had been engaged, the analyst often made a defense interpretation. (The analyst agreed that the patient was angry with his father for leaving but wondered whether his more immediate anger wasn't addressed to the analyst, who had recently returned from vacation.) At first the patient engaged the interpretation vigorously. ("You always think it's you. You, you, you! But you don't think it's you enough not to go on your stupid vacations!) Then the patient began a much less affective, more intellectual discussion of why he had used the identified defense. ("I wonder why I use displacement so much. That is the right term, isn't it?") As the session grew to a close the patient often felt it was urgent that he finish the discussion before the session's end. Frequently he tried to get out a few more sentences as he left. The analyst encouraged him to leave and assured him that the topic could be addressed more fully in the next session.

Analytic Minutes

Attending closely to the patient's speech revealed that it was marked by constant interruptions either as dysfluencies or interrupting self-reference.

"I hate my er father because he uh he uh he uh he kinda doesn't, I mean didn't. I find this hard to say. He didn't uh do uh. He didn't do what sorta what er he needed to do for me. Pause. You're going to ask what that was. Well he didn't uh do it! I can't describe it. You know! He kinda didn't!

The obsessional phenomena described here are familiar to all analysts. No one of them is more essential than another. They can all be seen as aspects of the same self-similar structure view with differing temporal magnification.

Robert M. Galatzer-Levy

Applying the idea of self-similarity to psychoanalytic data addresses one of the major problems of research—the intractable amount of data. The work of people like Dahl (1988), Bucci (1993), and Luborsky (Luborsky and Crits-Christoph, 1990), confirms our own clinical experience, that psychoanalytic data is highly self-similar. This is not alien from the common clinical observation that careful enough attention to the material of single hours or even fragments of hours commonly reveals the way in which patients approach and work out difficulties on a larger scale, inside and outside of analysis. The "red thread" of a patient's interests and concerns and style, is detectable in very small fragments of material because of the widely redundant self-similarity of the personality. It is common clinical wisdom that certain points in the analysis are particularly revelatory of the patient's underlying approach to issues; for example, the hour in which the first dream is reported, or the hour in which a termination date is set seem to be particularly informative. From this model, we can interpret this as reflecting times when we have chosen the right framework which reveals a major chunk of a self-similar structure at once, rather as though we had hit upon an area of the Mandelbrot set which was just right to include in one of the interior Mandelbrot sets.[8]

It remains uncertain to what extent it will be possible to find in the self similarity of analytic materials elements that can be used to explore those materials in an empirically rigorous yet manageable fashion. However, we welcome the discovery of a conceptual framework that allows us to think about and formulate the clinical wisdom that much more information is packed into brief fragments of an analysis than one might guess. Currently the discovery of self similarity in natural systems occurs when researchers familiar with patterns of fractals and chaos recognize these patterns, often in the visual representation of their data. There is much to recommend analysts playing around with these ideas, which is easy to do using home computers, to get a feel for this sort of material. More sophisticated

---

[8]It should be noted that other factors may contribute to making such a strategy effective. The redundancy of analytic material mentioned earlier may reflect aspects of ordinary human communication in which the importance of getting across affectively important ideas results in their being communicated with high redundancy.

means of recognizing fractal patterns and chaos are emerging and these will be applicable to psychoanalytic data.

CONCLUSION

Over the past quarter century, a new paradigm of scientific explanation has arisen that encompasses a far wider range of phenomena than had been capable of exploration using the Newtonian model of scientific explanation, including its variations such as quantum mechanics and relativity theory. This group of explanations, which has globally been referred to as chaos theory, involves a qualitative as opposed to quantitative view of nature, and addresses questions in a wholly different fashion from a traditional physical science investigation. Its capacity to deal with the intricacies of nature and the complexities of real systems, albeit in a different way from classical physics, makes it a promising candidate for a different form of theorizing than has previously been used in psychoanalysis. It brings a whole different meaning to the concept of prediction, one that is more in tune with what we as analysts expect, involving stable configurations over time as the unit of study, as opposed to instantaneous snapshots of static situations. In categorizing the sources of configuration that are mathematically possible, it may well suggest an empirically explorable psychoanalytic hypothesis. A major feature of aspects of chaotic systems, the quality of self similarity, suggests empirical approaches to the analytic situation that relieve us of the burden of analyzing intractable amounts of data, while still carrying the possibility of addressing genuinely psychoanalytically significant ideas.

Recent developments in the study of dynamical systems provide new ideas abut the description and understanding of the evolution of complex systems. They provide a new vision of what it means to predict the evolution of a system. Rather than predicting that the system will be in a particular state at a particular moment in time, they predict the form that this evolution is likely to take. This description of a system's evolution is close to the kind of prediction most interesting to psychoanalysts, who wish to understand characteristic patterns of response and coping rather than specific instances. The study of dynamic systems also suggests a theoretical grounding for the common psychoanalytic view that much information is contained in even small fragments of analytic material.

REFERENCES

ABRAHAM, R. & SHAW, C. (1992). *Dynamics: The Geometry of Behavior,* 2nd ed. Redwood City, CA: Addison-Wesley.

BARNSLEY, M. (1988). *Fractals Everywhere.* Boston: Academic Press.

BASCH, M.F. (1976). The concept of affect: A re-examination. *J. Amer. Psychoanal. Assn.,* 24:759–777.

——— (1985). Interpretation: Toward a developmental model. In *Progress in Self Psychology,* Vol 1, ed. A. Goldberg. New York: Guilford, pp. 33–42.

BOWLBY, J. (1982). Attachment and loss: Retrospect and prospect. *Amer. J. Orthopsychiatry,* 52:664–678.

BUCCI, W. (1993). The development of emotional meaning in free association. In *Hierarchical Conceptions in Psychoanalysis,* ed. J. Gedo & A. Wilson. New York: Guilford.

DAHL, H. (1974). The measurement of meaning in psychoanalysis by computer analysis of verbal contexts. *J. Amer. Psychoanal. Assn.,* 22:37–57.

——— (1988). Frames of mind. In *Psychoanalytic Process Research Strategies,* ed. H. Dahl, H. Kächele, & H. Thömä. New York: Springer-Verlag.

——— TELLER, V.; MOSS, D.; & TRUJILLO, M. (1978). Countertransference examples of the syntactic expression of warded-off contents. *Psychoanal. Q.,* 47:339–363.

——— KÄCHELE, H., & THOMÄ, H., eds. (1988). *Psychoanalaytic Process Research Strategies.* New York: Springer-Verlag.

EDELSON, M. (1983). Is testing psychoanalytic hypotheses in the psychoanalytic situation really impossible? *Psychoanal. Study Child,* 38:61–112.

——— (1988). *Psychoanalysis: A Theory in Crisis.* Chicago: Univ. Chicago Press.

FEYNMAN, R. (1985). *QED.* Princeton, NJ: Princeton Univ. Press.

FREUD, S. (1920). Group psychology and the analysis of the ego. *S. E.,* 18.

GALATZER-LEVY, R. (1976). Psychic energy: a historical perspective. *Annual of Psychoanal.,* 4:41–64. New York: Int. Univ. Press.

——— (1983). The regulatory principles of mental functioning. *Psychoanal. & Contemp. Sci.,* 6:255–289.

——— (1984). Perspectives on the regulatory principles of mental functioning. *Psychoanal. & Contemp. Thought,* 6:255–289.

——— (1988). On working through: A model from artificial intelligence. *J. Amer. Psychoanal. Assn.,* 36:125–151.

——— (1991). Computer models and psychoanalytic ideas. *Soc. Psychoanal. & Psychother. Bull.,* 6:23–33.

——— & COHLER, B. (1990). The developmental psychology of the self: A new worldview in psychoanalysis. *Annual Psychoanal.,* 18:1–43.

GILL, M. (1982). *Analysis of Transference, Vol 1: Theory and Technique*. New York: Int. Univ. Press.

———— & HOLZMAN, P., eds. (1976). *Psychology versus Metapsychology. Psychol. Issues,* Monogr. 36. New York: Int. Univ. Press.

GOLDBERG, A. (1988). *A Fresh Look at Psychoanalysis*. Hillsdale, NJ: Analytic Press.

GRIBBIN, J. (1994). The prescient power of mathematics. *New Scientist,* 14:256.

GROTSTEIN, J. (1991). Nothingness, meaninglessness, chaos, and the "black hole": III. Self- and interactional regulation and the background presence of primary identification. *Contemp. Psychoanal.,* 27:1–33.

KILERT, S. (1993). *In the Wake of Chaos*. Chicago: Univ. Chicago Press.

KLEIN, G. (1976). *Psychoanalytic Theory: An Exploration of Essentials*. New York: Int. Univ. Press.

KLINE, M. (1972). *Mathematical Thought from Ancient to Modern Times*. New York: Oxford Univ. Press.

KLUMPNER, G. & FRANK, A. (1991). On methods of reporting clinical material. *J. Amer. Psychoanal. Assn.,* 39:537–551.

LORENZ, E. (1963). Deterministic nonperiodic flow. *J. Atmos. Sci.,* 20:130–137.

LUBORSKY, L. & CRITS-CHRISTOPH, P. (1990). *Understanding Transference the CCRT Method*. New York: Basic Books.

MORAN, M.G. (1991). Chaos theory and psychoanalaysis. *Internat. Rev. Psychoanal.,* 18:211–222.

MORRISON, F. (1991). *The Art of Modeling Dynamic Systems: Forecasting for Chaos Randomness and Determinism*. New York: Wiley.

OTT, E. (1993). *Chaos in Dynamical Systems*. New York: Cambridge Univ. Press.

PRAGIER, G. & FAURE-PRAGIER, S. (1990). Un siecle apres l'Esquisse: nouvelles metaphores? Metaphores du nouveau? *Revue francaise de psychanalyse,* 54:1395–1529.

PETERFREUND, E. & SCHWARTZ, J. (1971). *Information, Systems, and Psychoanalysis: An Evolutionary Biological Approach to Psychoanalytic Theory. Psychol. Issues,* Monogr. 24/25. New York: Int. Univ. Press.

REISER, M. (1984). *Mind, Brain, Body: toward a Convergence of Psychoanalysis and Neurology*. New York: Basic Books.

———— (1985). Converging sectors of psychoanalysis and neurobiology: Mutual challenge and opportunity. *J. Amer. Psychoanal. Assn.,* 33:11–34.

RICOEUR, P. (1970). *Freud and Philosophy*. New Haven, CT: Yale Univ. Press.

———— (1977). The question of proof in Freud's psychoanalytic writings. *J. Amer. Psychoanal. Assn.,* 25:835–872.

ROSENBLATT, A. & THICKSTUN, J. (1977). *Modern Psychoanalytic Concepts in General Psychology, Psychol. Issues,* Monogr. 42/43. New York: Int. Univ. Press.

SARGENT, H.; HORWITZ, L.; WALLERSTEIN, R.; & APPELBAUM, A. (1968). *Prediction in Psychotherapy Research: A Method of the Transformation of Clinical Judgments into Attestable Hypotheses. Psychol. Issues,* Monogr. 2/6. New York: Int. Univ. Press.

SASHIN, J. (1985). Affect tolerance—A model of affect-response using catastrophe theory. *J. Soc. & Biolog. Structures.,* 8:175–202.

———— CALLAHAN, J. (1990). A model of affect usisng dynamical systems. *Annual Psychoanal.,* 18:213–231.

SCHAFER, R. (1976). *A New Language for Psychoanalysis.* New Haven, CT: Yale Univ. Press.

———— (1980). Narration in the psychoanalytic dialogue. *Crit. Inqu.* 7:29–53.

———— (1992). *Retelling a Life: Narration and Dialogue in Psychoanalysis.* New York: Basic Books.

SCHAFFER, S. (1993). Comets and the world's end. In *Predicting the Future,* ed. L. Howe & A. Wain. Cambridge, U.K.: Cambridge Univ. Press.

SPENCE, D. (1982). On some clinical implications of action language. *J. Amer. Psychoanal. Assn.,* 30:169–184.

———— (1987). *The Freudian Metaphor.* New York: Norton.

———— (1989). Narrative appeal vs. historical validity. Scientific Symposium: Clinical controversies and the interpersonal tradition. *Contemp. Psychoanal.,* 25:517–524.

SPRUIELL, V. (1993). Deterministic chaos and the sciences of complexity. *J. Amer. Psychoanal. Assn..* 41:3–44.

STEWART, I. (1989). *Does God Play Dice?* New York: Blackwell.

STOKER, J. (1957). *Water Waves. Pure and Applied Mathematics Series.* New York: Wiley.

THOM, R. (1975). *Structural Stability and Morphogenesis: An Outline of a General Theory of Models.* Reading, PA: Benjamin.

TOULMIN, S. (1990). *Cosmopolis: The Hidden Agenda of Modernity.* New York: Free Press.

TYLER, B.; WEGNER, T.; PETERSON, A.; & BRANDERHORST, P. (1990). Fractint, Version 15.0 (a computer program). Cleveland, OH: Compuserve Information Service.

WAELDER, R. (1963). Psychic determinism and the possibility of predictions. *Psychoanal. Q.,* 32:15–42.

WALLERSTEIN, R. (1964). The role of prediction in theory building in psychoanalysis. *J. Amer. Psychoanal. Assn.,* 12:675–691.

WIGNER, E. (1960). The unreasonable effectiveness of mathematics in the natural sciences. *Comm. Pure & Appl. Math.,* 13:1–14.

180 North Michigan Avenue
Suite 2401
Chicago, Illinois 60601
e-mail: gala@midway.uchicago.edu or 72255.1101@compuserve.com

THE EARLY HISTORY OF BOUNDARY VIOLATIONS IN PSYCHOANALYSIS

The notion of professional boundaries is a relatively recent addition to psychoanalytic practice. Freud and his early disciples indulged in a good deal of trial and error as they evolved psychoanalytic technique. The study of these early boundary violations illuminates the study of the evolution of the concepts of transference and countertransference. The recent publication of the correspondence between Freud and Jung, between Freud and Ferenczi, and between Freud and Jones has provided us with extraordinary insights into the boundary transgressions that occurred in the early days of psychoanalysis. The boundary violations of the analytic pioneers have contributed to the legacy inherited by future generations of analysts. Institutional resistance to addressing these difficulties in contemporary psychoanalytic practice may relate in part to the ambiguities surrounding boundaries in the training analysis itself.

In a letter of December 31, 1911, Freud wrote to Jung about a matter of concern:

> Frau C— has told me all sorts of things about you and Pfister, if you can call the hints she drops "telling"; I gather that neither of you has yet acquired the necessary objectivity in your practice, that you still get involved, giving a good deal of yourselves and expecting the patient to give something in return. Permit me, speaking as the venerable old master, to say that this technique is invariably ill-advised and that it is best to remain reserved and purely receptive. We must never let our poor neurotics drive us crazy. I believe an article on "counter-transference" is sorely needed; of course we could not publish it, we should have to circulate copies among ourselves [McGuire, 1974, pp. 475–476].

Bessie Walker Callaway Distinguished Professor of Psychoanalysis, The Menninger Clinic; training and supervising analyst at the Topeka Institute for Psychoanalysis.

The author gratefully acknowledges the helpful comments of John Kerr, Eva Lester, and Arnold Richards. Submitted for publication October 11, 1994.

Over eighty years later, similar concerns about countertransference enactments and sexual boundary violations still haunt the psychoanalytic profession. However, unlike Freud, most contemporary analysts agree that discussions of countertransference no longer require a shroud of secrecy. Our journals regularly publish scientific contributions that feature frank disclosures of countertransference issues in the author's work. The analyst's countertransference enactments are widely regarded as both inevitable and useful to the process (Chused, 1991; Jacobs, 1993; Renik, 1993; Gabbard, 1994a). The concept of countertransference enactment is of considerable heuristic value in understanding boundary violations. Most instances of such transgressions involve a countertransference action that reflects in part the patient's efforts to actualize a transference fantasy (Chused, 1991). In other words, the enactment is a joint creation involving a fit between what the patient has projected and the analyst's preexisting self- and object-representations (Gabbard, 1995).

Much of the enthusiasm for the concept of enactment, however, stems from the assumption that enactments are *partial*, and that the analyst catches himself before the enactment leads to a gross and unethical boundary violation. Indeed, enactments occur on a continuum from subtle changes in body posture to frank sexual involvement with the patient. More profound enactments that involve significant violations of the analytic frame are less likely to appear in the pages of our journals and in the public forums of our scientific meetings.

Every psychoanalytic institute and society has seen the ravages of severe boundary violations. It would be tempting for us to attribute these transgressions to a small handful of corrupt colleagues who suffer from severe character pathology and a propensity to act rather than reflect. This point of view allows all of us to projectively disavow our own vulnerability to boundary violations and see them as the province of a few who have nothing in common with the rest of us. The facts are otherwise. In my experience both of evaluating and treating individuals charged with sexual misconduct and consulting with psychoanalytic groups about problems in their midst, it has become increasingly clear that all of us are potentially vulnerable. Indeed, institutes and societies are often paralyzed in their efforts to take action when such cases surface because the analyst charged is frequently a leader in the field both locally and nationally. Even essentially ethical and apparently well-analyzed practitioners may suffer impairments in crucial ego functions (such as judgment) when they are in the midst of extraordinary life crises such as divorce, the death of family members, or other personal catastrophes.

Rather than condemn and moralize about our impaired colleagues, we need to acknowledge and examine our universal vulnerability that is inextricably linked to the psychoanalytic enterprise. A reasonable starting point is to study the nature of boundaries and boundary violations among the psychoanalytic pioneers as they struggled to define the parameters of the analytic relationship.

HISTORY OF BOUNDARY VIOLATIONS

The notion of professional boundaries is a relatively recent addition to psychoanalytic practice. Freud and his early disciples indulged in a good deal of trial and error as they evolved psychoanalytic technique. Like Josef Breuer, early analysts were often struck by the power of transference in the clinical setting. However, unlike Breuer, who managed to extricate himself from the treatment of Anna O. before disaster occurred, most of Freud's circle persevered in their efforts to define technique and were sucked into the vortex of a host of major boundary transgressions. As Freud noted to Oscar Pfister in a 1910 letter, "The transference is indeed a cross" (Freud/Pfister, 5.6.1910; Meng and Freud, 1963, p. 39). As Freud's 1911 letter to Jung suggests, the concept of countertransference had not been systematically elaborated, so many of the early analysts lacked a solid conceptual framework with which to understand what was happening to them.

The study of boundary violations in the history of psychoanalysis is also a study of the evolution of the concepts of transference and countertransference. As Haynal (1994) has pointed out, issues of transference, countertransference, and the optimal level of emotional involvement by the analyst were all forged in the context of triangles involving boundary violations. First, Freud was the third party in the Carl Jung–Sabina Spielrein relationship, and shortly thereafter he was enlisted to solve the problematic involvement between Sandor Ferenczi and Elma Palos. Finally, a similar triangle was created when Freud analyzed Loë Kann, Ernest Jones' common-law wife.

The recent publication of the correspondence between Freud and Jung, between Freud and Ferenczi, and between Freud and Jones has provided us with extraordinary insights into the underlying dynamics of boundary transgressions in psychoanalysis. The point I wish to stress is that we read these cases not only because of their historical value or because they provide titillating gossip. Rather, we study them to attempt to understand the fundamental vulnerabilities of the psychoanalytic situation. It is essential for analysts to study the history of boundary violations in order to avoid reenacting violations with their own patients.

Early on in his work with hysterical patients, Breuer and Freud (1893–1895) learned that patients often fall in love with the analyst and expect reciprocal feelings: "In not a few cases, especially with women and where it is a question of elucidating erotic trains of thought, the patient's cooperation becomes a personal sacrifice, which must be compensated by some substitute for love. The trouble taken by the physician and his friendliness have to suffice for such a substitute" (p. 301). As Friedman (1994) has stressed, the psycho-analytic situation involves an element of seduction. The patient is misled by the analyst to expect love while the analyst tends to provide an ill-defined substitute for love. Friedman acknowledges the fact that the exact nature of that substitute remains difficult to define.

The vicissitudes of love or substitutes thereof continued to haunt Freud throughout the development of psychoanalytic technique. Recognizing the power of transference love to keep the patient in-volved, he noted in a letter to Jung that "the cure is effected by love" (McGuire, 1974, pp. 12–13). A little over a month later, a comment in the Vienna Psychoanalytic Society minutes seemed to confirm this view: "Our cures are cures of love" (*Minutes I*, p. 101, cited in Haynal, 1994).

It should be noted that Freud's understanding of transference was rather rudimentary in the early years of psychoanalysis around the turn of the century. In his description of a patient who developed a wish that Freud would kiss her, he noted that such wishes arise through the phenomenon of transference, which he attributed to a "false connection" (Breuer and Freud, 1893–1895, p. 302). This was the first appearance of the term *transference* in Freud's writing. In an extensive footnote in his discussion of Frau Emmy Von N., Freud (Breuer and Freud, 1893–1895) elaborated on this notion. His meaning clearly refers to a rather restricted view of transference, namely, that when an unconscious connection is not apparent to the patient, the patient manufactures a conscious or false connection to explain his or her behavior. This idea that transference love was inherently "false" or "unreal" was revisited at some length twenty years later in "Observations on Transference-Love" (1915). A careful reading of that paper suggests that Freud has shifted his view a bit to acknowledge that there were "real" aspects of transference love in addition to those that stem from unconscious connections with significant figures in the patient's past. In his struggle to clarify whether transference love was similar to or different from love outside the analytic setting, Freud appeared somewhat equivocal (Schafer, 1993; Gabbard, 1994b), lending an air of ambiguity to the issue that persists to this day. In a postscript to the Dora case (1905), Freud recognized that transference involved an erotic reenactment of a drama from the past. If the past experiences had been of a positive nature, the patient would be suggestible and compliant in the transference. If they were negative, the patient would be resistant (Kerr, 1993).

Because Freud was influenced by figures like Bernheim, many observers have assumed that he regarded persuasion and suggestion as the active ingredients in psychoanalytic treatment. His position was actually a bit more complex. Freud regarded erotic attraction as the true vehicle of cure, whether the cure was by hypnotic suggestion or psychoanalysis. In his correspondence with Jung, he explained that the patient's erotic attraction to the analyst accounts for the patient's efforts to understand and listen to the analyst's interpretations.

Much of Freud's conceptual struggles with transference, countertransference, and the concept of love can be glimpsed in his correspondence with Jung. In 1904 Jung had analyzed Sabina Spielrein, his first analytic case, for a period of approximately two months (Kerr, 1993). Following termination, Jung and Spielrein developed a working relationship in Jung's psychology lab. When she became a beginning medical student, the friendship between the two intensified. In the midst of this friendship, there were intermittent interviews that revived aspects of the analyst–patient relationship. Four years after the original two-month treatment, Jung and Spielrein engaged in a tempestuous love affair that culminated in Spielrein's attacking Jung and drawing blood when he attempted to end the relationship. Her reaction to Jung's efforts to end the relationship is a common development in such affairs and has been described as "cessation trauma" (Gutheil and Gabbard, 1993).

The relationship between Jung and Spielrein is a cogent illustration of why so many "posttermination" romantic relationships present the same difficulties as those concurrent with analysis. Although the treatment had officially ended, the transference and countertransference dimensions of the relationship continued with a life of their own outside the formal confines of treatment.

Whether or not the two actually engaged in sexual intercourse cannot be established with certainty from the written correspondence and other documents remaining. However, the details of "did they or didn't they" are relatively unimportant in light of the pervasively boundariless relationship that characterized the period of years following the analysis. The scholarship of Kerr (1993) and Carotenuto (1982) has reconstructed the Jung–Spielrein relationship in sufficient detail that much can be gleaned from the data about the development of such relationships.

As Jung's first patient, Spielrein was extraordinarily special. Infatuated with Jung, Spielrein went on to attend medical school and move into the role of student and friend. The two of them soon began to view each other as soulmates who were connected through mystical, telepathic bonds. Jung, who was prone to an interest in the occult and parapsychology, became convinced that Spielrein and he could know what the other was thinking without verbalizing their thoughts. In most cases of sexual boundary transgressions in which there is intense infatuation between analyst and patient, the first boundary to disintegrate is the intrapsychic boundary between self and object. In other words, there is a kind of psychological fusion experienced prior to actual physical involvement.

Another striking feature of many instances when analyst and patient become sexually involved is that the analyst appears to take the transference at face value. In many cases it appears that the analyst approaches the relationship with one particular patient as though the transference feelings are an exception to other situations of erotic attachment in the analytic setting. It is noteworthy in this regard that Jung pointedly avoided using the term *transference*, even after the appearance of Freud's Dora case in 1905 (Kerr, 1993). He eventually used the term *transposition* instead. There is something inherently humbling in the psychoanalytic notion of transference. The analyst must reluctantly acknowledge that forces are at work that transcend his or her irresistible magnetism. If any other analyst were sitting in the chair, similar feelings would appear. Analysts who fall in love with their patients and become sexually involved with them often are longing to believe in the exclusivity of the patient's feelings toward them and cannot bear the pain of thinking that feelings of such intensity could be transferred to someone else (Gabbard, 1994a).

Another dimension to the Jung–Spielrein relationship was brought to light by Kerr's (1993) analysis of the psychological themes in their scientific writings of the time. Jung was preoccupied with the image of mothers as terrible and destructive. Apparently because of his intense resentment of his own mother, Jung dwelled on an image of a malevolent, incestuous mother who was responsible for man's mythological descent into hellish nether regions. At the same time, Spielrein's writings were concerned with the inevitability of destruction as a necessary accompaniment of love. As Kerr notes, "The two texts, his and hers, adjoin each other like severed halves of a forgotten conversation" (1993, p. 333).

Spielrein's long-neglected thesis deserves further study. Sexuality, in her view, always harbors an implicit threat of dissolution of the self. From a Darwinian perspective, the survival of the species is superordinate to the narcissistic investment of the individual. Part of her notion that sexuality involved dissolution was based on her view that fusion rather than pleasure might be the aim of the sexual act, a hypothesis that psychoanalytic clinicians often confirm in the exploration of patients' sexual fantasies. The ego, then, must always resist sexuality at some level, and Spielrcin suggested that the defenses against disintegration of the self most often took the form of inner images of death and destruction.

Connections between sexuality and death had been observed for centuries—in legend (Tristan and Isolde), in colloquial phrases (the French term for orgasm, *le petit mort*), and in verse (the poetry of John Donne). However, the particular connection forged by Spielrein seems to have had specific significance for the relationship she was involved in with her former analyst. Indeed, the relationship nearly destroyed Jung's career and brought Spielrein to the edge of despair. Jung tried to rationalize his way out of his unethical behavior by explaining to Spielrein's mother in a lengthy letter that he had never charged her a fee for his services: "I could drop my role as doctor the more easily because I did not feel professionally obligated, for I never charged a fee. . . . But the doctor knows his limits and will never cross them, for he is *paid* for his troubles. That imposes the necessary restraints on him" (Carotenuto, 1982, p. 94). In another letter he stated to Spielrein's mother that: "I have always told your daughter that a sexual relationship was out of the question and that my actions were intended to express my feelings of friendship" (Carotenuto, 1982, p. 94). He later described his correspondence with Frau Spielrein to Freud as a bit of "knavery."

Many modern cases of sexual boundary transgressions by analysts in some ways confirm Spielrein's thesis. One of the most striking aspects is the self-destructiveness in the analyst's behavior that is obvious to everyone but the analyst. It appears that the analyst unconsciously enacts a masochistic scenario that relates to childhood wishes of self-sacrifice. Often the details of this fantasy involve a wish to "go out in a blaze of glory" by acting on incestuous wishes for a parent and experiencing the retaliation and punishment for a forbidden act of pleasure. Sexual consummation with the patient offers a special means of actualizing such motives. The destructiveness inherent in libido may have been particularly apparent to Jung and Spielrein because of their constant struggle with boundaries and boundary violations.

Jung ultimately enlisted Freud's help in extricating himself from the situation, but Spielrein continued to feel that she had been used and deeply hurt by the relationship.

Freud later observed a similar turn of events in Ferenczi's treatment of Elma Palos. Ferenczi had previously analyzed Elma's mother, Gizella, a married woman, with whom he had had an affair. Ferenczi fell in love with Elma in the course of analyzing her and finally persuaded Freud to take over the case (Dupont, 1988; Haynal, 1994). What ensued was a rather remarkable series of boundary violations.

Freud made regular reports to Ferenczi regarding the content of the psychoanalytic treatment of Elma and specifically kept Ferenczi informed of whether or not Elma continued to love him. He also sent confidential letters to Gizella about Ferenczi. Ultimately, Ferenczi took Elma back into analysis, but she ended up marrying an American suitor while Ferenczi himself married Gizella in 1919.

It is clear from the Freud–Ferenczi correspondence (Brabant, Falzeder, and Giampieri-Deutsch, 1994) that Freud found the situation messy and highly disconcerting. In a letter to Gizella Palos in 1911, he made the following observation: "The main difficulty is this: Does one want to build this alliance for life on concealing the fact that the man has been her mother's lover in the fullest sense of the word? And can one rely on the fact that she will take it well and overcome it in a superior manner when she knows it?" (pp. 320–321).

Freud did not try to disguise his feeling that Gizella should be the preferred choice for Ferenczi. In his correspondence with Ferenczi, Freud made a number of disparaging comments about Elma, including that she had been spoiled by her father's lavish attention and was incapable and unworthy of love. Dupont (1994) explained this departure from neutrality as a reflection of Freud's concern that a young wife and children might have distracted Ferenczi from his devotion to the psychoanalytic "cause."

Ferenczi appeared to gain some perspective on the situation when he interrupted Elma's treatment and sent her to Freud. On New Year's Day of 1912, he noted to Freud, "I had to recognize that the issue here should be one not of marriage but of the treatment of an illness" (Brabant et al., 1994, p. 324). Later, on January 20 of the same year, he wrote to Freud, "I know, of course, that by far the greatest part of her love for me was father transference, which easily takes another as an object. You will hardly be surprised that under these circumstances I, too, can hardly consider myself a bridegroom any longer" (Brabant et al., 1994, p. 331).

The relationship between intrapsychic boundaries and the erotized countertransference of Ferenczi appears to have been pertinent. He viewed Elma as psychotic or near-psychotic and was fascinated by the apparent fusion of self and object and by her openness to him. A similar phenomenon occurred later in Jung's career with Toni Wolff, but the chapter in Jung's memoirs describing this episode was expurgated (Kerr, 1994, personal communication).

Despite this messy situation, Freud subsequently took Ferenczi into analysis, a process that occurred in a series of three meetings (some of which occurred during two- to three-week holidays) between 1914 and 1916. Actually, a more informal analysis took place in the summers of 1908 and 1911. He appeared to have some misgivings about jeopardizing the friendship by introducing an analytic relationship but nevertheless proceeded (Haynal, 1994). The ensuing analysis (I use the term advisedly) took place after Freud and Ferenczi had voyaged to America together for the Clark University lectures. On the ship they had done a bit of mutual analysis. Blum (1994) suggests that their subsequent periods of analytic work should be thought of as "analytic encounters." Freud would write Ferenczi letters addressed "Dear Son" in which he would suggest that they would have two analytic sessions a day while also having a meal together. Hence, the analytic relationship occurred in parallel with other relationships, including mentor-student, close friends, and traveling companions (Blum, 1994). Moreover, Freud apparently wished that Ferenczi would ultimately marry his daughter (Haynal, 1994).

To be fair to Freud, this blurring of the roles of friend and analysand had caused him to undertake Ferenczi's analysis with some trepidation. Indeed, the correspondence between the two of them suggests that Ferenczi placed a great deal of pressure on Freud to analyze him and that he finally capitulated only after expressing considerable reluctance. On the other hand, he had analyzed Max Eitingon during strolls through the streets of Vienna, and Kata Levy during summer holidays at her brother's house (Dupont, 1994). Ferenczi apparently entered the analytic process with bitterness that was masked by obsequious loyalty. In a letter of May 23, 1919, he made the following comment to Freud:

> from the moment you advised me against Elma, I developed a resistance against your person, that even psychoanalysis could not overcome, and which was responsible for all my sensitivities. With this unconscious grudge in my heart, I followed, as a faithful "son," all your advice, left Elma, came back to my present wife, and stayed with her in spite of innumerable attempts in other directions [quoted in Dupont, 1994, p. 311].

After the analysis, Ferenczi continued to have resentment toward Freud because he had not analyzed his negative transference. Freud defended himself in a letter of January 20, 1930: "But you forget that this analysis took place 15 years ago, and at that time we were not at all sure that this kind of reaction must happen in all cases. At least, I was not. Just think, taking our excellent relationship in account, how long this analysis would have had to go on to allow the manifestation of hostile feelings to appear" (quoted in Dupont, 1994, p. 314).

In that same letter, Freud seems to have come to the recognition that analyzing someone with whom one has a preexisting friendship is ill-advised: "I notice that, in connecting things with our analysis you have pushed me back into the role of the analyst, a role I never would have taken up again toward a proven friend" (quoted in Dupont 1994, p. 314).

Although Ferenczi renounced his wish to marry Elma, he went on to engage in other forms of boundary violations that were also problematic. After his break with Freud, deeply bitter about his "training" analysis, he began to experiment with mutual analysis. With four female American patients, he tried analyzing them for an hour followed by an hour in which he would let the patient analyze him. Entries in his diary at this time demonstrated his confusion of his own need to be healed with that of his patients: "Our psyche, too, is more or less fragmented and in pieces, and, especially after expending so much libido without any libido-income, it needs such repayment now and again from well-disposed patients who are cured or on the point of being cured" (Dupont, 1988, p. 13). A few months after this January 17, 1932, entry, he abandoned mutual analysis, apparently because of the obvious problems with confidentiality. If he stuck to the basic rule of saying whatever came to his mind, he would be telling one of his patients about the personal disclosures of other patients.

Another form that Ferenczi's wish to be loved and healed took was an effort to provide his patients with the love they had not received from their parents (Gabbard, 1991). He saw his patients as victims of actual sexual trauma and abuse, and he sought to repair that damage. His technique included kissing and hugging the patient like "an affectionate mother" who "gives up all consideration of one's own convenience, and indulges the patient's wishes and impulses as far as in any way possible" (Grubrich-Simitis, 1986, p. 272). He had grown up in a family with many siblings and never felt he received the love that he wished to have from his mother (Grubrich-Simitis, 1986; Blum, 1994). She was apparently harsh and cold, in Ferenczi's view, and he thus tried to give to his patients what he himself did not receive as a child (Gabbard, 1991). This pattern is a common one in which analysts desperately attempt to provide love to their patients, with whom they are overidentified as victims of mistreatment. When the love is not reciprocated, or the patient does not improve, the analyst may escalate his loving efforts in a defensive attempt to avoid his growing resentment and hatred of the patient (Searles, 1979; Gabbard, 1991, 1994c).

On December 13, 1931, Freud expressed his growing concern about Ferenczi's technique in a famous letter:

> we have hitherto in our technique held to the conclusion that patients are to be refused erotic gratifications. . . . where more extensive gratifications are not to be had milder caresses very easily take over their role. . . . A number of independent thinkers in matters of technique, will say to themselves: why stop at a kiss? Certainly one gets further when one adopts 'pawing' as well, which after all doesn't make a baby. And then bolder ones will come along who will go further to peeping and showing—and soon we have accepted in the technique of psychoanalysis the whole repertoire of demiviergerie and petting parties, resulting in an enormous increase of interest in psychoanalysis among both analysts and patients. . . . Father Ferenczi gazing at the lively scene he has created will perhaps say to himself: maybe after all I should have halted my technique of motherly affection *before* the kiss [Jones, 1957, p. 164].

Clearly, Freud was already aware of the well-known "slippery slope" phenomenon in which boundary violations that begin as minor and apparently harmless gradually escalate to major violations that are damaging to the patient in the process.

Freud was involved in another boundariless menage à trois when he undertook the analysis of Loë Kann. Ernest Jones and Kann had been living as husband and wife (although not technically married) since shortly after they met in London around 1905. Jones' comment in a June 28, 1910, letter to Freud suggests she apparently came to

him as a patient: "Now I have always been conscious of sexual at-
tractions to patients; my wife was a patient of mine" (Paskauskas,
1993). In 1908, when Jones moved to Canada, Kann joined him
there.

Jones' reputation in Canada was marred by rumors that he was
recommending masturbation to patients, sending young men to
prostitutes, and even showing obscene postcards to patients to stimulate their sexual feelings. A former patient threatened to charge him
with having had sexual relations with her, so Jones paid her $500 in
blackmail money to prevent a scandal. He explained this situation
in some detail to James Jackson Putnam in a letter of January 13,
1911 (Hale, 1971). He clarified that he had seen this patient four
times for medical purposes and that there was no truth to her claim
that she had had intercourse with him. She had also attempted to
shoot him, so he was protected by an armed detective. Jones described the patient as a hysterical homosexual woman who, after
leaving his care, went to a woman doctor of strict moralistic views
with whom she fell in love. Jones inferred that his female colleague
had encouraged the former patient to bring charges against him.
He felt he was foolish to pay the blackmail money because it would
be harmful either way. In a footnote to the Freud–Jones correspondence, Paskauskas (1993) suggests that the female doctor was Emma
Leila Gordon, an extremely religious member of the Women's Chris-
tian Temperance Union who frowned on alcohol consumption and
loose living.

Concerned that he would lose Kann, Jones asked Freud if he
would analyze her. She was afflicted with a number of somatic symptoms as well as morphine addiction. In 1912, Kann and Jones moved
to Vienna so Freud could begin his treatment of her. Freud was
evidently quite taken by her; he told Ferenczi in a letter of June 23,
1912, that "I will be pleased to be able to expend much Libido
on her" (Haynal, 1994). The bond between Freud and Kann grew
stronger as the treatment continued, even to the point where he
invited her to spend Christmas Eve with his family (Appignanesi and
Forrester, 1992). Freud made regular reports to Jones, apparently
without regard for confidentiality, just as he had done with Ferenczi
when he analyzed Elma. In fact, a major topic of the Freud–Ferenczi
correspondence was their parallel observations about Jones, who Ferenczi was analyzing, and Kann.

As Jones felt increasingly excluded from the process (more by Kann than by Freud), he became sexually involved with his maid Lina. Meanwhile, Freud steered Kann in the direction of Herbert Jones, a young American to whom she was drawn (Appignanesi and Forrester, 1992).

Freud clearly saw Ernest Jones as sexually impulsive, and the correspondence during this time reflects his disapproval of Jones' behavior. In a letter of January 14, 1912, he said to Jones, "I pity it very much that you should not master such dangerous cravings, well aware at the same time of the source from which all these evils spring, taking away from you nearly all the blame but nothing of the dangers" (Paskauskas, 1983, p. 124). Paskauskas suggests that the reference to his cravings as "dangerous" might have reflected Freud's concern about Jones' sexual boundary violations with patients. Paskauskas also quotes Jones' letter of April 1, 1922, regarding his analysis of Joan Riviere: "It is over twelve years since I experienced any [sexual] temptation in such ways, and then in special circumstances" (Paskauskas, 1993, p. 466). It is also significant that Freud's technique papers were written during this same time frame, which suggests that their emphasis on abstinence and objectivity may have grown out of concern for the boundariless behavior of his disciples (Barron and Hoffer, 1994).

Freud's need to place himself in the role of consultant to his male protégés regarding their women was clearly an overdetermined role that he found himself repeating again and again. Phillips (1994) notes that Freud appeared to take considerable glee in his ability to handle women that Jones found unmanageable, like Loë Kann and Joan Riviere. He also was patronizing to the point of condescension in his attitude toward Jones on these matters.

Freud's attitude about sexual relations between analyst and patient, however, was not nearly as cut and dried as implied by his correspondence with Jones and by his 1931 letter to Ferenczi. Although Jung expected a severe rebuke for his dalliance with Spielrein, Freud was surprisingly understanding and empathic. He wrote to Jung

> Such experiences, though painful, are necessary and hard to avoid. Without them we cannot really know life and what we are dealing with. I myself have never been taken in quite so

badly, but I have come very close to it a number of times and had *a narrow escape*. I believe that only grim necessities weighing on my work, and the fact that I was ten years older than yourself when I came to psychoanalysis have saved me from similar experiences. But no lasting harm is done. They help us to develop the thick skin we need to dominate "counter-transference," which is after all a permanent problem for us; they teach us to displace our own affects to best advantage. They are a "*blessing in disguise*" [McGuire, 1974, pp. 230–231].

Freud took a similar attitude of tolerance when a sexual transgression of Tausk came to light (Eissler, 1983). Eissler noted that in contrast to the high ethical standards we have today in psychoanalysis, Freud quite possibly felt less puritanical about sexual boundary transgressions. Freud, like Jung, appeared to blame female patients for the transgressions of analysts: "The way these women manage to charm us with every conceivable psychic perfection until they have attained their purpose is one of nature's greatest spectacles" (McGuire, 1974, p. 231). Despite this censure of women, however, Freud also expected the male analyst to be skilled enough to avoid the seduction (Eissler, 1983).

It is possible that Freud did not view ethics as a paramount concern to his new science. In a letter to the Protestant minister Pfister, who was a practicing analyst, Freud made the following comment:

Ethics are remote from me. . . . I do not break my head very much about good and evil, but I have found little that is "good" about human beings on the whole. In my experience most of them are trash, no matter whether they publicly subscribe to this or that ethical doctrine or to none at all. . . . If we are to talk of ethics, I subscribe to a high ideal from which most of the human beings I have come across depart most lamentably [Quoted in Roazen, 1975, p. 146].

There is no doubt that Freud was skeptical about the capacity to harness and sublimate the power of the drives. His letter to Pfister addressed boundary transgressions as inevitable miscues in the development of a new science. In another effort to reassure Jung about his fiasco with Spielrein, Freud drew an analogy in a letter of June 18, 1909: "In view of the kind of matter we work with, it will never be possible to avoid little laboratory explosions. Maybe we didn't slant the test tube enough, or we heated it too quickly. In this way we learn what part of the danger lies in the matter and what part in our way of handling it" (McGuire, 1974, p. 235).

Kerr (1993) frankly doubts that the revelation of Jung's relationship with Spieirein would have caused Freud much concern. He points out that sexual transgressions between analyst and patient were veritably ubiquitous among Freud's early disciples. Wilhem Stekel was well known as a "seducer." Otto Gross, who believed that the healthy solution to neurosis was sexual promiscuity, engaged in group orgies to help others relieve themselves of their inhibitions (Eissler, 1983). Jones had married a former patient. Even the clergyman Pfister was infatuated with one of his patients. Kerr (1993) emphasizes that disagreements with Freud's theories were much more troubling to Freud than sexual transgressions.

A more cynical view of Freud's attitude was that the advancement of psychoanalysis as a clinical and scientific endeavor was of such paramount importance in his hierarchy of values that it superseded considerations of ethics. Recent discussions of the Frink case (Edmunds, 1988; Gabbard, 1994b; Mahony, 1993; Warner, 1994) have made it clear that Freud was willing to lift his proscription against analyst–patient sexual relations if the cause of analysis might be advanced as a result. Frink's former patient, Angelica Bijur, was the heiress of a wealthy banking family, and clearly Freud saw the marriage between Frink and Bijur as potentially leading to a large donation to further the cause of psychoanalysis. In November 1921 he made the following comment in a letter to Frink:

> May I still suggest to you that your idea Mrs. B[ijur] had lost part of her beauty may be turned into her having lost part of her money . . . your complaint that you cannot grasp your homosexuality implies that you are not yet aware of your fantasy of making me a rich man. If matters turn out all right, let us change this imaginary gift into a real contribution to the Psychoanalytic Funds [Quoted in Mahony, 1993, p. 1031].

The results of this marriage were, of course, disastrous, and Freud's behavior can only be viewed as reprehensible. Mahony (1993) comments on the historical double standard applied to Freud and argues that Freud's way of comporting himself must be judged by the same set of standards used for other analysts.

A RETROSPECTIVE ASSESSMENT

One way to understand these historical events is to see them as the inevitable labor pains accompanying the birth of a new field. Personal and professional lives were intertwined in almost every conceivable way. Freud melded friendship and analysis in the treatment of Marie Bonaparte, during which he disclosed a good deal of personal information about himself. Bonaparte later was in treatment with Rudolf Loewenstein, only to ultimately become his lover (Appignanesi and Forrester, 1992). Jones sent the Stracheys to Freud for analysis as well as to be future translators of his work. On several occasions Jung analyzed Trigant Burrow aboard a sailboat. Rangell's (in press) view is that many of these early boundary violations must be viewed in the historical context of a new science struggling to define its parameters and should not be regarded as indications of lax technique or immoral character.

While this perspective undoubtedly has some validity, it is also true that complications surrounding a mother's labor may indelibly scar the child. Moreover, the early boundary transgressions of the pioneers in psychoanalysis can be viewed as a legacy inherited by future generations.

One of the main aspects of the legacy is a lack of clarity about the boundaries of the analytic situation. Certainly nonsexual boundary violations are far more pervasive than frank sexual relations between analyst and patient. Both Freud and Melanie Klein analyzed their own children. Anna Freud acknowledged later that she felt exploited by many aspects of this process, including her father having published accounts of her daydreams (Young-Bruehl, 1988). Klein also encouraged analysands to follow her to the Black Forest for her holiday, where she would analyze her patients while they reclined on her bed in her hotel room (Grosskurth, 1986). Winnicott held Margaret Little's hands through many hours as she lay on the couch, and on at least one occasion broke confidentiality by telling her about another patient he was treating and about his countertransference reactions toward that patient (Little, 1990). Judy Cooper (1993) reports that when she was in analysis with Masud Kahn, he continued to give her papers he had written and asked her to read them.

These transgressions were not limited to the field's pioneers practicing in Europe. Farber and Green (1993) have chronicled the history of a number of star-struck analysts in Southern California, who conducted boundariless analyses with their celebrity patients. Analysts served as technical advisors for films produced by their patients. Others collaborated on screenplays with their patients. Still others encouraged donations from their patients to various foundations with which the analyst was connected. Most of all, there was a general blurring of the boundary between an analytic and a social relationship.

The historical response of psychoanalytic organizations within the United States to boundary violations has been variable. In many cases the solution to any transgression of professional boundaries was to prescribe more analysis. We can speculate that one significant factor influencing the organizational and institutional responses to violations of professional boundaries has to do with the training setting itself. The training analysis may be viewed as the historical heir to the early violations in the field. There is a dual relationship—i.e., the treatment is both didactic and therapeutic—inherent in the training analysis. Moreover, following the analysis, the former analysand becomes a colleague to the training analyst and will be involved in committees, scientific meetings, and teaching alongside the former analyst. As Bernardi and Nieto (1992) observed, ''The paradox is that while no one would take a patient with whom such an enterprise was shared, in this case, this is precisely what is necessary'' (p. 142).

The problems arising from using one analysis for both educational and therapeutic purposes have been discussed exhaustively. As long ago as 1964, Kairys concluded, ''The problems of analyzing within a training program are intrinsically insoluble and no longer worth discussing'' (p. 485). Nevertheless, it is timely to reconsider the complexities of the training analysis lest we fall into the trap of a double standard, in which we are advocating one set of boundaries for nontraining analyses and another for candidates.

One of the most powerful resistances operating in training analyses relates to the analysand's fantasies about a posttermination relationship. In this regard the feelings of grief and mourning associated with termination may be short-circuited. The fundamental issue is that in reality, training analysts and analysand *will* have some form of ongoing relationship after termination. This feature makes the training analysis irrevocably different than other analyses (Novick, 1995; Weigert, 1955).

In nontraining analyses, boundary violations appear to be particularly problematic near the end of the process, as both analyst and patient wish to deny the painful feelings of loss associated with the ending of the analysis. As Novick (1995) stresses, there may be an inherent risk in the way we train analysts in that the analytic candidate's own termination in the setting of a training analysis may be taken as a model for conceptualizing *all* terminations.

As candidates terminate their own training analyses, they also may experience to varying degrees the impact of the training analyst's countertransference. Greenacre (1966) cited the training analyst's wish to maintain the candidate's allegiance after termination as one of the three main areas of countertransference in training analyses (the other two are overzealousness regarding the analysand's academic performance and active participation in training matters pertaining to one's analysand). She noted that rationalizations involving "saving" a promising younger colleague for the future of psychoanalysis may be conjured up to justify the training analyst's narcissistic need to control the candidate. Greenacre also observed that the training analyst's narcissistic needs may take the form of subtle indulgences that gratify instead of frustrate the patient's transference wishes.

The loyalty bind deriving from the training analyst's indulgences not only breeds discipleship in the posttermination period. It also establishes an intergenerational cycle that is difficult to break. Young analysts will repeat the behavior of their training analyst, even when they do not fully understand it or approve of it.

While the training analysis may be more inherently problematic, the supervisory situation has more recently become the focus of considerable concern. Sexual relationships between supervisors and supervisees have been called to the attention of education committees within institutes, and in some instances, nonsexual boundary violations have also been reported. While much has been written about the boundary between analysis and supervision, there is no consensus about more general boundaries of the supervisory setting. In the absence of any systematic discussion of supervisory boundaries, the candidate's own experiences of supervision become internalized and passed from one generation to the next.

Glen O. Gabbard

The intergenerational transmission of attitudes about the concept of boundaries, whether through supervision or training analysis, can be extraordinarily powerful. In the mid-1960s a training analyst in an institute was charged with sexual misconduct. Two decades later two analysts he had analyzed were also charged with sexual misconduct in the same city. What is scotomized in one analytic generation may well be scotomized in the next. Our emphasis on our historical legacy can be problematic, however, if we misuse it to blame our analytic parents rather than address basic challenges of the analytic situation that transcend time and place.

If we are to prevent destructive enactments of boundary violations, we must begin with a psychoanalytic understanding of how such enactments evolve. In addition, we must enrich our understanding of the impact these violations have on our patients. For too long institutes and societies showed greater concern for the protection of the transgressing analyst than for the patient who was deprived of an analytic treatment. This legacy of the "old boy system" is now being corrected by greater attention to the patient's suffering and appropriate reparation.

REFERENCES

APPIGNANESI, L. & FORRESTER, J. (1992). *Freud's Women.* New York: Basic Books.

BARRON, J.W. & HOFFER, A. (1994). Historical events reinforcing Freud's emphasis on "holding down the transference." *Psychoanal. Q.*, 63:536–540.

BERNARDI, R. & NIETO, M. (1992). What makes the training analysis "good enough"? *Int. Rev. Psychoanal.*, 19:137–146.

BLUM, H.P. (1994). The confusion of tongues and psychic trauma. *Int. J. Psychoanal.*, 74:871–882.

BRABANT, E.; FALZEDER, E.; & GIAMPIERI-DEUTSCH, P., eds. (1994). *The Correspondence of Sigmund Freud and Sandor Ferenczi.* Vol. 1, 1908–1914, tr. P.T. Hoffer. Cambridge, MA: Harvard Univ. Press.

BREUER, J. & FREUD, S. (1893–1895) Studies on hysteria. *S.E., 2.*

CAROTENUTO, A. (1982). *A Secret Symmetry: Sabina Spielrein Between Jung and Freud,* tr. A. Pomerans, J. Shepley, & K. Winton. New York: Pantheon.

CHUSED, J.F. (1991). The evocative power of enactments. *J. Amer. Psychoanal. Assn.*, 39:615–639.

COOPER, J. (1993). *Speak of Me as I Am: The Life and Work of Masud Kahn.* London: Karnac Books.

DUPONT, J., ed. (1988). *The Clinical Diary of Sandor Ferenczi,* tr. M. Baliant & N.Z. Jackson. Cambridge, MA: Harvard Univ. Press.

———— (1994). Freud's analysis of Ferenczi as revealed by their correspondence. *Int. J. Psychoanal.*, 75:301–320.

EISSLER, K.R. (1983). *Victor Tausk's Suicide.* New York: Int. Univ. Press.

EDMUNDS, L. (1988). His master's choice. *Johns Hopkins Magazine,* April:40–49.

FARBER, S. & GREEN, M. (1993). *Hollywood on the Couch: A Candid Look at the Overheated Love Affair between Psychiatrists and Moviemakers.* New York: William Morrow.

FREUD, S. (1905). Fragment of an analysis of a case of hysteria. *S.E.,* 7.

——— (1915). Observations on transference-love (Further recommendations on the technique of psycho-analysis, III). *S.E.,* 12.

FRIEDMAN, L. (1994). Ferrum, Ignis and Medicina: Return to the crucible. Plenary Address, Annual Meeting of the American Psychoanalytic Association, Philadelphia, PA, May 1994.

GABBARD, G.O. (1991). Commentary on "Dissociative processes and transference-countertransference paradigms" by Jody Messler Davies & Mary Gail Frawley. *Psychoanal. Dialogues,* 2:37–47.

——— (1994a). Sexual excitement and countertransference love in the analyst. *J. Amer. Psychoanal. Assn.,* 42:91–114.

——— (1994b). On love and lust in the erotic transference. *J. Amer. Psychoanal. Assn.,* 43:513–531.

——— (1994c). Psychotherapists who transgress sexual boundaries. *Bull. Menninger Clin.,* 58:124–135.

——— (1995). Countertransference: The emerging common ground. *Int. J. Psychoanal.,* 76:475–485.

GREENACRE, P. (1966). Problems of training analysis. *Psychoanal. Q.,* 35:540–567.

GROSSKURTH, P. (1986). *Melanie Klein: Her World and Her Work.* New York: Alfred A. Knopf.

GRUBRICH-SIMITIS, I. (1980). Sechs Briefe zur Wechselbeziehung von psychoanalytischer Theorie und Praxis. In *Zur Psychoanalyse der Objektbeziehungen.* G. Jappe und C. Nedelmann (Hrsg.). Stuttgart-Bad Cannstatt: Friedrich Frommann Verlag. (Translated in 1986 as Six letters of Sigmund Freud and Sandor Ferenczi on the interrelationship of psychoanalytic theory and technique, *Int. Rev. Psychoanal.)*

——— (1986). Six letters of Sigmund Freud and Sandor Ferenczi on the interrelationship of psychoanalytic theory and technique. *Int. Rev. Psychoanal.,* 12:259–277.

GUTHEIL, T.H. & GABBARD, G.O. (1993). The concept of boundaries in clinical practice: theoretical and risk management dimensions. *Amer. J. Psychiatry,* 150:188–196.

HALE, N.G., ed. (1971). *James Jackson Putnam and Psychoanalysis: Letters between Putnam and Sigmund Freud, Ernest Jones, William James, Sandor Ferenczi, and Morton Prince, 1877–1917.* Cambridge, MA: Harvard Univ. Press.

HAYNAL, A. (1994). Introduction to *The Correspondence of Sigmund Freud and Sandor Ferenczi,* Vol. 1, 1908–1914, ed. E. Brabant, E. Falzeder, & P. Giampieri-Deutsch, tr. P.T. Hoffer. Cambridge, MA: Harvard Univ. Press.

JACOBS, T. J. (1993). The inner experiences of the psychoanalyst: their contribution to the analytic process. *Int. J. Psychoanal.,* 74:7–14.

JONES, E. (1957). *The Life and Work of Sigmund Freud: Vol. 3. The Last Phase, 1919–1939.* New York: Basic Books.

Glen O. Gabbard

KAIRYS, O. (1964). The training analysis: A critical review of the literature and a controversial proposal. *Psychoanal. Q.*, 33:485–512.

KERR, J. (1993). *A Most Dangerous Method.* New York: Alfred A. Knopf.

LITTLE, M.I. (1990). *Psychotic Anxieties and Containment: A Personal Record of an Analysis with Winnicott.* Northvale, NJ: Jason Aronson.

MAHONY, P.J. (1993). Freud's cases: are they valuable today? *Int. J. Psychoanal.*, 74:1027–1035.

McGUIRE, W., ed. (1974). *The Freud/Jung Letters: The Correspondence Between Sigmund Freud and C.G. Jung.* Princeton, NJ: Princeton Univ. Press.

MENG, H. & FREUD, E.L. (1963). *Psychoanalysis and Faith: The Letters of Sigmund Freud & Oskar Pfister,* tr. E. Mosbacher. New York: Basic Books.

NOVICK, J. (1995). Termination conceivable and inconceivable. *Psychoanal. Psychol.* (in press).

PASKAUSKAS, R.A., ed. (1993). *The Complete Correspondence of Sigmund Freud and Ernest Jones 1908–1939.* Cambridge, MA: Belknap Press/Harvard Univ. Press.

PHILLIPS, A. (1994). *On Flirtation.* Cambridge, MA: Harvard Univ. Press.

RANGELL, L. (in press). Book review of *The Complete Correspondence of Sigmund Freud and Ernest Jones, 1908–1939. J. Amer. Psychoanal. Assn.*

RENIK, O. (1993). Analytic interaction: conceptualizing technique in light of the analyst's irreducible subjectivity. *Psychoanal. Q.*, 62:553–571.

ROAZEN, P. (1975). *Freud and His Followers.* New York: Knopf.

SCHAFER, R. (1977). The interpretation of transference and the conditions for loving. *J. Amer. Psychoanal. Assn.*, 25:335–362.

——— (1993). Five readings of Freud's "Observations on transference-love." In *On Freud's "Observations on Transference-Love,"* ed. E.S. Person, A. Hagelin & P. Fonagy. New Haven, CT: Yale Univ. Press, pp. 75–95.

SEARLES, H.F. (1979). *Countertransference and Related Subjects: Selected Papers.* Madison, CT: Int. Univ. Press.

WARNER, S.L. (1994). Freud's analysis of Horace Frink, M.D.: a previously unexplained therapeutic disaster. *J. Amer. Acad. Psychoanal.*, 22:137–152.

WEIGERT, E. (1955). Special problems in connection with termination of training analyses. *J. Amer. Psychoanal. Assn.*, 3:630–640.

YOUNG-BRUEHL, E. (1988). *Anna Freud. A Biography.* New York: Summit Books.

The Menninger Clinic
P.O. Box 829
Topeka, KS 66601-0829

THE AMERICAN PSYCHOANALYTIC ASSOCIATION
AND
THE PITTSBURGH PSYCHOANALYTIC COMMUNITY: INSTITUTE, SOCIETY AND FOUNDATION
ANNOUNCE

LISTENING:
HOW DOES A THERAPIST LISTEN?
WHAT DOES A THERAPIST HEAR?

PITTSBURGH/THE WESTIN WILLIAM PENN HOTEL
MARCH 16-17, 1996

A Workshop For Clinicians with:

Dr. Dale Boesky
Dr. Charles Brenner
Dr. Judith F. Chused
Dr. Arnold M. Cooper
Dr. Otto F. Kernberg
Dr. Anton O. Kris
Dr. Albert A. Mason
Dr. Evelyne Albrecht Schwaber

TO: HENRY F. SMITH, M.D., CHAIR, WORKSHOPS FOR CLINICIANS
THE AMERICAN PSYCHOANALYTIC ASSOCIATION
309 EAST 49TH STREET, NEW YORK, NY 10017 / (212) 752-0450, X28

SEND ME INFORMATION ABOUT THE MARCH 1996 WORKSHOP_____

NAME:_____

ADDRESS:_____

CITY:_____ STATE:_____ ZIP_____   C:\BBAD2

KARL ABRAHAM

KARL ABRAHAM, SIGMUND FREUD, AND THE FATE OF THE SEDUCTION THEORY

Even after Freud had turned his attention away from the seduction theory of neurosogenesis, his close pupil and colleague, Karl Abraham, initially sought to investigate child sexual trauma further. In two of the very first articles on child sexual molestation, Abraham proposed that sexual abuse was particularly common among neurotic and psychotic patients as a result of a "traumatophilic diathesis," a trauma-related conceptual precursor of the repetition compulsion. In their correspondence, Freud trenchantly criticized many aspects of Abraham's papers on the subject of sexual trauma, in contrast to his public endorsement of Abraham's work in this area. For largely transferential reasons that this paper attempts to elucidate, Abraham did not encourage dialogue regarding persistent questions on the seduction issue, ceased publishing on that topic, and for some time controlled his apparently deep rankle over Freud's criticisms and failure to acknowledge Abraham's contribution to the concept of the repetition compulsion. Despite their close friendship and shared intellectual enthusiasm, Freud's response to Abraham's 1907 papers, as well as Abraham's almost uniformly positive disposition toward Freud, apparently prevented Abraham from further developing his observations and ideas on seduction and also lent background to their later clash. Subsequently, there was virtually no further psychoanalytic investigation of the subject of child sexual abuse until the issue arose briefly with Ferenczi in the early 1930s, and only occasionally after that for the next fifty years. The death of Abraham, and then Ferenczi, shortly after disputes with Freud may be among the factors that had an inhibiting effect on an earlier reconsideration of the seduction theory by others. Abraham's previously unheralded concept of traumatophilia has relevance to current clinical controversy regarding constitution and sexual trauma.

> [A]t more than one important juncture in his [Karl Abraham's] life I have known him [to] risk the friendship of

---

Assistant Clinical Professor of Psychiatry, Harvard Medical School; Faculty, Psychoanalytic Institute of New England, East.
Submitted for publication July 7, 1994.

those very near to him by pursuing a course which seemed
to him the only right one, even when he knew it was one
that could readily lend itself to serious misinterpretation
E. Jones [1926].

Freud initially communicated doubts about the seduction theory
as early as September 21, 1897, in his letter to Fliess, which
noted that "one cannot distinguish between truth and fiction that
has been cathected with affect" (Masson, 1985, p. 264). By 1905 he
recognized that he had "overrated the importance of seduction in
comparison with the factors of sexual constitution and development" (p. 190). The creative, yet more recently controversial, shift
in Freud's thinking about the role of seduction in neurosogenesis—a
move toward an emphasis on psychic reality—was pivotal for the
development of psychoanalysis.

Along with subsequent reconsideration of the seduction theory
by others (Masson, 1984; Panel, 1988; Simon, 1992), the later role
of Ferenczi in questioning and countering Freud's theoretical
change has come into greater focus (Hoffer, 1991; Jacobson, 1994).
Less well recognized and explored is the truth-seeking but ambivalent role Karl Abraham played in what came to be the prematurely
foreclosed course of early thinking about the psychoanalytic significance of childhood seduction.

ABRAHAM ON SEXUAL TRAUMA

In 1907, the year Karl Abraham and Sigmund Freud first met, Abraham published his first psychoanalytic papers, "On the Significance
of Sexual Trauma in Childhood for the Symptomatology of Dementia Praecox" (1907a) and "The Experiencing of Sexual Traumas as
a Form of Sexual Activity" (1907b). An examination of these papers
illustrates how Abraham initially sought to investigate elements of
the seduction issue further. But despite his initial involvement with
these ideas, following Freud's response to his papers, he rather
abruptly discontinued his efforts and did not actively pursue the
subject. This cessation was uncharacteristic of Abraham and appears
to have been primarily due to transferential aspects of their friendship. A consideration of this and other developments in their relationship provides a perspective on the evolution of psychoanalytic

views and recent controversies regarding the subject of early childhood seduction and trauma.

Thirty years old at the time their friendship began, Abraham was an early, energetic, and enthusiastic adherent of Freud and the evolving theories of psychoanalysis. He had an interest in embryology, neurology, and development, and, like Freud, had written on the subject of aphasia. Abraham identified with Freud, just as he had with his own father (H. C. Abraham, 1974; Shengold, 1993). They shared what Abraham referred to as a "Talmudic way of thinking" (H. C. Abraham and E. L. Freud, 1965 [Letters], p. 36). Even their birthdays were close, only three days apart, although Abraham was twenty-one years younger than Freud. Considering himself one of Freud's pupils, Abraham, unlike later dissidents, remained almost unerringly loyal and devoted to the master. Even if Abraham had any early doubts on theoretical matters, over time he expressed still greater conviction about the correctness of Freud's conceptual views. By 1924, when Abraham became president of the International Psychoanalytic Association, he was Freud's heir apparent, his *rocher de bronze* (Letters, pp. 359–360). Although Freud was perhaps more intimate with Ferenczi, Abraham was the sounder, more objective, and more reliable Committee member (Schur, 1972, p. 386).

After Freud altered the original seduction hypothesis of neurosogenesis, Abraham readily agreed that the source of hysteria lay in constitutional factors. He also sought to demonstrate that infantile sexual trauma is not so much the cause of hysteria and dementia praecox as a determinant of the form of the disorder and the content of the patient's ideation. Even though Abraham's career revealed his capacity for deep psychological insights, his emphasis on constitution exemplified the strong biological perspective in background and training that he shared with Freud.

Abraham's 1907 papers were two of the earliest, and among the few until the 1980s, specifically on the subject of child sexual molestation (Good, 1994b). He was well aware that sexual trauma in childhood had significance. His papers do not question the actuality of reported seductions nor attribute them to false memories or fantasies. For him the question was *why so many neurotic and psychotic individuals reported sexual trauma in their histories.* Although Freud recognized that seductions occurred, Abraham's approach to this problem implicitly diverged from Freud's new theoretical emphasis in that Abraham still based his 1907 papers on the *actuality* of seduction, even though he retained homage to Freud by emphasizing the axiomatic importance of childhood sexuality. Abraham boldly proposed the arguable notion that certain children are predisposed to provoke sexual trauma, and that in many cases the child unconsciously desires the trauma, which may even come to be repeated over time ("traumatophilic diathesis") (1907b, p. 57). A constitutional predisposition to later neurosis or psychosis that accounted for some children's experiencing of sexual trauma would then explain the correlation of such trauma with mental disorder in later life. Abraham even asserted that there is no difference between children and grown-ups in terms of their provoking or complying with seduction. On the other hand, he distinguished those cases in which a child suffered sexual trauma without having been in any way responsive to it from those in which he considered the child predisposed to the sexual activity. "These children," he observed about the former, "can speak freely; they do not need to force out of their field of consciousness the recollection of that occurrence" (1907b, p. 55). In contrast, he believed the predisposed children were noncommunicative or secretive, having experienced guilt about the sexual experience.

Although they broke new ground when written, from current perspectives Abraham's papers are open to certain criticisms. His adultomorphic view of some children unconsciously seeking trauma would, by contemporary standards, not only be unfortunate medicolegally but also tragically harmful in social terms. (Compare the current issue of patient vulnerability to violations of treatment boundaries.) Abraham's traumatophilic hypothesis may be seen as implicitly blaming the victim and ignoring children's vulnerability. Given the then current state of knowledge of child development and the nature of European society at that time, however, Abraham most likely would not have anticipated these criticisms of his scientific endeavors. He was seeking to foster and elaborate on Freud's observations on the importance of childhood sexuality at a time when this notion was anathema to many. Even so, in further remarks that today would be considered prejudicial and offensive, his paper (1907b, p. 61) also refers to supposed characterologic behavior regarding pension claims of Polish workers employed in Germany. Perhaps such nationalistic comments illustrate why Freud sometimes found

Abraham to be "too Prussian" (Jones, 1955, p. 159; Gay, 1988, p. 461). Thus, Abraham's style in the 1907 papers may tend to detract from his focus on the meaning of actual seduction. Indeed, Masson (1984, p. xxii) apparently concluded incorrectly that Abraham advocated the view that the sexual events were imaginary. Nevertheless, as his titles and text convey, Abraham was dealing with the experiencing of actual sexual trauma. He even claimed, "The possibility cannot be ruled out that psychotics project their sexual phantasies back into childhood, but in none of the cases to which I have referred is there any cause for such a suspicion" (1907a, pp. 19–20)—in contrast to Freud's view about deferred action in hysterical patients (*Nachträglichkeit*) (LaPlanche and Pontalis, 1967, pp. 111–114).

FREUD'S REACTION TO ABRAHAM'S 1907 PAPERS

Abraham and Freud became close friends from virtually their first meeting (Grotjahn, 1966, p. 2). Given their mutual identification and common goals, Abraham most likely did not anticipate the degree of criticism he would receive from Freud, who diplomatically yet cogently took issue with Abraham regarding his 1907 interpretation of Freud's views on the problem of seduction. Spelling out his various objections to Abraham's work probably was not easy for Freud at that time. It was still a pioneering phase in the psychoanalytic movement, and Freud was grateful to have a psychoanalytic ally who so fully embraced his theories. Indeed, in the next year, 1908, at the age of 31, Abraham went on to found the Berlin Psychoanalytic Society. Freud's criticisms were thus preceded by, and interspersed with, praise. In his letter to Abraham dated June 25, 1907 (Letters, p. 1), for example, Freud wrote, "It is particularly gratifying to me that you have tackled the sexual side of the problem, which only very few are willing to approach." Nevertheless, in his letter of July 5, 1907 (pp. 1–4), again in response to the matter of seduction, Freud, after initially encouraging Abraham, admonished him about repeating his (Freud's) "first great error" regarding neurosogenesis. He went on to remind Abraham that "the sexual traumas reported by patients are or may be phantasies; distinguishing them from the so frequent genuine ones is not easy. . . ." He then explained that "the complication of this situation and the relationship of sexual traumas to forgetting and remembering is one of the chief reasons why I cannot persuade myself to undertake a conclusive account of them." Abraham, Freud was saying, has oversimplified the issue.

Later in the same letter, Freud again commended Abraham on some of his points but then cautioned, "only to me everything seems less clear-cut. . . ," and he expressed "reservations" or "uncertainties" of his own. Freud went on to mention the confusing factor of deferred action in the recollection of early traumatic experience. He then corrected Abraham's interpretation about unconscious purpose in seduced children, noting that "the dividing line between consciousness and unconsciousness has not yet been established in early childhood." Since Abraham had not dealt with the variable of children's ages, Freud also emphasized that, in his impression, the age of the child to which the determination of symptoms dates back is an important variable. He considered the ages of 3 to 5 years to be critical for later symptom formation. In contrast, he hypothesized that recollections of later traumas were usually genuine, and memories of prelatency seductions prima facie were doubtful. Yet he explicitly cautioned that these ideas still needed further observation and research.

On the issue of why some children report seduction and others do not, Freud agreed that a sense of guilt can interfere with a child's ability to talk about it, but he questioned why some children talk all the same. Freud noted that this difference cannot readily be ascribed to an abnormal constitution because such is the general infantile constitution. Rather than there being a sharp constitutional dividing line, he suggested that the sexual trauma develops its pathogenic effect "where the ground is well prepared for it by strong auto-erotism" (p. 3), an etiologic factor Abraham had not identified.

In a crowning correction of Abraham, Freud observed that in some environments the conditions for trauma of young children make such experiences more likely—so that it is not constitution alone that is operative in leading to sexual trauma—contrary to the thesis of Abraham's paper. (Although Abraham had briefly mentioned that there are sexual traumas in which constitution is not a factor, such as when the child is taken by surprise and is not tempted, compliant, or provocative [1907b, p. 49], these exceptions did not detract from his emphasis on constitutional factors.)

In the scientific meetings of the Vienna Psychoanalytic Society, virtually nothing was recorded regarding Abraham's 1907 papers (Nunberg and Federn, 1962). Abraham's name first appeared in the Minutes of the Society on November 27, 1907, when Freud mentioned (p. 248) a "short paper by Dr. Abraham in Berlin," not specifying which of the two titles on sexual trauma he was referring to, and apparently not discussing either one. Abraham was not at that meeting but did attend the meeting of December 18, 1907, as a guest, when the discussion was on the subject of "Sexual Traumata and Sexual Enlightenment." Underscoring the constitutional emphasis, Abraham is recorded (p. 272) as taking "a skeptical stand in regard to the opinion that traumata could be avoided through enlightenment" since "it does not help children who are so inclined." Freud followed in the minutes of the discussion, expressing his view then (prior to the formulation of a complemental series) that the sexual traumata were not important in the etiology of neuroses, other than in determining the form of the neurosis if a neurosis ensued, and that in that sense Abraham's work was an advance. None of the uncertainty or criticism found in Freud's correspondence with Abraham is reflected in these minutes.

ABRAHAM'S POSTSCRIPT

Abraham's initial response to Freud's incisive epistolary commentary, if he voiced one at all, is not included in their published letters. But, in 1920, thirteen years in the wake of Freud's critique, Abraham added a terse postscript to his second article:

> This paper, which was written in 1907, contains certain errors in its rendering of Freud's views. At the time of writing I had only recently begun to interest myself in the psycho-analytic method of thought. I consider it better to point out this fact in a general way than to make the necessary corrections in each place in the text, particularly since those errors do not invalidate the results of my investigations [Abraham, 1907b, p. 63].

Abraham's postscript illustrates how readily even someone remarkably sympathetic to Freud's ideas could erroneously interpret certain of them. Perhaps his zeal made him less judicious in applying the new insights. His acknowledged mistakes are all the more understandable given the complexity of the subject matter and the uncertainty, and even the contradictions, in Freud's writings. In 1907 Abraham saw himself as a psychoanalytic neophyte, even if he was an enthusiastic one. Yet we might wonder whether, in writing the postscript, Abraham succumbed to Freud's arguments, even while asserting, without explanation, that his errors did not invalidate his own conclusions. That it took thirteen years to write this ambivalently worded concession, which remains entirely vague on the specifics of his mistakes, is noteworthy. That he felt impelled to publish such an acknowledgment at all is remarkable. He was evidently in conflict over the matter.

Although Abraham was extensively occupied with his psychoanalytic activities in Berlin, along with the advent of World War I, he did manage to publish over two dozen more articles between 1907 and 1920 (the year of the postscript), none of which addressed the seduction issue more extensively. A partial exception is an unpublished paper entitled "Incest and Incest Phantasies in Neurotic Families. Case Contributions Concerning Actual Sexual Relations within Neurotic Families and Symptoms of Illness Based on Incest Phantasies" that was delivered in Berlin in 1910. It was a timely title on the fantasy versus reality issue, but unfortunately the paper was apparently lost (Simon, 1992) and is not included among his published papers and essays. Given Abraham's ambitions to see his work in print, its disappearance is remarkable. Would publishing it have gone too far at the time? As with Ferenczi's 1933 paper, "Confusion of Tongues between Adults and the Child," might there even have been an attempt to suppress it (Gay, 1988, p. 584)? The subject of sexual trauma remained on his mind, but he did not develop it. Perhaps Abraham drafted other papers on the subject, but it seems unlikely. Rather than pointing to later works with similar titles, his references to the paper "Sexual Trauma in Childhood" and "The Significance of Sexual Trauma" (Letters, pp. 9, 163) apparently refer to the same early article ("On the Significance of Sexual Trauma in Childhood for the Symptomatology of Dementia Praecox"), which was published in June 1907. But in his letter to Freud on January 15, 1914, in response to questions Freud had about dates he wished to clarify while writing "On the History of the Psycho-Analytic Movement" (1914b), Abraham appears to have misremembered the month of this 1907 paper, referring to its publication in November of that year, rather than June. His second paper on sexual trauma, the one criticized more extensively by Freud, was the work actually published in November 1907. For the November date, Abraham apparently unconsciously substituted the more acceptable paper! Since Freud was working on a history that might well revisit the seduction issue, there was all the more reason for this parapraxis. The slip suggests the persistence of Abraham's conflict over Freud's criticisms from seven years earlier.

His other references to the seduction issue are quite brief. In his paper on intermarriage (1909a), Abraham referred again to true incest, but then asserted that he would not go more closely into that problem. In his piece on the Prometheus myth (1909b), he briefly cited the 1907 papers in a footnote and restated his conclusion about the primacy of constitutional factors. He returned to the subject only in passing in his 1913 paper on neurotic exogamy, noting that at one end of the spectrum is true incest, which is "far less rare in psychopathic families than has been hitherto supposed."

We can wonder whether an explication of his acknowledged errors in the 1907 paper, or publication of his other, now lost, paper delivered orally on the subject of trauma and fantasy, might have helped to clarify certain ambiguities in Freud's own writings that have persisted to this very day—especially since Freud acknowledged that he could not persuade himself to make a conclusive account of the relationship of sexual trauma to forgetting and remembering. If an attempt at dialogue had come from an adherent like Abraham, might Freud have been further motivated to address questions about the modified seduction theory? Might he even have adduced illustrative case material on the problem of fantasy and reality in memories of early sexual trauma, of which there is such a paucity published even today (Good, 1994a)?

The trenchant response in Freud's letter regarding Abraham's 1907 papers is belied by his published commentary. Writing in 1914, in "On the History of the Psycho-Analytic Movement," Freud stated: "The last word on the subject of traumatic etiology was spoken later by Abraham, when he pointed out that the sexual constitution which is peculiar to children is precisely calculated to provoke sexual experiences of a particular kind—namely traumas" (p. 18).

At first his description would appear to be at least an endorsement of Abraham's paper. Is he also praising Abraham for issuing the up-to-date and complete "last word" ("Das letzte Wort") on the subject, even if he considered it flawed, or is he subtly, or even unwittingly, suggesting that Abraham's word should be the "last said" on the subject? It is surprising that it would be the last word at a time of such great psychoanalytic energy and investigation. Masson (1984, p. 131) found this comment of Freud's curious for a different reason. He noted that it is a misreading of Abraham's paper, the point of which is not that children in general are constitutionally predisposed to provoke sexual traumas, but that *certain* children are seductive and provoke them.

Although Abraham was one of Freud's most gifted and favorite pupils and among the staunchest of his supporters, he was not an idolater. According to Glover (Letters, p. xiii), Abraham could disagree with the master, such as in supporting the idea of a film on psychoanalysis. On theoretical matters, however, Abraham apparently did not differ with Freud. Near the end of his life, he remarked that the only differences he had with Freud pertained to judgments of personality (e.g., regarding the Jung situation). Glover, however, recalled Abraham confiding to him in 1921 that "he had to overcome resistances to ideas which, stated with complete conviction by Freud, he could digest and apply only after close searching of heart and head" (Letters, p. xiv). While writing to thank Freud for his encouragement, Abraham also explained on October 13, 1907 (Letters, p. 10), not long before embarking for Berlin, "I know how difficult it is to stand up against orthodox opinion in Berlin medical circles." Apparently, it was so for Abraham in Vienna as well (see also Abraham's slip regarding Schreber's "photophobia" about standing up in defiance to the sun, cited by Shengold [1993, p. 66] and described below).

Freud was well aware of transference in Abraham's relationship to him. For example, when Abraham wrote to him on May 4, 1917 (Letters, p. 251), that Freud was "as always, at work putting us younger ones to shame" with his Lectures (1916–1917), Freud answered (pp. 251–252), even while denying his own depressive tenor: "I see with dismay that you depreciate yourself in relation to me, building me up in the process into a kind of imago instead of describing me objectively. In reality I have grown old and rather frail and tired, and have more or less given up work" (p. 251).

In certain respects, Freud's opinion and wording on etiologic theory did oscillate between doubt and orthodox certainty. His earlier expression of reservations about modifying the seduction hypothesis lessened with time. By 1916, in the *Introductory Lectures on Psycho-Analysis*, on the subject of seduction memories from childhood involving the father, he stated that "there can be no doubt either of the imaginary nature of the accusation or of the motive that has led to it" (p. 370). And yet earlier on the same paper he said, "Phantasies of being seduced are of particular interest, because so often they are not phantasies but real memories. . . ." And later he went on to say, "Most analysts will have treated cases in which such events were real and could be unimpeachably established; but even so they related to the later years of childhood and had been transposed into earlier times" (p. 370). Freud's wording in 1933 is unequivocal: "In the period in which the main interest was directed to discovering infantile sexual traumas, almost all my women patients told me that they had been seduced by their father. I was driven to recognize in the end that these reports were untrue and so came to understand that hysterical symptoms are derived from phantasies and not from real occurrences" (p. 120). Later he qualified this postulate (Good, 1994a), reiterating the importance of historical truth and the complexity of the causation of neurosis. Even though he never abandoned the recognition of the importance of trauma, his focus did shift to the intrapsychic realm (Simon, 1992).

Abraham may thus have written his postscript in the face of more definitive theoretical statements from Freud against the seduction hypothesis. The brief postscript may have constituted a compromise solution for Abraham. It was a middle ground between, on the one hand, a more detailed, concerted investigation of the issue (pursuit of which may have represented, at some level, a rivalrous counterorthodoxy) and, on the other hand, a compliance with what was certainly viewed, even before 1920, as Freud's "abdication" of the seduction theory, such that it was no longer a subject of inquiry from within the psychoanalytic community, either by Freud or his exponents—except for Ferenczi in the late 1920s and early 1930s.

The focus on psychic reality and fantasy in neurosogenesis, as opposed to actual seduction, eventually even incorporated Abraham's 1907 writings, despite his emphasis then on actual experience.

For example, in her biography of Abraham, his daughter Hilda (1974) wrote, "In his second paper, 'The Experiencing of Sexual Traumas as a Form of Sexual Activity,' he takes up Freud's discovery of the way sexual experience may be utilized in neurotic illness and *how it may be a fantasy rather than a real experience*" (p. 33; emphasis added). Although Abraham had introduced the idea of a wish for sexual experience that may be unconsciously provoked (and thus may be *derived* from fantasy), he did not at all in that paper develop the notion that the sexual experiences were themselves fantasies. Hilda Abraham was, in effect, covering up her father's "error." Although Masson (1984, p. xxii), in his critique of Freud's "suppression" of the seduction theory, approached the issue from a different direction from Hilda Abraham, he also misconstrued Karl Abraham's emphasis by stating, "In particular, violent sexual crimes could be attributed to the victim's imagination, a position held by Freud's pupil Karl Abraham. . . ." Thus, Abraham's ground-breaking inquiry on the *actual* experiencing of sexual traumas was misrendered into its opposite by both proponents and opponents of the focus on fantasy.

TRAUMATOPHILIC DIATHESIS, THE COMPULSION TO REPEAT, AND PRIORITY

What became of Abraham's 1907 notion of a traumatophilic diathesis, the unconscious tendency to seek out or provoke repeated trauma? Abraham did not limit the concept to sexual trauma. His idea adumbrated what came to be known as the repetition compulsion, a principle Freud did not introduce as such until 1914 in "Remembering, Repeating, and Working-Through" (p. 150) and developed more fully in 1920 in *Beyond the Pleasure Principle*. It is remarkable that, even though Freud wrote Abraham that he was sending him *Beyond the Pleasure Principle* (Letters, p. 319), there is no further reference to, let alone discussion of, the repetition compulsion in their published correspondence. Grotjahn (1966, p. 9), moreover, observed that Abraham came close to anticipating Freud's later concept of the death instinct. The repetition compulsion is one of Freud's pivotal psychoanalytic concepts, yet Abraham's contribution to its evolution apparently was not acknowledged. Instead, Abraham (1907b, p. 57) credited Freud's 1901 work on the nature of unconscious purpose, *The Psychopathology of Everyday Life*, for his own idea of the traumatophilic diathesis. The term is no longer used in everyday psychoanalytic parlance, but the essence of the traumatophilic diathesis did not entirely fade. It was transformed and adopted by Freud, as might then have pleased Abraham. Not until shortly before Abraham's death did possible resentment about this appropriation become more overtly detectable.

Freud was ordinarily scrupulous about crediting others and assigning priorities, including Abraham's, on other subjects. He even asked colleagues to check his manuscripts for ideas he had inadvertently picked up from them (Grosskurth, 1991, p. 38). In his writings Freud made many references to Abraham's contributions, citing the influence of Abraham on his own ideas on several occasions. Another exception, however, is Abraham's 1912 paper on Amenhotep IV, in which some of Freud's conclusions about Moses and monotheism are prefigured (Shengold, 1993, pp. 62–65). In 1934, when Freud was working on his essay, "Moses and Monotheism," he must have "forgotten" Abraham's paper, even though he had originally greeted it with enthusiasm and had referred to it as late as 1923 (Letters, p. 334). Freud did not once mention Abraham's work on Amenhotep in "Moses and Monotheism" (1939). Amenhotep had erased his father's name, and Freud had erased Abraham's. In an expository analysis of this parapraxis, Shengold (1993) related it to the evocative associations of Karl Abraham's name, which connected Abraham for Freud with his biblical namesake. Biblical figures and identifications were especially meaningful and abundant among those who were closest to Freud professionally and emotionally, including his father, Jacob. Interestingly, in 1911 Abraham had also written a paper on the subject, "On the Determining Power of Names." Shengold (p. 71) speculated that the association of the primal father Abraham in relation to the sacrifice of Isaac and with circumcision, conditioned some of Freud's hostile attitudes toward Karl Abraham. In his later contact with Freud, Abraham, on the other hand, was often in the position of feeling *reluctantly* obliged to reproach the older man, who, with middle age and its inevitable reversal of parent–child roles, was reliving his own Oedipus complex (Shengold, 1993, p. 125).

Michael I. Good

Doria-Medina (1991) suggested the possibility that Freud forgot to credit Abraham's Amenhotep paper because he repressed the aspects of the relationship with the mother and the wet-nurse that Abraham emphasized in the life of the Pharaoh. Although Freud gave more attention to preoedipal and maternal factors late in his life, he tended to maintain a distance from these topics (Freud Study Group at PINE, 1991).

Abraham, on the other hand, consciously omitted Freud's name on one occasion. When his book of collected papers, *Klinische Beiträge zur Psychoanalyse aus den Jahren 1907–1920*, was published in 1921, he wrote to Freud: "You know best how much of the book stems from ideas you first put forward. I must say that, as I wrote each separate paper over all these years, I wanted to make readers aware of my gratitude and loyalty towards you. And because I thought these sentiments were clearly recognisable, I omitted dedicating the book as a whole to you" (Letters, pp. 321–322).

By the same token, as time went on, Abraham was less hesitant about lightheartedly correcting Freud. For example, on March 13, 1922, while mentioning his apposite paper on "Mistakes with an Overcompensating Tendency" (Abraham, 1922), Abraham related an "interesting misprint" in a footnote in Freud's "On the History of the Psycho-Analytic Movement" (1914b)—"discredit" instead of "discrete"—which Abraham thought of as an amusing allusion to discrediting Jung (Letters, p. 329). Some time later, on July 31, 1924, Freud corrected Abraham: "Forgive me one small comment of secondary importance. You charge Adler with responsibility for the connection between ambition and urethral erotism. Well, I have always believed it was my discovery" (Letters, p. 364).

Regarding the traumatophilic diathesis, Abraham clearly identified a tendency to experience sexual traumas repeatedly. However, his paper on this subject (1907b, p. 54) did not clarify whether certain children's "precocious sexual development," "premature occupation with sexual matters," and "abnormal desire for obtaining sexual pleasure," leading to sexual trauma that he considered attributable to constitutional factors, could be understood as due to earlier passive sexual, or other traumatic, experiences. (Compare this issue of infantile or early childhood experience, as contrasted with hereditary factors, with Freud's later use of the concept of the complemental series [Freud, 1916–1917, pp. 347, 362–364]). Although Abraham had particular interest in pregenital development, he did not pursue the subject of early sexual trauma. The subject lay fallow except for the efforts of Ferenczi, who, especially in 1932 to 1933, in contrast to Abraham, took more explicit issue with Freud on the matter of childhood sexual trauma, in particular regarding earlier developmental phases (Hoffer, 1991; Kirshner, 1993). Freud was deeply upset by Ferenczi's 1933 paper, "The Confusion of Tongues between Adults and the Child," and considered it a regressive return to the erroneous seduction theory about which he had warned Abraham in 1907. Freud urged Ferenczi not to present the paper and certainly not to publish it (Jones, 1957, p. 173). Ferenczi's persistence in pursuing his belief that what his patients told him about sexual trauma was actually true may have cost him his friendship with Freud, a price Abraham evidently did not wish to pay. There is question about how much Ferenczi's belief about Freud's supposed hostility was delusional (perhaps as a result of his pernicious anemia), and how much was related to Freud's actual forbiddance.

Ferenczi died in 1933, soon after he ran afoul of Freud. Thus opened and closed another, albeit brief, chapter on the seduction problem. In his "Confusion of Tongues," Ferenczi did not acknowledge Abraham's 1907 papers, even while observing early in this paper that "[i]nsufficiently deep exploration of the exogenous factor leads to the danger of resorting prematurely to explanations—often too facile explanations—in terms of 'disposition' and 'constitution' " (p. 156). Only in recent years has the seduction debate resumed (Simon, 1992; Good, 1992, 1994a, 1994b; Raphling, 1994; Esman, 1994), but Abraham's role has remained largely obscured.

ABRAHAM'S WRITINGS ON REBELS AND AUTHORITY

According to his daughter (H. C. Abraham, 1974), herself a physician and psychoanalyst, Abraham sublimated a good deal through his psychoanalytic writings. For him the mark of maturity was overcoming ambivalence, thus making reaction formation unnecessary and increasing the capacity for sublimation (Grotjahn, 1966). He was quite inclined to write about theoretical matters undisguisedly derived from his own family experience, including his papers on intermarriage (1909a) and on neurotic exogamy (1913), which reflected the fact that his own parents were first cousins (H. C. Abraham, 1974, p. 17). Similarly, his seemingly repressed opposition to paternal authority in the person of Freud, who apparently resembled Abraham's father (H. C. Abraham, 1974, p. 20), may have found partial, sublimated expression in his writing on Prometheus in "Dreams and Myths" (1909b) and Amenhotep IV (1912). As described by Hilda Abraham (1974):

> It may have been an unconscious part of his love and gratitude to his own father transferred to Freud which inspired him to grapple with the theme of "Dreams and Myths." He used this paper to fight on an intellectual level for the new science of psychoanalysis and its founder. . . . The choice of the myth of Prometheus as his central subject cannot be accidental and may well have sprung from his feelings of gratitude, both to his father and to Freud, for their trust and support [p. 37].

In this way she identified his ambivalent opposition to paternal authority, about which she then made a sanguine, but not entirely convincing, interpretation: "It is obvious that he was able to work on the myth of Prometheus, the rebel against paternal authority, because he had worked through his own ambivalence towards his father and towards Freud" (p. 37).

In "Dreams and Myths IV: The Analysis of the Prometheus Myth" (1909b), Abraham returned in passing to the topic of his 1907 papers:

> Although many of the child's experiences arise from external causes and are thus not rooted in his personality, others derive from his own individual makeup. In two shorter papers [footnoting the 1907 articles] I have attempted to prove this for certain sexual experiences of childhood. We can here formulate the conclusion reached as follows: the child owes part of his experiences, and probably the most impressive part, to his innate impulses [p. 179].

Abraham was still trying to reconcile his ambivalent conflict over the seduction problem. He reiterated his earlier view about the dominant role of constitution in the nature–nurture dichotomy, qualifying his position with "probably," but again he did not elaborate on the issue. Prometheus was the firegiver, but Abraham did not play with the fiery subject of seduction.

Similarly, Hilda Abraham observed (1974) that his work on Amenhotep IV, a historical essay about an Egyptian father–son conflict in which the son broke away from the father's polytheistic beliefs and established the sun god as the only god, "deals with a son's relationship to his father, picking out the post-pubertal hostile feelings towards the father and comparing these with the behaviour of the neurotic" (p. 43). Abraham was identified with the rebellious Amenhotep, who called himself "the king who lived for the truth" and "exalted truth above a mere ethical principle" (Abraham, 1912, p. 283). Amenhotep was a "revolutionary, but not in the usual sense of the word" because he "sublimated his aggressive instinctual impulses" (p. 287). Freud, an Egyptologist, eagerly awaited Abraham's paper on Amenhotep, a precursor of Moses and his monotheism, but questioned Abraham on whether the Egyptian son was actually neurotic (Letters, pp. 118–119). Hilda Abraham (1974, p. 45) felt that Freud knew or suspected a defensive motive in Abraham's exposition of Amenhotep as a neurotic, and that something of Abraham's own conflicts had slipped into the paper. She reminded readers of the fact that Abraham "never had any personal analysis and that his understanding of his own conflicting feelings and reactions was hard-won and slowly achieved" (p. 33).

Shengold (1993, p. 66) noted the connection of Amenhotep, who established the sun god as the only god, with Freud's 1911 Schreber case. Schreber defied the sun, with its paternal significance, by staring into it. Abraham wrote to Freud (Letters, p. 117) about patients he had seen who could stare into the sun without flinching, demonstrating what Abraham called "photophobia," rather than "photophilia." Shengold considered this slip as perhaps showing the ambivalence of the usually unflinching Abraham when he faced Freud as the father figure.

In 1925, the year in which he and Freud were at odds over the making of a film on psychoanalysis and in which Abraham became terminally ill, Abraham published a paper on a patient who was an imposter and confidence man, "compelled by unconscious drives to ruin every favourable situation." Because the patient's pattern of social behavior underwent a "complete transformation," Abraham considered the case to illustrate "how important it is not to overestimate the part played by heredity." Earlier it had been Abraham who, like Freud, had undergone a transformation away from the seduction theory, in which he had overestimated the part played by heredity. Perhaps the paper also foreshadowed the negative transformation that was occurring in Abraham and Freud's relationship.

THE FILM AFFAIR: ILLNESS, REENACTMENT, AND DEATH

Although he did not explicitly reopen the seduction issue, Abraham's usual identification with Freud's views on psychoanalytic matters strikingly changed shortly before he died. Writing to Freud on June 7, 1925, while abed with a feverish bronchitis due to a pharyngeal injury from a fishbone—the first sign of his fatal illness—which went on to a septic bronchopneumonia, lung abscess, and terminal subphrenic abscess (Letters, p. 382), possibly bronchogenic carcinoma (Schur, 1972, p. 388), he described plans for sponsoring a documentary film about psychoanalysis. The film was entitled *Geheimnisse einer Seele* ("Secrets of a Soul," Clark [1980, p. 463]; Gabbard and Gabbard [1987]; Ries [1995]; see also *Geheimnis der Seele* or "Secret of the Soul" [Letters, p. 382]; "The Mystery of the Soul" [Jones, 1957, p. 115]). Abraham was well aware of Freud's displeasure over the idea of such a film, but he persisted. Freud was virtually adamant in his objection (Jones, 1957, p. 114ff; Clark, 1980, p. 462), despite the fact that such a film might have generated needed funds for the psychoanalytic publishing house (Letters, p. 385). Although he was an avid and pioneering interpreter of the arts, Freud was no movie fan (Gabbard and Gabbard, 1987). His feelings went deeper than fear that the subject to which he had devoted his life would be vulgarized and trivialized for popular consumption; he believed it was impossible to explain psychoanalytic concepts properly on the silver screen (Clark, 1980, p. 462; Letters, p. 384). According to Glover (Letters, p. xiii), documentary films in those days were rather simple minded, and this particular film was naive, verging on the ridiculous. At a deeper level, a film about "secrets" may have struck a sensitive chord in Freud about his own motivation to unveil nature's secrets

(Freud Study Group at PINE, 1991). The director of the film was to be G. W. Pabst, whose film on the desperate poverty in Vienna had been profoundly influential; that film was entitled, as if now to ridicule, *Freudlose Gasse* ("Joyless Street" [Clark, 1980, p. 462]; see also *Die Freudlose Strasse* [Ries, 1995, p. 767]). Freud, in recent years, had become more than joyless himself. In January 1920 he was dealt two grievous blows: Anton von Freund, a friend and lavish benefactor who had generously contributed to the establishment of the psychoanalytic publishing house, died of cancer at age 40 (Gay, 1988, p. 391), followed five days later by the unexpected death of his dear daughter, Sophie, due to pneumonia. Within three weeks of her death he had introduced the concept of the "death instinct" for the first time in his writing. Then, in addition to the friction with Rank, not only was it discovered early in 1923 that he had cancer of the jaw, necessitating numerous, extensive, and painful surgeries, but also in June 1923 his favorite grandson, 4-year-old Heinele (Sophie's son), died of miliary tuberculosis. Freud was extremely upset by the loss of this beloved grandchild, and he declared that life had lost all meaning (Gay, 1988, p. 421).

These developments had meaning and implications for Abraham. The film dispute, in particular, was a new expression of a conflict. This time it was not another disagreement about a third party or "sibling rival" in the Committee but had to do more directly with Abraham and Freud himself. It also involved the old issue of Freud's theories and how these ideas were interpreted, as if Abraham wanted another chance to render Freud's theories correctly, now in an expanded, cinematic version of his short 1920 postscript.

On October 27, 1925, responding to Freud's "reproach of harshness" regarding the film affair, Abraham complained of Freud's pattern of "blame" and "criticism" of him again, in which "the same sequence of events repeated itself each time." On November 5, 1925, with an echo of the traumatophilic diathesis, Freud objected to Abraham's interpretation and wrote reprovingly:

> Let us not give too much play to repetition compulsion. You were certainly right about Jung, and not quite so right about Rank. That matter took a different course, and would have passed over more easily if it had not been taken so very seriously in Berlin. It is still quite possible that you may be even less right in the matter with which we are concerned now. You are not

necessarily always right. But should you turn out to be right this time too, nothing would prevent me from once again admitting it.

With that let us close the argument about something that you yourself describe as a trifle. Such differences of opinion can never be avoided, but only quickly overcome [p. 399].

Differences of opinion were not avoided, and, ironically, Abraham himself was quickly overcome. The next, and last, published letter is a condolence note from Freud to Abraham's wife (Letters, pp. 399–400). Abraham had died that Christmas Day. Freud had not been one to mince words. As he wrote to Jones in 1922 (Clark, 1980, p. 450), "You know it is not my habit to suppress my true judgment in relations of friendship and I am always prepared to run the risk attaching to that behavior." Freud, of course, was distraught at the loss of his devoted paladin. After sending Frau Abraham a telegram upon receiving the news of Abraham's death, he "put off" writing to her until January 17, 1926. Explaining his delay, Freud wrote: "It was too difficult, and I hoped it would become easier. Then I fell ill myself, became feverish, and have not yet recovered" (Letters, pp. 399–400). Citing an interview of Sandor Rado by Bluma Swerdloff on November 27, 1964, in the Columbia Oral Archives, Grosskurth (1991) quoted Rado's comments on Freud's "refusal" to mourn Abraham: "I remember that [Abraham] was just on the verge of conflict with Freud. And my theory, at that time, was that he killed himself to avoid the conflict" (p. 175).

In his biography of Freud, Schur (1972, p. 388) attempted to reconcile Freud's pique at Abraham with his concern and supreme gentleness in situations where his younger friends were seriously ill. Schur considered that Freud's angry remarks may have been a displaced response to Abraham's periodic comments in preceding letters (Letters, e.g., pp. 395, 397, etc.) about Fliess, who had been treating Abraham and whom Freud had never quite forgiven. Schur believed that Abraham was expecting some response from Freud about Fliess, but Freud was silent except for a sarcastic remark in a circular letter (Jones, 1957, p. 116). (But see also Abraham's much earlier sanguine comment about Fliess in his letter of February 26, 1911 [Letters, p. 102], and Freud's bitter-sounding response on March 3 [Letters, p. 103].) While Schur's interpretation may account for part of Freud's feelings, the fact that his reaction came when it did probably also had something to do with the direct provocation by Abraham regarding the film itself, in combination with whatever annoyance and guilt Freud may have felt over Abraham's illness. Freud preferred to face facts about his own health and insisted on being told the full truth (Schur, 1972, pp. 357, 391; Gay, 1988, pp. 424–425), whereas Abraham was inclined to minimize illness, both in Freud's case and in himself. Freud called Abraham an "Incurable Optimist" and advised him to "get used to the idea of my mortality and frailty" (Letters, pp. 336, 342). At the time of his last letter to Abraham, Freud probably already suspected that Abraham's illness was a serious one, and Freud may have been irritated by the possibility that Abraham was trying to mislead or fool him (Schur, 1972, p. 388). Because Abraham, in turn, knew how much Freud relied on him, particularly in view of Freud's own illness and the curtailment of his work, Abraham may have been trying to minimize additional worries, including financial concerns, for Freud. The film venture may have been partly a defensive activity for Abraham, which Freud could not condone. He considered "poor Abraham" to have been "deceived by euphoria" (Schur, 1972, p. 390). Freud, moreover, had yet other reasons for irritability: in addition to his own illness, other losses, and worries about death, his early mentor and paternal friend, Josef Breuer, died June 20, 1925 (Jones, 1957, p. 110; Letters, p. 386), the same year that his early, close friend from adolescence, Eduard Silberstein, also died (Grosskurth, 1991, p. 30).

In the last months of his life, Abraham's relations with Freud were more troubled than at any other time (Jones, 1957, p. 114). To Abraham their terminal clash, although ostensibly a dispute about a film, must have echoed seemingly repressed themes from their earliest communications about his 1907 papers and from the postscript. Unresolved matters involving the seduction theory, child sexual trauma, and the traumatophilic diathesis now could be heard in terms of strong feelings about criticism, the significance of repetitions, and who was right. Not directly discussed but clearly festering, these early themes had become embedded in their mutual transferential tendencies, augmented by the intense stresses of illness, loss, and mourning. It had taken years for the earlier themes to be played out again, especially with the strong professional and personal rapport and friendship they shared. Abraham, the eternal optimist, was hardly a hostile person. Jones (1926, p. 180) considered him to be incapable of hating and "even at times curiously oblivious to the strength of hostile emotions in other people." That, too, is possibly why Abraham responded so little to Freud's 1907 critique. (His daughter, on the other hand, mentioned his occasional explosive outbursts of temper coming out of the blue [H. C. Abraham, 1974, p. 20]. Also, when Freud had a fainting spell in 1912 while he and Jung had been discussing Abraham's paper on Amenhotep, Abraham himself reportedly mentioned in passing that though not epileptic, he had had fits as a boy [Thornton, 1984, p. 236, citing Jung, 1963].)[1] Although Jones described seeing Abraham "cheerfully reasoning with someone who was glowering with anger and resentment, apparently blandly ignoring the emotion and full of hope that a quiet exposition would change the situation" (1926, p. 180), there is virtually no indication that he tried to reason with Freud on the seduction issue. This absence of dialogue on the subject is in contrast with Jones' [1955] description of Abraham having "no hesitation in saying when he had not yet been able to confirm this or that point from his own experience" (p. 156). Jones believed that Freud had a higher opinion of Abraham's intellectual powers than of any other of his colleagues and therefore welcomed confirmation of his ideas from Abraham most of all.

But in the end, perhaps unwittingly, Abraham challenged Freud more directly than he ever had in the past. In the course of this seeming reenactment, he felt blamed, receiving not just scientific criticism but now Freud's overt anger as well. Regretting the situation, but still standing by his correctness and effort to clarify facts—much as he had done in the postscript—Abraham closed his last published letter, dated October 27, 1925, with these words: "It gives me pain to have aroused your displeasure once again, although I am certain that this time, as on previous occasions, you will one

---

[1]As Shengold observed (1993, p. 74), in Jung's account of his argument with Freud over the question of death wishes and the significance of the son's erasing the name of the father, Jung, too, completely neglected to mention the name of Karl Abraham, neither in that context nor anywhere else in his autobiography. This "brother figure" with whom Jung was overtly in conflict had the very name Jung himself was nicknamed ("Father Abraham") by his childhood classmates after having been accused of plagiarism by his teacher (Jung, 1961, pp. 82–85)! In addition, Abraham's only sibling was, in fact, an older brother (Jones, 1926), a transferential role Jung must have filled.

day reconsider your judgement of me; but *I on my part wanted to do everything to get the facts clear.* I am, with kindest regards to you and your family, in unaltered and unalterable sincerity, Yours, Karl Abraham" (p. 398; emphasis added).

In eulogizing Abraham, Freud described him as a "model leader in the pursuit of truth, led astray neither by the praise or blame of the many nor by the *seductive illusion of his own phantasies*" (1926, p. 277; emphasis added). These words echo the sense that Abraham, in Freud's view, might have been, but was not, led astray by the seduction theory, which had once been Freud's own "seductive illusion."

DISCUSSION

Abraham was the first psychoanalytic "rebel," albeit an ambivalent and tentative one. His earliest psychoanalytic contributions on sexual trauma are still relevant in the current controversy over the significance of childhood seduction and its repression in causing neurosis. Much of the recent debate has arisen from outside of psychoanalytic circles (see, for example, Esman, 1994), a phenomenon that echoes Freud's early conflict over the seduction theory. It is as if Freud's ambivalence about the seduction theory, which in more recent years has been "rediscovered," is now voiced by clinical factions that take opposing stances originally struggled over internally by Freud and then briefly with Abraham and Ferenczi (for instance, compare Brenneis [1994] with Person and Klar [1994]).

Currently, Abraham's conceptualization of the role of constitutional factors and a "traumatophilic diathesis," which might include very early childhood experience, highlights questions about the causes and consequences of child sexual molestation and repetitive sadomasochistic phenomena that are not so well understood even today (Grossman, 1991). That it has taken half a century or more for these questions to regain considerable psychoanalytic attention is a topic for investigation in the history of psychoanalytic knowledge.

The overall hiatus in thinking on the subjects of incest, sexual abuse, and their intrapsychic consequences (Simon, 1992; Good, 1994b) may be attributed to various factors. Among these factors is the cogent influence of Freud's thinking and personality, the nature of "discipleship," and the "politics" of psychoanalysis (Roustang, 1976a; Grosskurth, 1991). Even since Freud's death, in an enduring sense, the very depth, breadth, imagination, and strength of his psychoanalytic ideas, together with the social-intellectual Zeitgeist (see, for example, Decker [1991, pp. 168–189, 256 n. 6]) of the subsequent forty years or so, contributed to what can be viewed as an overly intrapsychic emphasis—even if such a delimited emphasis restricts or distorts what Freud actually intended psychoanalysis to be (Good, 1994a). Simon (1992), for example, has noted how important psychoanalytic textbooks subsumed "incest" under "Oedipus complex," and how the internal history of psychoanalysis was simplified by the omission and suppression of material that increases the complexity and confusion regarding Freud's early discoveries and their vicissitudes. Kuhn's (1970) work on paradigms in science adds perspective to the issue of shifts in theoretical dominance. To expand upon all of these influences, however, would exceed the objective of this paper, which is to explore more specifically the relationship of Abraham and Freud as it reflects the fate of the seduction theory. Viewing this fate from the perspective of their mutual transferences—and the extension of themes of authority, idealization, identification, loyalty, and dependency into group psychological processes (Freud, 1913, 1921; Blum, 1994) within the succeeding psychoanalytic community—is useful in understanding both the prolonged absence of more extensive interest in incest and the ways in which renewed interest has recapitulated earlier controversies.

For instance, writing on the relationship between Freud and his "savage horde" (wilden Heer) of followers, Roustang (1976a) concluded that "the consistency of the fantasies of Freud's disciples and the irrepressible regularity of their reactions are no doubt related to their own neurosis, but at the same time their reactions must also have been induced by Freud" (p. 11). Notwithstanding Roustang's frequently censorious tone, he suggested that, in the countertransference, his followers were supporting some part of their master's diffracted desire. Thus, without the Jung affair, we would probably have neither *Totem and Taboo* (1913) nor "On the History of the Psycho-Analytic Movement" (1914b). Rank's disaffection was associated with Freud's writing *Inhibitions, Symptoms, and*

Anxiety (1925), and Ferenczi's works inspired him to write "Analysis Terminable and Interminable" (1937).

But Abraham, the model disciple, was not represented in this trend of reaction by essay. Was Abraham's objectivity always subordinated to his leader's interests (Roustang, 1976a, p. 15)? Roustang emphasized the dependence of Freud's followers on him for financial help and patient referrals as a price for loyalty (pp. 11–12). Yet Abraham readily established a practice after his move to Berlin (Pines, 1972), so that it is doubtful that he was in reality any less independent than other early analysts who explicitly questioned and challenged Freud (Letters, pp. 310–320). Indeed, even though Roustang (p. 2) documented Abraham's recognition of his (at times) unconscious, yet effective, tendency to provoke hostility in others, such as Jung (Letters, p. 36), Roustang did not identify the clear extension of this tendency into Abraham's later, direct relationship with Freud. Such an omission is perhaps understandable, because Abraham did not actively reopen the seduction issue or the matter of the traumatophilic diathesis. Nor did Freud acknowledge Abraham regarding the repetition compulsion in *Beyond the Pleasure Principle* (1920), in which he addressed the problem of trauma and repetition—but not explicitly sexual trauma. Certainly, sexual trauma in its various forms and reactions would have been a subject worthy of an essay comparable to Freud's responses to Jung, Rank, and Ferenczi. It appears, however, that what was overtly challenging to Freud in his relationship with the latter men could, in the case of Abraham and Freud, remain for the most part either mutually suppressed or unconscious. But, as Shengold concluded (1972), Abraham, like Freud's father and his younger brother Julius, became a "victim" of Freud's death wishes.

Abraham and Ferenczi each died soon after confrontations with Freud. That is a remarkable repetition also, if not mere coincidence. It even may have affected other analysts and, in the psychoanalytic group unconscious, further inhibited reconsideration of the seduction theory and the significance of actual incest, in contrast to an emphasis on the importance of fantasy. It is certainly possible that their deaths reinforced attention to Thanatos and metapsychological–philosophical matters, as was the case for Freud. The emphasis shifted to topics more remote from early developmental vicissitudes and traumas. It is thus less surprising that another half-century had to pass before the subjects of incest and sexual trauma in child-hood—and the question of the truth of their later recall—could more fully reenter the psychoanalytic arena.

To suggest that the deaths of Abraham and Ferenczi in the context of direct or indirect disputation with Freud over the seduction theory may have inhibited its further pursuit by others is, of course, hypothetical. As I have noted, there were other factors that also affected this part of the course of psychoanalytic history. But the influence of Freud's ideas and personality, the nature and course of the relationship of Abraham and Ferenczi with Freud, and the relevance these had to the early course of the seduction theory are evident. The early deaths of Abraham and Ferenczi may be seen, in part, as a culmination of a mythic saga in the development of psychoanalysis, an oedipal struggle, as it were, in which the seduction theory represented both the female object (to which it primarily applied) and the psychic reality of the possibility of incest. The seduction theory, Freud's "error," became taboo. Just as Freud's initial conflict over the seduction theory (Blass and Simon, 1994) related to his own oedipal conflicts, so his "renunciation" of the seduction theory followed not only from a scientific reassessment of data but also from a working through and "dissolution" of oedipal remnants in his own makeup by means of cognitive advances (Mahon, 1991). Freud replaced the problematic notion of incest as *the* cause of neurosis with an oedipal theory that *stood for*, and contained, the possibility of incest. The oedipal theory was thus not only a conceptual development with clinical applicability but also a more intellectualized psychic representation of incest for Freud himself. Actual incestuous fantasies or impulses, tempered by superego influences (cf. Krüll, [1979]), were transformed by cognitive means into a theory of oedipal fantasy. And, while the idea of incest was not strictly repressed, there was a "reactive reinforcement," to use Freud's term (see Blass, 1992, p. 166), by means of a theoretical emphasis on fantasy and psychic reality.

Viewing the shift from the seduction theory to the oedipal theory in terms of the theorizer's ongoing psychological *development*, as opposed to defensive *motivation*, may clarify some of the controversy over whether Freud's discovery of psychoanalysis was entirely a creative solution (see, for example, McGrath [1986, pp. 197–198] for a summary of various other views on reasons for Freud's shift away from the seduction theory and whether the shift was an advance or a retreat). Historically, many psychoanalysts apparently could identify with the creative aspects of these theoretical developments, not only intellectually but also as a means of dealing with countertransference pressures of a seductive nature, like those with which Freud himself had been struggling (Blass and Simon, 1994) and that we now identify more commonly and openly in terms of possible "boundary violations." Ferenczi's boundary experiments in technique, for example, were clearly worrisome and even alarming to Freud.

Further evidence for a "group reactive reinforcement" that worked against attention to seduction is contained in Anna Freud's statement (Masson, 1984, p. 113) that keeping up the seduction theory would mean abandoning the Oedipus complex and the whole importance of conscious and unconscious fantasy. I find this statement puzzling (for why could there not be a reconsideration of seduction without sacrificing intrapsychic perspectives?), unless her statement is heard in terms of the problem of regression from a developmental advance that is essential to psychoanalytic neutrality. Recently, Blum (1994) underscored the dramatic impact of the disagreement between Freud and Ferenczi on the wider psychoanalytic community, such that some analysts were afraid that any threat to the importance of psychic reality might undermine the psychoanalytic movement. To the extent that to find "incest" later analysts had to "see under oedipus complex" (Simon, 1992), not only were incest and the Oedipus complex conflated theoretically but also the reality of actual oedipal transgression was superseded by the oedipal theory in a quasi-developmental or adaptive sense for the greater body of psychoanalysts, as it was for Freud. As Roustang (1976b, pp. 58–59) and others have suggested, theory can be studied in terms of the fantasies and desires that gave rise to it (or that support it), like the text of a dream or myth.

Would Abraham himself have returned to the subject of child sexual trauma if he had lived beyond 1925? If so, would such a reversion have helped obviate any of the Freud–Ferenczi dispute over the role of early trauma? Where then might the subject have stood today? We can only speculate. What is striking, in any event,

Michael I. Good

is the parallel in Abraham's and Ferenczi's experiences with Freud in the first third of this century and the continued "latency" of the seduction theory for nearly fifty more years. Perhaps now, with the "rediscovery" of incest, we can say that in this area psychoanalysis has passed through its "latency" phase and entered into its "adolescence." As in adolescence, there is still more to learn. The interplay of constitution, development, environment (including traumatic experience), fantasy, and memory remains an area for further clinical discovery.

REFERENCES

ABRAHAM, H.C. (1974). Karl Abraham: An unfinished biography. *Int. Rev. Psychoanal.*, 1:17–72.

———— FREUD, E.L., eds. (1965). *A Psycho-Analytic Dialogue: The Letters of Sigmund Freud and Karl Abraham.* New York: Basic Books.

ABRAHAM, K. (1907a). On the significance of sexual trauma in childhood for the symptomatology of dementia praecox. In *Clinical Papers and Essays on Psycho-Analysis.* New York: Basic Books, pp. 13–20, 1955.

———— (1907b). The experiencing of sexual traumas as a form of sexual activity. In *Selected Papers of Karl Abraham.* New York: Brunner/Mazel, 1979, pp. 47–63.

———— (1909a). The significance of intermarriage between close relatives in the psychology of the neuroses. In *Clinical Papers and Essays on Psycho-Analysis.* New York: Basic Books, 1955, pp. 21–28.

———— (1909b). Dreams and myths. IV. The analysis of the Prometheus myth. In *Clinical Papers and Essays on Psycho-Analysis.* New York: Basic Books, 1955, pp. 172–176.

———— (1911). On the determining power of names. In *Clinical Papers and Essays on Psycho-Analysis.* New York: Basic Books, 1955, pp. 31–32.

———— (1912). Amenhotep IV: A psycho-analytic contribution towards the understanding of his personality and of the monotheistic cult of Aton. In *Clinical Papers and Essays on Psycho-Analysis.* New York: Basic Books, 1955, pp. 262–290.

———— (1913). On neurotic exogamy: A contribution to the similarities in the psychic life of neurotics and of primitive man. In *Clinical Papers and Essays on Psycho-Analysis.* New York: Basic Books, 1955, pp. 48–50.

———— (1921). *Klinische Beiträge zur Psychoanalyse aus den Jahren 1907–1920.* Internationaler Psychoanalytischer Verlag.

———— (1922). Mistakes with an overcompensating tendency. In *Clinical Papers and Essays on Psycho-Analysis.* New York: Basic Books, 1955, pp. 76–79.

———— (1925). The history of an impostor in the light of psycho-analytic knowledge. In *Clinical Papers and Essays on Psycho-Analysis.* New York: Basic Books, 1955, pp. 291–305.

BLASS, R.B. (1992). Did Dora have an Oedipus complex? A reexamination of the theoretical context of Freud's "Fragment of an Analysis." *Psychoanal. Study Child*, 47:159–187.

―――― SIMON, B. (1994). The value of the historical perspective to contemporary psychoanalysis: Freud's 'seduction hypothesis.' *Int. J. Psychoanal.*, 75:677–694.

BLUM, H.P. (1994). The confusion of tongues and psychic trauma. *Int. J. Psychoanal.*, 75:871–882.

BRENNEIS, C.B. (1994). Belief and suggestion in the recovery of memories of childhood sexual abuse. *J. Amer. Psychoanal. Assn.*, 42:1027–1053.

CLARK, R.W. (1980). *Freud: The Man and the Cause.* New York: Random House.

DECKER, H.S. (1991). *Freud, Dora, and Vienna 1900.* New York: Free Press.

DORIA-MEDINA, R. (1991). On Freud and monotheism. *Int. Rev. Psychoanal.*, 18:489–500.

ESMAN, A. (1994). "Sexual abuse," pathogenesis, and enlightened skepticism. *Amer. J. Psychiat.*, 151:1101–1103.

FERENCZI, S. (1933). On the confusion of tongues between adults and the child: The language of tenderness and passion. In *Final Contributions to the Problems and Methods of Psycho-Analysis.* New York: Basic Books, 1955, pp. 156–167.

FREUD, S. (1901). The psychopathology of everyday life. *S.E.*, 6.

―――― (1905). Three essays on the theory of sexuality. *S.E.*, 7:123–243.

―――― (1911). Psycho-analytic notes on an autobiographical account of a case of paranoia (dementia paranoides). *S.E.*, 12:1–79.

―――― (1913). Totem and taboo. *S.E.*, 13:1–162.

―――― (1914a). Remembering, repeating, and working-through (Further recommendations on the technique of psycho-analysis, II). *S.E.*, 12:145–156.

―――― (1914b). On the history of the psycho-analytic movement. *S.E.*, 14:1–66.

―――― (1916–1917). Introductory lectures on psycho-analysis. *S.E.*, 16.

―――― (1920). Beyond the pleasure principle. *S.E.*, 18:1–64.

―――― (1921). Group psychology and the analysis of the ego. *S.E.*, 18:65–143.

―――― (1925). Inhibitions, symptoms and anxiety. *S.E.*, 20:75–172.

―――― (1926). Karl Abraham. *S.E.*, 20:277–278.

―――― (1933). New introductory lectures on psycho-analysis. *S.E.*, 22:1–182.

―――― (1937). Analysis terminable and interminable. *S.E.*, 23:209–253.

―――― (1939). Moses and monotheism: Three essays. *S.E.*, 23:1–137.

FREUD STUDY GROUP AT THE PSYCHOANALYTIC INSTITUTE OF NEW ENGLAND, EAST (PINE): BARRON, J.W.; BEAUMONT, R.; GOLDSMITH, G.N., GOOD, M.J.; PYLES, R.L., RIZZUTO, A.-M.; & SMITH, H.F. (1991). Sigmund Freud: The secrets of nature and the nature of secrets. *Int. Rev. Psychoanal.*, 18:143–163.

GABBARD, K. & GABBARD, G.O. (1987). *Psychiatry and the Cinema.* Chicago: University of Chicago Press.

GAY, P. (1988). *Freud: A Life for Our Time.* New York: Norton.

GOOD, M.I. (1992). Witnessing pornography and the reconstruction of suspected child sexual molestation (letter). *J. Amer. Psychoanal. Assn.*, 40:630–633.

―――― (1994a). The reconstruction of early childhood trauma: Fantasy, reality, and verification. *J. Amer. Psychoanal. Assn.*, 42:79–101.

———— (1994b). Differential constructions of trauma in cases of suspected child sexual molestation. *Psychoanal. Study Child*, 49:434–464.

GROSSKURTH, P. (1991). *The Secret Ring: Freud's Inner Circle and the Politics of Psychoanalysis*. Reading, MA: Addison-Wesley.

GROSSMAN, W.I. (1991). Pain, aggression, fantasy, and concepts of sadomasochism. *Psychoanal. Q.*, 50:22–52.

GROTJAHN, M. (1966). Karl Abraham, the first German psychoanalyst. In *Psychoanalytic Pioneers*, ed. F. Alexander, S. Eisenstein, & M. Grotjahn. New York: Basic Books, pp. 1–13.

HOFFER, A. (1991). The Freud-Ferenczi controversy—A living legacy. *Int. Rev. Psychoanal.*, 18:465–472.

JACOBSON, J.G. (1994). Signal affects and our psychoanalytic confusion of tongues. *J. Amer. Psychoanal. Assn.*, 42:15–42.

JONES, E. (1926). Karl Abraham, 1877–1925. *Int. J. Psychoanal.*, 7:155–189.

———— (1955). *The Life and Work of Sigmund Freud*. Vol. 2. New York: Basic Books.

———— (1957). *The Life and Work of Sigmund Freud*. Vol. 3. New York: Basic Books.

JUNG, C.G. (1961). *Memories, Dreams, and Reflections*, rec. & ed. A. Jaffe; tr. R. Winston & C. Winston. New York: Random House.

KIRSHNER, L.A. (1993). Concepts of reality and psychic reality in psychoanalysis as illustrated by the disagreement between Freud and Ferenczi. *Int. J. Psychoanal.*, 74:219–230.

KRÜLL, M. (1979). *Freud and His Father*, tr. A.J. Pomerans. New York: Norton, 1986.

KUHN, T.S. (1970). *The Structure of Scientific Revolutions*. 2nd ed. Chicago: University of Chicago Press.

LAPLANCHE, J. & PONTALIS, J.-B. (1967). *The Language of Psycho-Analysis*. New York: Norton, 1973.

MAHON, E.J. (1991). The "dissolution" of the Oedipus complex: A neglected cognitive factor. *Psychoanal. Q.*, 60:628–634.

MASSON, J.M. (1984). *The Assault on Truth*. New York: Farrar, Straus, & Giroux.

———— ed. & tr. (1985). *The Complete Letters of Sigmund Freud to Wilhelm Fliess, 1887–1904*. Cambridge, MA: Belknap Press/Harvard University Press.

MCGRATH, W.J. (1986). *Freud's Discovery of Psychoanalysis: The Politics of Hysteria*. Ithaca, NY: Cornell University Press.

NUNBERG, H. & FEDERN, E., eds. (1962). *Minutes of the Vienna Psychoanalytic Society. Vol. 1: 1906–1908*, tr. M. Nunberg. New York: Int. Univ. Press.

PANEL (1988). The seduction hypothesis. A.E. Marans, reporter. *J. Amer. Psychoanal. Assn.*, 36:759–771.

PERSON, E.S. & KLAR, H. (1994). Establishing trauma: The difficulty distinguishing between memories and fantasies. *J. Amer. Psychoanal. Assn.*, 42:1055–1081.

PINES, N. (1972). Hilda Abraham (1906–1971). *Int. J. Psychoanal.*, 53:331.

RAPHLING, D.L. (1994). A patient who was not sexually abused. *J. Amer. Psychoanal. Assn.*, 42:65–78.

RIES, P. (1995). Popularize and/or be damned: psychoanalysis and film at the crossroads in 1925. *Int. J. Psychoanal.*, 76:759–791.

ROUSTANG, F. (1976a). The savage horde. In *Dire Mastery: Discipleship from Freud to Lacan*, tr. N. Lukacher. Washington, DC: American Psychiatric Press, 1986, pp. 1–16.

—— (1976b). On the transmissibility of analytic theory. In *Dire Mastery: Discipleship from Lacan to Freud*, tr. N. Lukacher. Washington, DC: American Psychiatric Press, pp. 55–75.

SCHUR, M. (1972). *Freud: Living and Dying.* New York: Int. Univ. Press.

SHENGOLD, L. (1972). A parapraxis of Freud's in relation to Karl Abraham. In *Freud and His Self-Analysis*, ed. M. Kanzer & J. Glenn. New York: Jason Aronson, 1979, pp. 213–244.

—— (1993). Fliess, Karl Abraham, and Freud. In *"The Boy Will Come to Nothing!" Freud's Ego Ideal and Freud as Ego Ideal.* New Haven, CT: Yale Univ. Press, pp. 59–94.

SIMON, B. (1992). "Incest—see under Oedipus complex": The history of an error in psychoanalysis. *J. Amer. Psychoanal. Assn.*, 40:955–988.

THORNTON, E.M. (1984). *The Freudian Fallacy: An Alternative View of Freudian Theory.* Garden City, NY: Dial Press.

74 Craftsland Road
Brookline, MA 02167

THE RECONSTRUCTION OF A REPRESSED SEXUAL MOLESTATION FIFTY YEARS LATER

The current public concern about childhood molestation and abuse has fueled the debate in psychoanalysis about historical versus narrative truth, a subject that has implicitly and explicitly been an important theme since the origin of psychoanalysis. The evocation of false memories by suggestion has had significant social consequences. This raises important questions about the role of real trauma as contrasted with fantasy in the genesis of psychic conflict.

This paper explores the conditions for the emergence of long repressed trauma. It is argued that such traumatic memories emerge only after significant structural change has occurred, in particular modifications in the representational world (self and object representations). This substantive change may be viewed as a macroscopic way station in the evolution of the analysis. This is demonstrated in the description of the analysis of a patient born with a congenital anomaly. The analysis of her unconscious fantasies about her deformity, her identifications with defective people, and of a negative paternal transference had to occur before the development of an erotic transference. It was then that fragments of the memory of the sexual trauma emerged. Details of the reconstruction are presented. The successful integration of this painful experience is described. Six years after termination of the analysis, the patient wrote a letter describing a confirmation of the event, now sixty years past, from the sole other survivor of the period who had knowledge of what had happened.

Psychoanalytic theory from its inception has involved a dialectic about the relative pathogenic influence of trauma

Professor of Clinical Psychiatry, Cornell University Medical College; Training and Supervising Psychoanalyst, Columbia Psychoanalytic Center.

This paper was presented at the meeting of the International Psychoanalytic Association, San Francisco, August 1, 1995, and at the Association for Psychoanalytic Medicine, December 5, 1995.

I would like to express my appreciation to Drs. Robert Michels and Alain de Mijolla for their helpful critiques of this paper.

Submitted for publication August 8, 1994.

versus drive, conflict, and fantasy. Although the concept of psychic reality in 1897 marked Freud's theoretical focus on drive rather than experience, his interest in external experience and trauma re-emerged with the development of the structural hypothesis and its elaboration in ego psychology, although innate factors continued to dominate his view. One form that contemporary discussion takes is the debate about historical and narrative truth (Spence, 1982). In its purest form, the narrative view insists that truthfulness regarding early experience is not the domain of psychoanalysis properly speaking and only meaning and coherence are pertinent.

This theme has taken on special social significance in the context of renewed attention to childhood incest and abuse. How might one conceptualize psychoanalytic material that would suggest an actual incident, contrasted with an organizing fantasy? What are the conditions for the emergence of such material, previously repressed? How might one evaluate the patient's success in integrating the recovered traumatic past in a way that promotes growth? This paper will address these questions; namely, the structural conditions for the recovery of memories of traumatic events, the stimulus and motivation for the recovery of such memories, and the manner they are integrated into the patient's life. This latter aspect has to do with the complex problem of responsibility for one's life, the view that one is an agent in creating one's life rather than the passive recipient of external experience. In the case of trauma this involves a transformation from a view of oneself as victim to a view of oneself as actor and creator of life. This has much to do with maturity as well as the successful termination of analysis.

This theme will be elucidated by the description of a patient who, two years into analysis, reconstructed with intense affect the memory of a molestation fifty years earlier of which she had no awareness before. One of the important contributing factors to the initial repression was the atmosphere of disbelief and denial that surrounded her attempts to tell others of what had happened. All of the protagonists with one exception were long since dead. As the analysis progressed, it became clear that the patient needed to integrate the experience, not to establish blame but to have a clearer idea of who she was. Six years after the end of analysis there was a touching confirmation of the reality of the event by an old family friend on her deathbed.

The details of the analysis were recorded not only in process notes but in a diary that the patient maintained during her analysis and which she offered after the analysis was over. The patient gave permission to use this material and was pleased to have been given a copy of this paper to read.

HISTORY

The patient was a 52-year-old married mother of three who presented with a moderate depression in the context of a number of distressing experiences, foremost among them her sense of rejection by a younger male artist for whom she had been a mentor and who had been treated as a surrogate child in her family. Though depressed and inclined to control her feelings, she was an expressive woman, articulate, intelligent, and sensitive, trying her best to maintain a "stiff upper lip." It was easy to empathize with her and to communicate understanding of the distress that she was experiencing. An additional burden was the poor communication that existed between her and her well-meaning husband who was emotionally isolated and psychologically naive. During our initial encounter I noticed a certain asymmetry of her face, but it was only in the second session that she revealed in an offhand way that she had been born without an ear on the left side, deafness, and a slight asymmetry of the face. She had had a reparative surgical correction during adolescence. She affirmed, however, in a clear and loud voice that she had worked out any difficulties about this. She could say "with certainty" that the abnormality caused her no current problems. She emphasized that her childhood had been basically a happy one. These two themes, of course, were to be the subject of important parts of the analysis.

The patient indicated that while she had been quite shy as a child, her relationship with her attentive and emotionally responsive mother had been extremely positive, although mother was subservient to the patient's father who was domineering, demanding, and rigid. The patient, the middle child of three, had an older brother who became the pariah for the father when he failed to meet father's expectations in school and in sports. A younger brother, cut to the father's mold, was the preferred sibling. The family was a prestigious one that traced its roots on both sides through many generations in this country. The patient's beloved maternal grandmother had been an important presence in the patient's life. Her approbation gave the patient a sense of special value.

Generally a compliant child, adolescent, and young adult, the patient had a successful career in the best schools and colleges, married, and enjoyed her role as mother to her three daughters. But she felt bereft as they moved to greater independence, this accentuated by the sense of rejection by the young artist mentioned above. The patient became very active in important roles, both at her college and in charitable organizations.

THE INITIAL EVALUATION AND TREATMENT

Although the patient was intelligent, introspective, and highly motivated, she hesitated to accept the recommendation for formal analysis, and the initial contact was an analytic therapy twice a week vis-à-vis for six months before a more formal analytic arrangement four times a week on the couch began.[1] Over the course of this period it became apparent that she was fearful of losing control over her feelings, "becoming crazy," and was also fearful of challenging the structure of the life that she had constructed so carefully over the years. In particular she was fearful of examining the wall that she had built to protect herself from awareness of the impact of the congenital anomaly. There was no awareness of the traumatic event of her childhood.

The patient's initial response to the couch was to focus on the positive aspects of change that had occurred since she had begun treatment. She spoke of the relief of depression and the sense of belonging in many areas of her life, particularly in the professional areas where she took great responsibility.

[1] Although I call this psychotherapy to avoid a debate at this point about the nature of psychoanalysis as a therapy, our interaction during this period had all the qualities of what would be called psychoanalysis. I will reserve this discussion for another paper in anticipation of a panel at the 1996 Spring meeting of the American Psychoanalytic Association on psychoanalysis less than four times a week.

As the initial positive response to analysis was elaborated, she began to move into revelation of conflicts as they pertained to her congenital abnormality. These themes evolved for the most part in a context of a benevolent and trusting transference. Stormier periods were to follow. In discussing the imbalance between her personal and marital life and her increasing sense of success in the outside world, she stated, "Why do I feel so lopsided, that part of me has grown and developed and that another part of me has not?" She was shocked when I directed her attention to the physical implications of the metaphor, and the patient began to recognize her rage at her parents for having created her in a defective way. She recognized a feeling that her parents had been very relieved when her husband had chosen to marry her, although she had been indecisive about the marriage and felt that it was her role to please her parents. It was never clear to her what her husband had felt about her infirmity. She recognized that this "lopsided sense" pertained to many aspects of her life. On the one hand she had felt safe and protected as a child by her parents, but this at the cost of being the good child, the angel. On the other was the difficult world outside in which she felt less sure of herself. This dichotomy was expressed in the difficulty the patient had in leaving sessions, and a ritual that she evolved in which she would first sit up, silently wait for a few minutes, then gradually swing her legs over the side of the couch, sit silently, turn to direct her gaze at me, and then slowly leave. She lived in a world of both lightness related to her accomplishments, which generated a good sense of herself, and heaviness that surrounded her personal life and other feelings about herself. Identifications with defective people began to emerge more clearly in her fantasy life. She was powerfully moved by and identified with the victims of the Holocaust, victims of physically deforming diseases, individuals with elephantiasis (then in the news), and homosexuals who had been discriminated against. The overprotection by her mother was a proof of her defectiveness, and only her nanny and her grandmother "allowed her to develop in her own right." These figures were positive figures in her life and were the prototype for the positive and trusting transference. The transference in both its positive and negative aspects often became more manifest after the emergence of pertinent genetic material rather than before it.

As a new view of self was consolidated through the uncovering of the fantasies of the damaged self, she became much more comfortable with her body, purchased earrings proudly for the first time in her life. One day she began by sitting on the couch, turning to me and stating, "I think it is time to show you my ear," which had been covered by her hair. She revealed at this time an ear that had been reconstructed, though it did not have the perfection of the right ear. This was a nodal point in her acceptance of her physical self as she was. The consolidation of self also involved the interpretation of a secret fantasy of identification with the *Scarlet Pimpernel*, the highly idealized man who was hidden and when exposed would be admired and loved. When I interpreted this secret identification as reflecting her sense that her successes were compensations for something missing rather than solid bricks on a solid edifice, she began to recognize that she had had a secret reparative fantasy of being a little boy, and that she had been tempted to give up her interest in art to maintain this fantasy. This coincided with the realization of a negative identification with the older "defective and unsuccessful brother," by which I mean that the patient's ideal self representation was the inverse of the representation of the devalued brother.

In a context of her consolidation of a new sense of self, an angry paternal transference developed as she outlined her father's distance and lack of attention to her. When I interpreted her resentment at my not taking note of her accomplishments, she began to sob and describe with bitterness the sense of deprivation from the ungiving father who had "put her in the institution of marriage" to be rid of her. As her hostility was progressively analyzed, she began to have memories of erotic fantasies about her plastic surgeon and his resident assistant. This led to the recovery of memories of good moments with father, of shared experiences on the ski slopes, and periodic moments of communication. There was a diminished intensity of displaced angry feelings directed toward her husband. It was in the context of an increasingly positive and defined sense of femininity that an erotic paternal transference developed. This led to the emergence of dreams and fragmented memories that only later would be understood as related to a sexual trauma.

In tandem with the development of erotic transference was the emergence of memories of her powerful, supportive grandmother, an ideal object and an object of identification. This grandmother, who was a professional well ahead of her time, had been a bedrock of strength for the patient in her early development. Grandmother had given her the sense that she was different rather than defective (Lussier, 1980), and was to be a major figure in the drama that was to unfold about her sexual molestation.

The analysis of the resistance to a developing erotic transference permitted an examination of sexual inhibitions and the emergence of fragments of memories and fantasies connected with the molestation. The emergence of erotic feelings was consistently associated with a fear of abandonment.

A premonitory dream took place in her grandmother's house.

> I was in her bedroom. It seemed to be mine. There was an open door looking at in the hall. A man came by either in his underpants or clad with a towel and I was aware of the fact that he was virtually naked. We had only verbal contact not physical contact.

The patient's associations pertained to her grandmother's house and the ghost of men. Her grandfather had abruptly abandoned his wife for a younger woman. Grandmother had maintained his study in the state it was left, with all of his books, photographs of paintings, and paintings (mummification; Viederman, 1988), an indication of unresolved mourning. The patient's uncle, a strange man, disapproved of by the grandmother, spent much time in this room. Shame and guilt about sexuality were associated with grandmother's remonstrations about the importance of keeping private parts clean. Periodic anxiety would emerge with fragmented dreams and memories, the sources of which were unclear. In one dream she was outside a door in the upstairs landing of a house in the country, wanting something in the room but unable to get in. What was in the room?

Sexual feelings became more intense as the patient dreamt of being fitted with a diaphragm by two younger men in a hospital associated with the plastic surgeons who had done reparative work on her ear. The patient became concerned about her body. During the period of surgery she had felt that her body didn't belong to her. "They would do what they wanted to me and all I could do was complain." This was a feeling she experienced in lovemaking.

Frightening memories came to mind of Nazi concentration camps where tormentors exerted tyrannical control over other people's bodies and selves. She recognized her macabre identification with "the victim," and realized that an initial fear of analysis on the couch was that her mind and body would be taken over. She remembered her rage at her intimidating mother-in-law who exerted control by spanking the patient's daughter for a minor infraction. Her oldest brother's child had been born defective, and she recoiled at the thought that the doctors had recommended that they let it die. She acknowledged her wish to be like her adored little brother so loved by the father. She dreamt of an inconsolable and very plain baby whose sex was unclear and who didn't want to reveal whether it was a boy or a girl. The patient mourned the loss of an idealized perfect self that included the fantasy of being a boy. This was followed by a reassuring dream of the resumption of menstrual periods connected with the experience of being complete in her femininity. Periodic eruptions of anger in a paternal transference related to frustration of erotic wishes and my failure to confirm her feminine self. As she relinquished the wish to be a perfect boy child and began to accept her femininity, memories of a fantasy world of herself as a beautiful girl emerged. An oedipal theme developed and she spoke of competition with her mother for the attention of the highly admired plastic surgeon. This was accompanied by erotic feelings in the transference.

THE EMERGENCE OF THE TRAUMATIC MOLESTATION

Over the course of a month and a half, new material began to emerge that ultimately crystallized into the extremely painful and agonizing memory of having been molested by her uncle. Immediate external stimuli had to do with the social climate when this was being examined in analysis. The newspapers at that time were describing in considerable detail Masson's attack on Freud and his contention that Freud had abandoned the traumatic theory of neurosis for political and personal reasons. The patient was incensed by the idea that a person could be confronted with the disavowal of a real seduction in those around, and frequently referred to it with anger during this phase of the analysis. Material about the molestation appeared in dreams and associations which only gradually took on definable form.

A series of dreams ushered in this new phase.

> I am off with a group of people who are friends, and in particular a man who was important to me. I want to be embraced by him and kissed by him but it is important not to show how I feel. I had slippers on and took them off and when I came back they were gone.

> A dream with M in it (her daughter)—she is leaning over a fence and stated that she wanted to know about . . . the patient's . . . uncle. She leaned over so far and fell down into a ravine with water at the bottom. I had a sense that she couldn't survive and then she turned around and came up and I woke up crying.

> Michel came back. This time I would not let the opportunity pass to sleep with him.

The patient felt there was great danger in asking about her uncle. Michel, a colleague, was associated with Richard Chamberlain in the *Thorn Birds*, a priest who fell in love and had an illicit affair with a young woman. The young girl, named M, with whom she identified, was an adolescent when seen by the priest and was clearly attracted to the older, unavailable man. Why had her maternal uncle come to mind? He was a romantic figure, a drinker, irresponsible, and a black sheep in the family. Characteristic was his sudden decision to marry a girl of a different social class. To the patient's surprise she had been asked to be the flower girl at the wedding. Later his wife became psychotic and had finished her life in a mental institution. The patient's mother would send her packages of soap and slippers, an element in the dream in which she was embraced. Wasn't it curious that when the patient went on trips she always brought soap, and was particularly attentive to footwear? Some strange identification was operating.

The patient entered the next session in a panic about a dream which she had remembered during a board meeting. In this and at a previous meeting she had experienced a newfound sense of competence.

Milton Viederman

Entry from the patient's diary: [2]

Date. A breakthrough session—and most unexpected. I arrived in a state—coming from a meeting with tremendous urgency to get there. It was difficult to get it all out to him—why I was so relieved to get there. All a little incoherent and confused. Thank goodness he is patient and understanding. Giving it to him—the sequence all confused. Here I will do it in sequence as it happened.

Woke up thinking again.—No dreams but a strange bit flashed through my mind dressing—I remembered I was in a dark "space"—a van was there—and I was lying down—there was some kind of metal contraption that went from my vagina to my rectum—I didn't seem upset about it—just there. This flash startled me but hardly thought about it again. At meeting—they brought up how "special" I was—completely accepted. Later I took taxi to another board meeting—I thought I can really accept something like that now—can realize what I am capable of and what I do without feeling apologetic, unworthy, or even puffed up—this is a change. Made me feel a little tearful, didn't know why.

During board meeting suddenly image of dream came up again—as though it had some connection with my thoughts about accepting my abilities. Wondered but let my thoughts go—and other images came up—the old garage at the country house—meeting Bill [parents' handyman] for the first time (I was about 6 or 7) all very strange and very intense. Realized the force of all of this—and had urgent sense about getting to Dr. V. yet wanting to stay with that group—safety even though they knew nothing.

Left and took taxi—experienced real panic about getting there and seeing him.

All of this came pouring out along with tears. The actual dream came out at the end—this painful.

---

[2]The presence of the diary and full process notes will offer the opportunity at a later date to examine discrepancies in the two texts and to consider their implications. It was apparent early in the analysis that she was writing a diary which she had also done in the past. Clearly this had multiple meanings which were analyzed. It permitted a continuing dialogue with me when I was not there and therefore a reminder of my presence in the face of anxiety about separation. It was a method of organizing her experience, thereby containing her anxiety. Important was the sense of the diary as a "secret sharer," a person with whom she could have a most intimate dialogue when she was alone. Not least in importance was her wish to document her experience as the trauma revealed itself in the face of the public debate on the existence of childhood molestation. This became apparent only later in the analysis.

Other thoughts coming up. It all had to do with the hired man before Bill—no image of him—think he was Jack. Left under a cloud—don't remember him.

Image of Bill rescuing me from bathroom where I was locked in—through window—there always had been trouble with the lock since.

So much unclear. Dr. Viederman: "What about the van?" Don't know but image—when Bill retired he went to live in a trailer—I always thought it was awful to live in one. I loved Bill.

Told him [Dr. V.] my feeling as I woke that my vagina was "wide-open," had same feeling as I walked to get the taxi. "It didn't come from me." He asked me where Bill slept—told him wasn't sure when he first came, later in the house, but the other man slept over the garage.

I finally came to the point, I have the feeling—but no image—that it has to do with "Jack"—he must have exposed himself to me—or something—I can't get any more but this is my sense.

I told him—at board and coming over, so frightened as I realized something important and new, the surface—afraid of it but didn't want to lose it—have it stuck back again—kept thinking—calm down and it will go away—he interpreted and said this sounded like sexual excitement. I don't know. Do know I wanted to keep it till I saw him.[3]

The fear I have had so many times—that I will lose him—he will disappear—there is such urgency—he said why—I said if this had been there for fifty years and now the chance to get it out—so afraid I will lose him who is my chance to do this.

He [was] concerned something like "exposure" must have happened. Other thoughts coming up—the time in Rochester for my grandfather's funeral—my father's pajamas open, leaning over—his penis coming out.

Told him like hunting for pieces of a puzzle to all go together—so difficult and painful—many tears. Then time was up and I told him that it was terrible to have to go—he said he knew that—the hardest time yet—oh, yes! kept crying—told him whatever this was—it had scared me all my life. More tears I know. It has a connection with my feelings about accepting my abilities—as though this had given all that had been repressed a push that sent it up toward the conscious (to get it out).

---

[3]This was a premature interpretation. The patient's experience was fear, not desire. The disruption of empathic communication not only led to the fear that she would lose me but was consistent with her fear that erotic feeling would lead to abandonment.

He—when you realized that you weren't "a fuzzy think-er"—yes I feel I am getting to know that.

Sitting up—found that I was physically shaking—feet on floor, I still couldn't stop sobbing. He "It is all right to cry." When he said I had to go I said, "I feel like a baby and you are going to say you mustn't cry." I just cried harder and said, "I feel I am crying about this for the first time. When all this happened someone must have said, 'Don't cry that is being a baby.' "

Also said, you don't know what it is like to be able to cry about it. I have been frightened all my life. It has kept me from feeling good about myself.

He was wonderful. Took time to let me get through this. Sweet and gentle. Finally able to leave with him telling me that we did have time, we would find all the pieces of the puzzle. I know there is more. I don't feel that I am at the bottom and I always know when I am. He told me I could stay as long as I wanted in the waiting room and he gently checked up on me a few times in the next fifteen minutes.[4]

It has been an extraordinary experience—to find that there was something so hidden I had been totally unaware of all these years and only gradually have hints of it these last months. I left totally wrung out and exhausted and still very tearful—to meet . . . husband . . . for cocktails! I did manage to pull myself together pretty well."

On the following day on Saturday she called with fear and panic and I again reassured her about the intense feeling what had so long been repressed.

On Monday the patient indicated that she had been very reassured by my presence over the weekend and emphasized the love

---

[4]A brief comment about technique is indicated here. Each of the reviewers of this article commented on this issue but in markedly divergent ways. The first indicated that my supportive behavior manifested by touching the patient, asking her to sit up, giving her my telephone numbers, checking on her in the waiting room, and my direct reassurance, were puzzling and required a discussion of their rationale and impact (see pp. 1181–1182, footnote 5). The second reviewer believed that I was too apologetic about this behavior and that I was "backing away from a fuller exploration and possible reappraisal of traditional concepts of neutrality and abstinence in working with patients who have suffered sexual abuse," a view with which I concur. The third viewed these behaviors as parameters and wondered whether they were subjected to analytic scrutiny. It is clear from these contradictory views that psychoanalytic technique is changing and is the subject of vigorous debate. Bibring (1964) treats the subject with much less self-consciousness in emphasizing that all therapies include elements of suggestion, abreaction, manipulation, clarification, and interpretation in different degrees. This will be addressed in a subsequent paper.

and respect that she had received from so many people, including those outside her family. The diary response:

> I could believe him and accept that—just as last Thursday I accepted what had been said to me about my work at the board meeting—this seemed to be the nudge that started every-thing—Dr. V. had said something about beginning to accept how people feel about me. I want to go back to that, to find out what he said. I feel it has to do with believing in myself. It has taken all this time because, "They didn't believe me back when this happened and so I grew up not believing in myself."
>
> A lot of thoughts came up over the weekend. I am very sure now that two events took place. One in the cellar and one in the garage. I have such strong feelings about both places, I never liked going into that cellar—didn't feel that way apart from the old cellar. All dark and concrete—don't like going into any cellar even in my country house. Felt the same way about garage even when it was redone into my father's study.
>
> I think he must have exposed himself to me in the cel-lar—but more in his room in the garage—I don't think it was his penis but his hands.
>
> Thoughts came up about *Sophie's Choice*, the incident when she is "finger-fucked" in the subway. It horrified me—feel the same way about rape too, though it has some terrible fascina-tion—then at . . . grandchild's . . . birthday Sunday—one of the mothers said she thought I would find lots of little toys in the sofa later, and I laughingly said I would have to run my fingers around the cracks, and this whole incident came up so strongly I told him it was horrible. Another image—the time I was in the bathroom at 12 or 14 looking at myself—I realize now it was to see if I had a hymen—had just read about this in a book.
>
> I do keep wondering about Jack. He is still so hazy and I think about Bill, but my feelings for him were so strong and good. I loved him and he was one of the people who sustained me and treated me as I was—a little girl. Dr. Viederman broke in and said, "This is what you were, you were just a little girl." He then said he thought I should sit up before I had to go. I couldn't believe it was time, but I knew I needed some human contact. I told him how terrible it was to leave.

The patient then spoke about her anxiety about my impending departure for a meeting and I offered my telephone number at the hotel where I was staying.[5]

[5]Anxiety about separation had been manifest from early in the analysis and related to the expectation of abandonment for unacceptable impulses and fantasies of both an erotic and aggressive nature. The emergence at this time of erotic feelings

I had told him I felt like a baby. He said, and I repeated, "You have nothing to be ashamed of in many different ways." I had so many mixed feelings going on in my head. He said, "Little by little all of this would be put in perspective and in its place and we will work it through." I left with a pat on the shoulder from him. All of this has been very hard, but knowing that I will come out of it eventually, and his strong support and sympathy, has made it possible to keep at it. It would have been easier not to go over all the details, but I have the sense that if I don't I will just have to go back to them and they are so painful. I hope I have the strength to keep at it and not just collapse under the weight of it all.

The sessions over the week before I left for a week-long meeting were charged with tension and anxiety. The patient cried repeatedly, but new memories emerged and old memories took on new significance. For the most part she was extremely anxious to come to the sessions where she found relief in spite of the continuing and painful emergence of new material. At the same time she was relieved at the weekend to be able to avoid the confrontation. She speculated about Bill and Jack and repudiated the idea that it was Bill who exposed himself. She remembered going into the bathroom with a sense that she had gone in there to do something that she shouldn't have done. She locked herself in by mistake, and it was her nanny who discovered her and Bill who released her. She must have looked at herself in the mirror and thought of herself again as "damaged goods," the old feeling she had experienced with her father. She would never have gone to her father to tell him about the molestation, but certainly must have spoken to her beloved nanny. Nonetheless there was the feeling that she had not been believed. The nanny felt she had done all she could do by informing the grandmother, and the patient had to make the best of it. The patient was aware of the fact that fantasies could be very strong, but she was sure that this wasn't fantasy, even though she couldn't yet get a clear image of

---

and fragmented memories of the molestation coincided with the impending separation, and by confirming the patient's fears led to extreme anxiety and some derealization. It is also possible, although it was not obvious in the material, that the impending separation evoked elements of the molestation with the wishful expectation of a reassuring enactment with me. I felt that the situation required that I assert my presence by having her see me briefly at the end of the session and by offering my telephone number. I believe that this supportive and reassuring mode is necessary in the context of the emergence and analysis of a disorganizing traumatic situation.

what had happened. At the end of one session she again sat in the waiting room and other images kept coming up. When I found her unable to leave I called her back into the office and she stood there sobbing. She told me that she couldn't go, that it made her feel as if I didn't believe her, that she couldn't go back there alone the way she had in the past and start all over again. She sat down and talked and said that she knew that I hadn't sent her away but it was the way she felt. She was fearful of leaving me. She told me of the images—the garage: "It wasn't a van but a room upstairs, Jack's room, and I was screaming. He said if you don't tell I will give you ice cream. My feelings about ice cream—I had loved eating it but since then I really couldn't." I told her that I would be at home during the weekend and I offered my home number. In response to her question I indicated that it was not unusual for someone to react so intensely over something that had been repressed for so many years. She felt she had really touched the bottom and I told her that this wouldn't disappear, that she wouldn't have to forget this, that she was no longer the child to which it had happened. She ended her diary note, "A harrowing session—thank goodness for him and his willingness to see me through it. A warm handshake at the end. He told me be careful about locking the bathroom door, and we were both able to laugh."

This spontaneous remark reflected my countertransference need to diminish anxiety, which was successful in that it led to shared laughter, and that we could deal with the material on another level. On later reflection, it appeared that I was communicating a concern about the patient's shutting me out and was suggesting that she be careful to keep the erotic channel open.

Another important theme in the sessions before I left related to the patient's fear and anger about abandonment. This was manifested clearly in the transference, but had its roots in the sense that everyone had abandoned her during this period, that no one had believed her, or acknowledged that anything had happened.

Upon my return it was apparent that she had developed a mild phobia about going down into the subway. The recognition that this was related to the fear of cellars relieved her and the phobia disappeared. Her anxiety about being crazy was related to a feeling of unreality about the experience and the failure of the adults to confirm what had happened. The central theme became the disbelief that had surrounded her which evoked derealization with mild dissociation.

Over the next few months the intensity of the patient's anxiety diminished and she began to recognize how the congenital anomaly *and* the molestation had crystallized her sense of defectiveness. This had accentuated her need to be the good girl. The patient had an angry dream in which I was sitting back in a chair with my hands on my head. She associated with the indifference of her father. She was fearful that her rage would alienate me.

Over the next six months the patient became calmer as what she now called "the incident" was integrated with her familiar sense of herself. As we examined guilt and anxiety about sexual feelings she became freer sexually and experienced gratification with her husband. The realization that the two important themes—her anomaly and the incident—were connected in her mind was liberating.

Then something disturbing arose having to do with physical sensations which were sexual. This made her fearful of lying on the couch. "This trauma was becoming more and more intense as I found myself letting myself go—words were coming up but at the same time the battle was going on to subdue all of it. Words 'Stop all of this ridiculousness'; 'Pull yourself together'; Thoughts of Nana, also of husband." The patient began to sob. As the intensity of her feelings increased, the patient began to experience panicky confusion and needed reassurance that she wasn't crazy, that people weren't laughing at her, that it wasn't all her imagination. She gradually calmed with the assurance that she wasn't going crazy. She remembered with anger the vision of her nanny, Nana, telling her to stop the nonsense and wondered whether it was all in her head. She realized that it was Nana and her father who were saying stop the nonsense and also that she should not tell her mother. I asked why not? Suddenly she had the fragmented memory of a mustached man in the dream and said with great feeling 'It was my uncle; my mother's brother. The one who didn't like me. I could never understand why he had asked me to be a bridesmaid at the wedding. (She sobbed.) It was for this reason they were protecting my mother, and I had to go it all alone." What emerged was that her uncle on two occasions had fondled her genitals and had her touch his penis.

There had been no penetration but the patient had been very frightened and had been offered ice cream not to tell.

It was with the realization that her uncle was the culprit that the threads of the drama came together. Most traumatic was the atmosphere of disbelief and the insistence that the mother be protected. She remembered being summarily contradicted about whether anything had happened and criticized by her beloved grandmother for "having such thoughts and not telling the truth." This had been the most traumatic aspect of the entire incident. The patient turned and with great anxiety confronted me with the question as to whether I believed her. I replied that I did.[6]

A great mystery in the family was thereby solved. The grandmother had left her entire house with furnishings to her in her will, this to the surprise of the entire family since there were many grandchildren. The patient realized that her distaste for ice cream, her need to carry slippers and soap on trips, reflected an identification with the uncle's psychotic wife. Her fear of cellars also had its origin in the incident. Gradually the intensity of the feeling diminished and the incident was integrated.

Years after the analysis, a conversation with a now dying, extremely aged friend of the grandmother, confirmed that she knew of the event that had occurred years before.

DISCUSSION

Conditions for the Emergence of the Repressed Memory

Freud used the onionskin metaphor to allude to the progressive analysis of defense, with revelation of unconscious fantasy and its interpretation, with a repetition of the cycle as analysis deepens. This pertains to the microscopic evolution of an analysis. If, however, one

---

[6]The patient realized that I had no special knowledge. My response was authentic. The patient revealed later, that she felt that my response was necessary to keep her from pushing all underneath again. I shall not address the issue of narrative versus historical truth (Spence, 1982), although I will discuss the question of belief below. My position is a constructionist one, so elegantly described by Gill (1994), in which he regards experiences described as an amalgam of innate and experiential elements. I also recognize that the analytic method does not lend itself or for the most part occupy itself with the distinction between event and fantasy, both ingredients of memory.

takes a macroscopic view, one might view process from a point of view of intermediate goals which when achieved, permit the emergence of a new domain of previously repressed material. Inferences about transitional goals that precede nodal points in the analysis may be possible if one examines the state of the patient before particularly significant, painful, and frightening repressed material emerges. One might examine the transference situation, and in particular modified aspects of the self representations and object representations, these to be viewed as way stations that signal the potentiality for the emergence of new material.

Levine (1990), Raphling (1990), and Bernstein (1990) indicate that before traumatic sexual material can emerge in analysis, an atmosphere of safety and trust must be developed. Important to emphasize in the analysis of this patient was that the benevolent transference evolved after the analysis of negative paternal and fraternal transferences. Although these transferences had not been entirely resolved, an important negative aspect had come to the surface and been interpreted. The patient's long-standing fear that her anger would drive her father away had been partially worked through with the emergence and interpretation of transference to me as the disinterested and uncaring father. As this was examined the patient modified her self representation and she began to see herself as a person worthy of attention and care. This permitted the emergence of more benevolent trusting transferences related to early figures in her life such as her nanny, her mother, her grandmother, and the surgeon who had been so supportive during her reparative surgery. Moreover, our consistent work together had permitted the emergence of an ideal parental transference (to be distinguished from idealized [Viederman, 1991]) that solidified the sense of protection and safety.

Of special importance was the significant change in her self representation as a damaged, unworthy, and vulnerable figure who had been a burden to her parents. Her more positive sense of self emerged as she recognized and dissociated herself from her identifications with the grotesque, the victim, the devalued homosexual, and so on, though she remained compassionate toward them. It was with an increasingly confident sense of self, a sense of self worthy of attention and less fearful of abandonment, that she could approach

the traumatic sexual molestation. The consolidated new self representation with its strength and defined identity was a necessary pre-
lude to permit her to withstand the disorganizing emergence of the
traumatic past experience. This could occur only in the context of
the security and sense of personal value that gave her the confidence
to allow an erotic transference to develop. The emergence of the
erotic transference, a major step in the analysis itself, led to the
terrifying emergence of the memory. It is of particular interest that
the patient remembered the initial dream that ushered in the phase
of reconstruction at a time when her sense of confidence had been
officially confirmed by those about her and she was feeling particularly good, having consciously noted her newfound sense of comfort
in this important role with peers.

Important to note as well is the fact that the patient's wish to
be a boy, her phallic identification, had been a defense against her
own devalued sense of femininity, and that the analysis of this defensive operation permitted the emergence of more secure femininity
that was to participate in the development of the erotic transference.
An important change in her self representation had preceded this
next phase of the analysis.

Hence, internal releasing factors and external stimuli related to
the Masson–Freud debate, which was covered extensively in *The New
York Times* and weekly news magazines, converged to create a fertile
field for the emergence of fragments of memories pertaining to the
initial sexual molestation and ultimately to the reconstruction. An
additional element was the supportive role that I played as the material emerged, which is discussed below. She clearly experienced me
as a partner in her struggle to overcome the pain of the traumatic situation.

THE NATURE OF RECONSTRUCTION

Although reconstruction is often viewed as a function of the analyst,
this was not the case here. Not only was the patient a primary actor
in the reconstruction but the reconstruction was accompanied by
powerful affects and involved a reexperience that was of a different
order than an intellectualized explanation (Viederman, 1994).

Although the use of the terms *construction* and *reconstruction* is not consistent in the literature, Blum (1994) defines construction as the organization in the mind of the analyst of a view of the childhood antecedents of conflict; whereas reconstruction is a complex form of interpretation that involves a coherent and integrated statement of early life experience as it relates to current behavior. He distinguishes reconstruction from genetic interpretation which he sees as more limited and particulate, involving the suggestion of an impulse or a fear at a moment in past time.

> Reconstruction, however, applies to those genetic interventions where the patient does not specifically recapture and recall infantile fantasy and experience. Using all the data of the analysis such as transference, dreams, screen memories, and fragments of memory, the analyst synthesizes the analytic evidence to reconstruct a piece of the patient's past . . . as an integrated act [Blum, 1994].

In his view, reconstruction is a statement, a type of interpretation by the analyst that integrates fragments of past life experience and fantasy which the patient may or may not remember. Hence the reconstruction of which Blum speaks may be intellectual and function to give coherence rather than emotional conviction. Emphasis is, of course, placed on the complexity of memory with the recognition that memory is modified by fantasy and changes throughout life and during analysis.

I distinguish this point of view from my use of the term *reconstruction*. Here I refer to the gradual recovery and beginning awareness of memory of a specific traumatic event as the patient struggles to integrate material from dreams, fantasies, and memories. In this situation, it was the patient who reconstructed the trauma, although this was facilitated by interpretation of defense or questions pertaining to feeling states. The emergence of this material was accompanied by intense painful affect, particularly anxiety, and in itself seemed like a secondary trauma (a point made by Blum) accompanied by some derealization. That the patient did not experience depersonalization may be a tribute to work already done in the analysis reflected in a stable self representation. The experience of derealization related to the regressive disturbance of the sense of reality, which was generated by the unwillingness of those who surrounded her to accept the reality of what had happened. Once exposed, what had happened became an important focal point for the patient's under-standing of conflicted behavior and symptomatic acts. Important also was the contribution of fantasy to experience as memories are formed and changed throughout life. Blum addresses the issue of conviction by analyst and patient, but belief which involves an emo-tional component seems to be minimized by Blum whose view of reconstruction often seems intellectual and explanatory. Admittedly, the search for meaning and coherence is important and character-izes human experience. However, does it directly lead to structural change if the experiential element in the recovery of the past (which I see as central) is not present? Freud himself (1937) spoke of "the explanations," emphasizing that it is "the analyst's task to make out what had been forgotten from the traces which it has left behind or, more correctly, to construct it" (pp. 258–259). Freud's archaeologi-cal metaphor is curiously undynamic in that it rests on inert frag-ments of the past rather than on living remains. Freud's regression model of a repressed dynamic past is more appropriate in consider-ing the therapeutic aspects of the reworking of the past in psycho-analysis (Viederman, 1994).

It is important to note that the important emphasis on transfer-ence as the primary therapeutic modality, relates to the view that it is the only sure method of reexperiencing the past, albeit in modified form. Analysts such as Kris (1956) doubted whether "the seduction of the staircase" could be accurately reconstructed. The experience with my patient belies his view if by "seduction of the staircase" Kris means traumatic events, recovered as memories with feeling.

MEMORY OR FANTASY: THE QUESTION OF BELIEF

It was only years later that the patient was able to confirm from external sources that a real incident had occurred. Clearly, in the absence of external confirmation it was impossible to determine whether fantasy or memory of actual trauma was emerging. In prac-tice, the analyst often has the luxury of ignoring this distinction, and indeed it generally is not considered his task to make such a judg-ment. However, it has been noted that analysts frequently develop views about the reality or truth value of what patients tell them.

As the patient and I groped to understand what was painfully emerging we began to be suspicious that an incident had occurred. By the time she became aware that it was her uncle who had been involved, I believed that an incident involving her uncle had in fact occurred. Gradually I had been coming to believe that the patient was reconstructing a real event. Important were the prolonged and painful circumstances of its appearance and the degree of panic, disorganization, and derealization that the material was creating. Moreover a thesis of this paper is that in stable personalities important traumatic memories emerge only after structural change has a bearing on the question. Is it possible that one criterion related to the truth value of a significant traumatic memory has to do with the requirement that substantial structural change anteceded the recovery of the memory in the form of a modification of the representational world? Other elements contributed to my belief. As the story became more complete, many seemingly incomprehensible behaviors of the patient and circumstances of her history became clear. Her dislike for ice cream, her fear of cellars, her need to take soap and slippers on trips, reflective of her identification with her uncle's psychotic wife, became clear. Of special importance was the understanding of the grandmother's gift to her of her valued house upon her death. This was an implied recompense for the grandmother's unwillingness to acknowledge the uncle's behavior. Admittedly none of this proved the reality of the event and both the patient and I were aware of this.

Person and Klar (1994) suggest that traumatic memories tend to be dissociated rather than repressed, as is the case with wishful unconscious fantasy. "The impermeability of the boundary of the dissociated memory works primarily in one direction; the memory appears to be intact from revision, but it continues to influence other products of the mind" (p. 1072). Moreover they emphasize that, "trauma may be encoded primarily at the sensory-motor level rather than in symbolic linguistic forms, whereas fantasy is encoded primarily but not exclusively, in symbolic linguistic forms," and therefore undergoes all of the transformations characteristic of the primary process. They go on to indicate that, as was the case with my patient, many individuals "recovered traumatic memories when they hear or read about others' accounts of abuse" (p. 1073), and that their awareness of the dilemma of others tends to facilitate the recovery of their own memories since "the stigmatization that they have applied to their own experience is to some degree mitigated" (p. 1072). The authors go on to point out that these memories appear to be more intensely charged and more visual or sensory in their presentation than do other memories, and it is this vividness that marks them as veridical. Moreover, as they emerge in analysis, they seem to be out of the main flow of transference reactions. Although this was the case with my patient, she did not reveal the significant splitting and defined alternate ego state described by Davies and Frawley (1991). Many factors contributed to a higher level of integration, including positive aspects of her background, probably innate constitutional factors, and the fact that the person who molested her was less central in her life. The betrayal by grandmother had a more powerful impact than the incidents themselves.

An important aspect of the continuing elaboration of the traumatic event for this patient and for many others has to do with the problem of belief in the reality of the event. One of the most traumatic aspects of the patient's experience, and an important contributor to the repression, was the unwillingness of otherwise trusted members of the family to acknowledge that the event had occurred. This was to lead to an important moment in the analysis when the patient in a panic turned to me and asked whether I believed her. I did believe that an event had occurred and I acknowledged this in response to her imperative request. She was immensely relieved and then remembered her grandmother's refusal to acknowledge the incident. On a number of occasions after this and in a contact long after the analysis was over, she expressed her gratitude and stated her conviction that had I not acknowledged the actuality of the event, it all would have gone underground once again only questionably to reemerge. Although my action was a transference–countertransference enactment I believe that it was in the service of furthering the analysis.

INTEGRATION OF THE INCIDENT

How might one understand the ultimate integration of the incident? I am treating the "incident" as a presumed fact rather than a fantasy.

Moreover before the configuration of the "incident" became clear to the patient the memories had elements that ultimately changed, in particular the identity of the perpetrator. Hence they were screen memories. But at what point does a screen memory become a real memory? Clearly it is impossible to know since one psychic element may at any time defend against and conceal another. This presents the same problem as the truth value of memory and is theoretically unresolvable in the psychoanalytic situation.

This patient had many assets. The molestation, though traumatic, was not manifestly violent, occurred on only two occasions, and did not involve direct penetration. The patient was surrounded by many warm and supportive people ("a magic circle"), though their unwillingness to acknowledge the incident contributed strongly to the traumatic effect. Yet the patient integrated the experience in a highly adaptive way. Although it had had profound repercussions on her life experience, it was not utilized as a central organizing theme to explain the patient's life or to justify neurotic behavior. It did not redefine her as the victim but freed her the burden of being an outcast. Unlike those situations in which the false "recovery of memory" is used to indict relatives (Wright, 1994) or to justify a sense of bitter victimization, it enriched the patient's self-understanding and freed her from the sense of defectiveness and unworthiness. She did not become the narcissistic exception (Freud, 1916) as has been described by Kramer (1983) in cases of sexual abuse.

CODA

Five years after the end of the analysis a letter sent by the patient to me put the final period on the event.

> I'm sending you the enclosed to go with my notebooks as I think it is an appropriate part of the material.
>
> It was a very important conversation for me and writing it down in this way has helped me put it together in the right context and now I can leave it. I do marvel that it took place and that it came out the way it did, but then we know amazing things happen!
>
> It has always puzzled me that no one ever referred to this incident to me over the years, particularly as an adult. Perhaps

those who knew of it repressed it, just as I did, and perhaps only a few knew. By the time I became aware of it only two people remained who I thought might have known; my god-mother in her nineties and a close friend of my family's, in her eighties. My godmother has died and as her health and then her mind began to fail, I never asked her about this. However, during my years of analysis . . . the friend . . . was vigorous and I saw her frequently. She was the head of my grandmother's office for years, has known five generations of my mother's family, and was certainly living at the summer residence and office at the time of the traumatic confrontation there between grandmother and me, some time after the incident which took place at my parents' home.

She knew my uncle well, which meant knowing both his good and his dark side. At some point during analysis, I alluded to the probability of my uncle doing something devastating to me as a child that I had become aware of in my analysis, to get her reaction. She is a reticent maiden lady, down to earth and practical, and doesn't set much store in therapy. If something is wrong in your life, figure it out yourself, is her motto. How-ever, she is a caring person and we have been close since I was a little girl. She was one of the people who made a lot of differ-ence in my childhood and still does; one of that special circle that helped me so much.

When I brought this up, she said very little except that she didn't remember anything like that, and immediately changed the subject. I was disappointed; she could have shed some im-portant light on what I was going through, but decided she just might not have known.

Her reaction did not diminish my belief in all that came up over the incident, the confrontation and deep repercussions of those events. However, it has always nagged at me that she apparently knew nothing. Something was wrong with that picture.

Quite a few years have gone by and she is now in a Vermont nursing home where I visit her every few months. She has no family, only us and another nonfamily near her. Almost 90, she is very frail and not always lucid, but when she is, she is "right on" and we have good conversations. Realizing that this may change at any time, I decided to try again the last time I was there about a month ago.

She was very clear that morning and we talked about things we did together in the past and the family. Then I brought up my uncle and she made a few remarks about him. I said to her, "You know, my uncle did a terrible thing to me when I was a little girl and it is very hard for me to have any good feelings about him." She was quiet for a minute, giving me a very penetrating look. Then she looked away and said, "Uncle Ian was afraid of you."

I found myself saying "I know he was," and thinking mine was a surprising answer, but it seemed natural. I realized he was, but I had never put it in words before.

She continued, with some agitation, "I was so young at the time and I didn't know anything about such kind of things happening, but now I have read about them. I was so young and didn't know." There seemed to be a hint of apology and sadness in her voice, but she stopped talking. I was so taken aback I just sat there. Then she started again, this time on an entirely different subject, and I knew that was all that was going to be said about the incident.

As we talked about inconsequentials, I realized that she had been young; probably about 32, a not very sophisticated Ohioan, and it was a long time after 1935 that people acknowledged much about child molesting. She too must have found it more comfortable to forget it.

Later when I had time to focus on this brief but riveting conversation and have it all sink in, I felt a tremendous sense of relief and was very tearful. Though the rest of the two-day visit was pleasant, Sally was more hazy than not, and it would have done no good to go back to this. Besides, it was unnecessary. My nagging question was finally answered and I was very glad for both of us that it had all come out.

The relief and release remain. It is as though the end of unearthing this saga has finally come, that began almost exactly nine years before in analysis when I first had intimations that there was something buried and terrible in my childhood. Once the details of the incident and confrontation finally surfaced, I have never doubted that it all happened, but for me this was the final piece of the puzzle; small but important. Since that conversation I have felt stronger in myself and freer and even sense that I feel less "involved" when I read or hear of child molesting, something that has continued to haunt me. It all seems to have settled more firmly into my past and I can now finally let it go.

REFERENCES

Bernstein, A.E. (1990). The impact of incest trauma on ego development. In *Adult Analysis and Childhood Sexual Abuse*, ed. H.B. Levine. Hillsdale, NJ: Analytic Press, pp. 65–91.

BIBRING, E. (1964). Psychoanalysis and the dynamic psychotherapies. In *Psychiatry and Medical Practice in a General Hospital,* ed. N.E. Zinberg. New York: Int. Univ. Press, pp. 51–71.

BLUM, H.P. (1994). *Reconstruction and Psychoanalysis: Childhood Revisited and Recreated.* Madison, CT: Int. Univ. Press.

DAVIES, J.M. & FRAWLEY, M.G. (1991). Dissociative processes and transference and countertransference in the psychoanalytically oriented treatment of adult survivors of childhood sexual abuse. *Psychoanal. Dial.,* 1:5–36.

FREUD, S. (1897). Letter to W. Fliess (#69). In *The Origins of Psychoanalysis,* ed. M. Bonaparte, A. Freud, & A. Kris. Garden City, NY: Doubleday, 1957, pp. 218–221.

———— (1916). Some character-types met with in psychoanalytic work. *S.E.,* 14:309–333.

———— (1937). Constructions in analysis. *S.E.,* 23:255–269.

GILL, M. (1994). *Psychoanalysis in Transition: A Personal View.* Hillsdale, NJ: Analytic Press.

KRAMER, S. (1983). Object-cohesive doubting. In *Defense and Resistance,* ed. H.P. Blum. New York: Int. Univ. Press, pp. 325–352.

———— (1990). Residues of incest. In *Adult Analysis in Childhood Sexual Abuse,* ed. H.B. Levine. Hillsdale, NJ: Analytic Press, pp. 149–172.

KRIS, E. (1956). The recovery of childhood memories in psychoanalysis. *Psychoanal. Study Child,* 11:54–88.

LEVINE, H.B., ed. (1990a). *Adult Analysis in Childhood Sexual Abuse.* Hillsdale, NJ: Analytic Press.

———— (1990b). Clinical issues in the analysis of adults who were sexually abused as children. In *Adult Analysis in Childhood Sexual Abuse.* Hillsdale, NJ: Analytic Press, pp. 197–218.

LUSSIER, A. (1980). The physical handicap and the body ego. *Int. J. Psychoanal.,* 61:179–193.

PERSON, E.S. & KLAR, H. (1994). Establishing trauma: The difficulty distinguishing between memories and fantasies. *J. Amer. Psychoanal. Assn.,* 42:1055–1081.

RAPHLING, D.L. (1990). Technical issues on the opening phase. In *Adult Analysis in Childhood Sexual Abuse,* ed. H.B. Levine. Hillsdale, NJ: Analytic Press, pp. 45–64.

SPENCE, D.P. (1982). *Narrative Truth and Historical Truth.* New York: Norton.

VIEDERMAN, M. (1988). Pathological grief response. In *Phenomenology of Depressive Illness,* ed. J.J. Mann. New York: Human Sciences Press.

———— (1991). The impact of the real person of the analyst on the psychoanalytic cure. *J. Amer. Psychoanal. Assn.,* 39:451–489.

———— (1994). The uses of the past and the actualization of a family romance. *J. Amer. Psychoanal. Assn.,* 42:469–489.

WRIGHT, L. (1994). *Remembering Satan.* New York: Knopf.

525 East 68th Street
New York, NY 10021

PSYCHOANALYSTS AT WORK

PSYCHOANALYSTS TALK. By *Virginia Hunter.* New York: Guilford
    Press, 1994, xviii + 456 pp., $35.00.

Eleven noted psychoanalysts talked and talked and talked to
Virginia Hunter, a California psychoanalyst and psychothera-
pist who videorecorded their remarks and has now presented
them verbatim in this unique and enriching volume. Each analyst was also presented with a brief summary of the psychoanalytic treatment of a 45-year-old borderline woman, together
with brief excerpts from two sessions spaced 5 years apart. The
diverse comments of the 11 analysts follow their videorecorded
interviews. Five of the interviews have already appeared in *The
Psychoanalytic Review.*
    The volume contains an excellent foreword by León Grin-
berg, who notes that although this interview format (i.e., providing similar data to a number of practitioners) has been used
before, what makes Hunter's work valuable are the extensive
in-depth interviews that leave the reader anticipating and even
predicting the analysis of the case.
    Hunter has given us a valuable resource for historians of
contemporary psychoanalysis and a statement of the variegated
psychoanalytic enterprise. Hunter comments:

> Each of these outstanding individuals has a personal his-
> tory and personal integrity that necessarily mark his or
> her works. Each has a personal way of working, of evolving
> an analytic relationship, and of stimulating the emergence
> of analytic and other interpersonal relatedness. The frame
> I presented, although left as open as possible, was still
> mine. The video camera was mine; the final editing, al-
> though mine to complete, had to be approved for publica-
> tion by each subject. This mode of response to analytic
> material was not as easy for some as for others, since peo-
> ple obviously relate, think, and present in their own spe-
> cial ways. Time and many other factors may have
> influenced in the light in which some are seen. It may be
> that the light cast on some was a result of the nature of
> the study and the case chosen. Several participants were
> frank in saying they generally do not treat patients as dis-

turbed. . . . Some simply stated that they were not referred such patients even though they might wish to treat them. None canceled or withdrew from participation after receiving the case material, which is, perhaps, why they are considered special in their field. All possessed that quality of mind that is necessary to engage undefensively in sharing and exploring the study of the human mind and heart [p. 8].

The 11 analysts interviewed are André Green, Hanna Segal, Frances Tustin, John Bowlby, Ernest Wolf, Peter Giovacchini, Arnold Goldberg, Rudolf Ekstein, Robert Wallerstein, Arnold Modell, and Jacob Arlow. It might have been useful to know how many had declined to be interviewed. The analysts who did volunteer are certainly to be commended for their honest self-revelations.

Hunter describes four subjective elements or combinations of factors that she feels influence analysts. They are transference to theory, personal myth, personal history, and cultural and sociopolitical factors. Hunter does not regard these influences as necessarily negative, but sees them simply as inescapable personal influences. If one doubted that analysts bring all of themselves into the consulting room, no matter how "neutral" they believe they may be, this book should forever explode the illusion of neutrality. Hunter herself had different "transference" responses to each of the interviewees. For example, her interview with Hanna Segal, one of only two female analysts in the group, begins with a discussion of jewelry. All of the interviews dealt with motivations for becoming a psychoanalyst, their own analysts, childhood influences, and roles within psychoanalytic organizations and politics. There is juicy gossip, a bitchy tone, disappointments, hurts, slights, and an expressed feeling of having had it with the politics of psychoanalysis. There is a recording of enemies and multiple analyses, but overall an enthusiasm for psychoanalytic practice.

The interview with André Green included his real journey from Cairo to Paris and his intellectual journey from Lacan and bullying tactics to object relations and Winnicott. Green commented that Lacan made "very nasty, but veiled, allusions. That was the method he used. Lacan never attacked someone, I mean, one of his people, openly and directly. He openly attacked his enemies, but as far as the people of his herd were concerned, he used to make allusions and afterwards the seminar people talked together, 'Who do you think he meant?' 'It is probably Mr. So and So' and I reacted to this very vigorously . . . and finally I decided not to go to his seminar any more" (p. 29).

Hunter's interview with Robert Wallerstein has an interrogating quality, and Wallerstein, to his credit, answers her provocative questions openly and undefensively, particularly about his role as President of the IPA during the "lawsuit." Wallerstein's childhood wish to become a United States senator seems to have been sublimated in his having been president of both the International and the American, thus satisfying early political ambition.

Hanna Segal told of her struggles to get medical training after she left Poland. She wanted to set the record straight about the Grosskurth biography of Klein and what a positive experience an analysis with Melanie Klein was really like. Segal's struggle to give up smoking is also charmingly documented. Perhaps of greater importance is a poignant comment about Melanie Klein: "I learned from her not to break the parameters. Analysis is about analyzing. Analysis is not about helping, not about reassuring, and not about advising" (p. 50).

Bowlby, in a charming interview, claimed that there is too much emphasis on fantasy and not enough about reality. He remarks about the current emphasis on fantasy: "I think it's not only untherapeutic, it's antitherapeutic. It has a very adverse effect on the patient if you doubt his story. I believe it is far better to believe a story even if you subsequently find it isn't quite true than the reverse. I think one should always believe what a patient tells you if there's a huge amount of evidence that it is valid" (p. 114).

In Hunter's interview with Bowlby as well as her interview with Peter Giovacchini, there is an effort to pathologize childhoods seemingly free of trauma. She comments to Giovacchini that "it doesn't sound as if there was enough pain in that background to cause you to have all this awareness of the deeper structures" (p. 202). Giovacchini asks if a troubled background is required to be an analyst. Giovacchini, like a number of others, complains of analytic rigidity, mechanistic interpretations, and the tyranny of exclusiveness in psychoanalytic institutes. This need to find a troubled childhood, I felt, was generally excessive, particularly since Giovacchini came from a warm and loving family and Bowlby from a caring one with multiple "attachments."

Ernest Wolf, a well known Kohutian, described movingly his battle with tuberculosis and equally movingly his disappointment with his first analyst. "He was highly respected. When I complained to people about my terrible analysis, they used to look at me as though there was something wrong with me. 'You have one of the best analysts in the world!' they would say. 'Everybody would like to be in analysis with him! What are you complaining about?' I believed it. I thought there was something wrong. I really did. I thought there was something terribly wrong. I became more and more depressed and more and more fragmented. I felt terrible all the time" (p. 160). Fortunately for Wolf, he went on.

Arnold Goldberg, critical of the guru phenomenon in psychoanalysis, described the first Milton Erikson conference in Arizona: "Seven thousand people came, and all the geniuses were there—Szasz, Victor Frankel, and just a whole body of them. Each was more impossible than the next. One of them, Carl Whitaker, said that he would only treat people for his own good. He only treats people to help himself. He's someone who supposedly does family therapy. These are all very disturbed, narcissistic, megalomaniac characters who act out and then say, 'I think I'll form a cult or a theory or a school or something like that' " (p. 229). And he further advises: "We have to get away from knowing things for certain. We have to get away from the heroes that we have had. We have to get away from the knowing how to train people and knowing who to train and knowing what's right. . . . We're having to train people we didn't use to train. We're having to consider alternate ways of treating people. We've got to loosen up all around, or else it will be death of us. You know it's a dying field as it is" (p. 246).

Arnold Modell's interview focuses on the role of the human relationship in psychoanalysis and documents a kind of psychoanalysis that hopefully is dead. In commenting on Felix Deutsch, he remarks, "The thing I recall, if the patient's name was Anna, Felix Deutsch might say, 'Anna, that's like anus. She has an anal complex of some sort because her name is Anna' " (p. 359).

Hunter's interview with Jacob Arlow, conducted during a period of personal tragedy for him, nevertheless saw Arlow forceful, self-contained, and open. He spoke movingly of his childhood and of his extended family with acute clinical observations. Arlow was critical of the role of the charismatic leader, of the current emphasis on countertransference and of the departures from standard method. He spoke movingly of his struggles for curriculum revision at the New York Psychoanalytic Institute and of his disinclination to be president of the International. Of nonmedical analysis, he remarked: "I feel that it behooves the well trained medical analysts to see to it that the nonmedical analysts get the best possible training. I also advise young people against studying medicine as an introduction to psychoanalysis. I suggest that they rethink their priorities. . . . Medical education today is not the best introduction to psychoanalysis at all" (p. 393).

In an appended digest and synoptic chart, Hunter categorizes responses to the case presentations into a main focus, a genetic and dynamic focus, comments on transference and countertransference, and treatment recommendations.

Comments about the case material yielded few surprises. Green focused on the split between external and internal world; Segal on the patient's attack on the functions of the therapist and on how the patient was lacking a container; Tustin on the autistic bits; Bowlby on the role of real events such as childhood abuse and the importance of the mother and the mother transference; Wolf on faulty selfobject relationships; Giovacchini on the psychotic and assaultive role of the mother, which makes the patient vulnerable to states of disintegration because of an insufficient holding environment; Goldberg on the need for an idealizing transference; Ekstein, a child analyst, on the need to separate from a destructive mother; Wallerstein on hysterical character structures; Modell on faulty internalized psychic attunement and faulty affect processing; and Arlow on the importance of fantasies.

While each analyst brought enormous sensitivity and understanding of the case, the fact that one anticipates responses highlights the stereotyped and preprogrammed aspect of psychoanalytic interpretation. It should be noted that several analysts remarked that they do not treat really sick patients. A better case, a case with less severe trauma, abuse, and damage, might have elicited more interesting responses, although the responses might have been just as stereotyped.

Perhaps Dr. Hunter will make her videotapes available for conferences since they are an invaluable historical document. I had met, heard, or knew all but two of the analysts and I could often hear them speaking in my mind. More books like this are needed, but meanwhile we have Virginia Hunter's splendid contribution.

Joseph Reppen
211 E. 70 Street
New York, NY 10021-5207
FAX: 212 628 8453
e-mail: psabooks@datagram.com

WOMEN ANALYZE WOMEN: IN FRANCE, ENGLAND AND THE UNITED STATES. By *Elaine Hoffman Baruch* and *Lucienne J. Serrano*. New York: New York Univ. Press, 1988, xxiv + 409 pp., $40.00.

Reading this book is a thrilling intellectual adventure at times, and at other times a frustrating, puzzling, even tedious experience. Perhaps this is inevitable in a book that reports 19 interviews, with a variety of prominent women. The authors/interviewers are psychoanalytic feminists and literary critics. These interviews stem from the authors' mutual interest in exploring alternative ways to organize psychoanalytic data. They believe that women analysts in particular are engaged in this effort, which ideally will keep analysis evolving as an area of inquiry and avoids its being reduced to a doctrine to be defended. In addition, they observe women who have been energized by the women's movement turning to psychoanalysis to explain women's condition in society.

Thus, their interviewees include women clinicians who sought analytic training as a means of enhancing their skill in the healing arts, such as Enid Balint, Hanna Segal, and Marianne Eckardt; others whose personal analysis changed the way they used a previous discipline, such as Muriel Dimen (anthropology) and Jessica Benjamin (social theory); and those who combined literary or philosophical training with psychoanalytic training, as is more usual in France. The interviewers include several generations of women: Diana Trilling and Enid Balint are in their eighties, the others are middle aged except for Jessica Benjamin and Donna Basin who are young women with young children. The vocabulary changes with the generations, the questions become more trenchant and infused with feminist thinking, but the need for women to find their own voice and to recapture their intrinsic sense of agency remain central issues.

The interviews are not chronologically arranged. The first two, recorded in 1980, of Julia Kristeva and Luce Irigaray, are in the middle of the French section. The other interviews were completed between 1985 and 1987, most in one sitting, some in two. Most are transcribed in 12 to 18 pages, with a few shorter (fortunately the most arcane) and two longer ones. Monique Schneider, my favorite of the French analysts, has 35 pages, and the feisty, charming Diana Trilling, 30. The book is tripartite, with a French, English, and American section. The nine French psychoanalytic scholars fill the first half, followed by four English and five American interviewees.

I tried to experience the book in a variety of ways: (1) as a psychoanalyst interested in female psychological development, (2) as a clinician, and (3) as a woman looking for greater understanding of myself.

The interviewers' clearly stated intent was to provide a bridge between the continents—between French theoretical preoccupations, especially in response to Lacan, and British and American clinical concerns, currently influenced by object relations and self psychology. It was an exciting prospect, but my excitement dropped to frustration, then became irritation, as I struggled through the beginning chapter. I was disoriented by the labyrinth of the French intellectual style, faithfully preserved in translation by the authors, and mystified by the use of the unfamiliar and unexplained Lacanian argot.

The French group is comprised predominately of scholars; one does not often sense the presence of a real patient. The clinician in me loses interest, the patient in me feels competitive, inferior. The scholarly authors/interviewers are at home here and do their best to provide structure by asking similar questions of each interviewee and questioning each on some aspect of her writings.

Here and there in these Byzantine French webs are sparkling drops of refreshing dew: for example, Dominique Guyomard stating that "analysis should always be a creation" (p. 43) or that anxiety keeps the phobic patient from falling into psychosis; Monique David-Minard commenting that "biological sex is only raw material for the unconscious" (p. 59). Joyce McDougall's instructive thought that the mother seduces, induces the child to want to live; Julia Kristeva's idea that human beings live in language, not just biology, and therefore can love each other, that is, be open to the other in the *symbolic* dimension, not simply for narcissistic gratifications; Luce Irigaray's demand that women reenter culture and become co-creators of this world, not simply reproducers; and Monique Schneider's point that Freud denied the importance of the womb and its cyclic activities in women's lives. What Schneider sees as specifically feminine is "the power of improvisation," not the lack of maleness (p. 203).

Certain philosophical themes and assumptions appear repeatedly in these thinkers: it is language, that manifestation of the human capacity for symbolization, which creates psychic structure, not biology—thus, the link to literature. Through language, the symbolic dimension or register, the inner and outer worlds become meaningful, "the universe of signification" (Chassequet-Smirgel, p. 125).

The unconscious, drenched in language, is the same for all speaking people (Françoise Petitot). Language, which provides a means of discriminating, categorizing, thinking, ordering, is linked in the unconscious with the father. It is the phallus that permits language to exist (Petitot). The French believe the father has not been sufficiently emphasized in his necessary role as the rescuer of the infant from maternal engulfment.

For the French theorists the *first* differentiation, which makes all later differentiation and individuation possible, is the sexual difference between mother and father (not the difference between self and object, not the difference between inner and outer). The oedipal organization refers to the structure of law and order, and since this is derived from the father, the superego is genderized. Thus, alterations in gender roles, shared parenting, and single parenting all carry with them, for the French interviewees, the fear of raising children who have impaired psychic structure.

Yet despite this insistence on language as the psychic organizer, clearly a cultural event, the French group seems more invested in instinctual drives than the British or American groups. They emphasize the importance of "desire" and the phallus as its signifier for both sexes. The phallus represents both male and female elements since its erection results from the presence of the female genital (McDougall). The phallus, unlike the penis, is always erect, always successful, always desirable. Therefore, the first phallic object is the breast (McDougall), and for the mother the infant is the phallus. For the man the woman is the phallus; he needs her attached to him.

Castration is related to the phallus, not the penis (McDougall). There is a phallic mother in the unconscious that is more structured than the archaic mother, but is omnipotent and does not need the father to be creative. The feminine resolution of the oedipal is the identification of the woman as the object of man's desire (C. Millot).

Women, unlike men, combine the image of seducer and instructor in their image of lover. Men split the image into the Madonna/whore; thus, they have more difficulty integrating tender and erotic feelings. Since women's pleasure in sex (*jouissance*) is not limited to the genital organ, but is without limits, like the abyss, it frightens men (C. Millot).

It is unclear why the phallus is chosen as the "master signifier." Petitot's explanation is that the penis is what is *seen*. But considering the myriad of bodily differences between the child and the adult, this does not appear satisfactory unless one posits an essential instinctual "valorization" (a favorite word in the French interviews) of the genitals.

French feminists—though many of these writers shun the term *feminist* for fear that it implies antipathy toward men—are preoccupied with recovering or discovering feminine discourse (language or writing equals "ecriture feminine"). They hope to encourage the expression of what lies below or is at least unformed by the phallic language of symbols and logical order. This feminine (not differentiated from female among the French analysts) register is closer to the bodily experience, the mystical, the creative.

This idea, if not the vocabulary, resonates with feminist ideals in all three countries. For the French it seems more problematic since the mother is seen as a danger rather than a resource. The amorous state (a state of endless desiring of the unattainable bliss) is seen as a dangerous desire to lose oneself in the primitive chaos of the archaic mother. Female analysts who are asked to help their women patients complete separation/individuation must be seen as fathers in the transference, according to this formulation. The very use of language in the analysis seems to doom the enterprise. The French feminists' interest is in preserving singularity (separation and individuation) from being lost in intimacy, rather than in enhancing one's self though intimacy in a nurturant relationship. On both sides of the Atlantic, women appear to seek the same renewal of identity and empowerment of self, but see different dangers and remedies.

The British group present quite a different picture. They show little enthusiasm for biting the theoretical bait. Even Juliet Mitchell, the one literary scholar among those interviewed, is not tempted to stray far from clinical experience. She disagrees with the French suggestion that there is a presymbolic language that is feminine. She sees a different history of the use of language by the two sexes, but not a different formation.

The other English analysts, Enid Balint, Hanna Segal, and Dinora Pines, found their way to analysis out of an interest in patients under their care, which is evident in their response to questions. Their text is clearly their clinical experience, providing a refreshing open-mindedness. The language is unassuming, compassionate, and cautious. The clinician and the patient in me felt revived and hopeful. There were provocative moments, such as Balint's description of her analysis with Winnicott, of his way of listening in an intense and caring way, which led to her belief that it is the quality, not the quantity, of mothering that benefits the child and her emphasis on communication as central.

Segal describes her analysis with melanie klein as providing enormous stability in the frame of the analysis. Her discussion of the Anna Freud-Melanie Klein disagreement is illuminating, thoughtful, and generous. While she believes there is some "innate" sense of one's "composition" (gender), she sees the mother's reaction to the baby as decisive. She suggests that the baby's interest in the world begins with mother's body (the first body of knowledge). This can lead to destructive fantasies toward mother's body. The boy can make reparation by giving mother babies; the girl cannot use this route, so makes reparation by identification. She, like the French, fears single parenting as an expression of the mother's narcissism.

Pines, a member of Anna Freud's group, arrived at analysis through an interest in women's psychosomatic expression of pain, while working as a dermatologist. Her feminist attitudes are intrinsic to her personality and seem free of guile or intellectualizing. She feels women's confidence in themselves is deeply influenced by the mother's handling of the baby's body and her attitude toward her own. The little girl needs an experience with a responsive father to establish a belief in her body as exciting to men.

While the British analysts interviewed caution against militant feminism and fear changes in parenting responsibilities, as did the French, they were more modest in their prophecies. Their comments on sexual life came from clinical observations: for some women tender feelings are more important than orgastic experiences (Pines); some women have difficulty combining a lover and the father of their children in one man (Balint); "art is like a successful love-affair. When there's too much idealization it breaks down, but if there's none, it may not take off at all" (Segal, p. 255).

By now I had more understanding and sympathy for the organization of this book. I needed the tantalizing, intellectually provocative beginning to appreciate the comforting repose in the gentle laps of the English.

Mariane Eckardt, an analyst in New York and Karen Horney's daughter, presented a clarifying account of her mother's shift of interest from feminine development, including the interpersonal and cultural roots of penis envy, to the formation of a nonlibidinal theory of character formation and neurosis. Eckardt is reluctant to generalize about sexual differences, and emphasizes her interest in what is unique in each person.

Dorothy Dinnerstein reiterates her eloquent plea for a controlled application of technology with the aim of cherishing rather than exploiting the earth. Her concern with the way conventional gender roles sustain coercive and exploitative sociopolitical and economic institutions leads to very different conclusions about child-rearing practices. She believes an increase in shared parenting would help men become more intuitive and sensitive to vital connections, channel aggression into life-preserving activities and provide children with models of equal and mutual parental concern.

Jessica Benjamin, Donna Bassin, and Muriel Dimen bring both the conceptual rigor and the content of their earlier disciplines to the psychoanalytic inquiry. They draw new and exciting music from old saws. Benjamin, in particular, entering the psychoanalytic world to find a means of integration between personal and political life, is able to live in both the theoretical and the clinical world while recognizing the gap between them.

Her theorizing illuminates experience with the intensity of thunder and lightning. For example, too much despair in infancy results in an inchoate experience, a terror which cannot be communicated or understood. The oedipal father, she suggests, may represent not the rescuer from maternal chaos, but a regressive pull toward an incestuous state. The mother becomes the principle of separation, just as the experience of feminism for many women has renewed the individuality they had lost in their relationship with men. This loss occurs readily in cultures that endorse masculinity by turning the mother into the passive baby, the object of desire, thus splitting her from her subjectivity, that is, her experience of herself as an agent (subject) of desiring.

It is in this discussion of subjectivity and desire that French and American interests begin to dialogue. For Benjamin, it becomes an issue of dominance-submission, which leads to the question, is sexual tension dependent on a sense of power differential? Is sexual activity interesting if it does not represent a reparation of trauma, envy of the other, desire to be rescued by the power of the other and so forth?

For Bassin, Benjamin's colleague and co-discussant, these questions lead to a stimulating discussion of the development of subjectivity: "we have no symbols or carriers to articulate the origins or pathways of the development of subjectivity and agency other than the penis and phallic strivings" (p. 348). Thus, femininity requires suppression of active strivings. Failing the integration of these active strivings, separation/individuation is compromised, as is the sense of an *active creative* inner space.

Dimen brings up the fear daughters may feel if they achieve in ways that were unavailable to their mothers. As each generation of women is permitted more use of their active strivings than the previous generation, guilt and fear of retaliation from the internally perceived envious mother may dampen the daughter's pleasure in her own success.

The authors/interviewers invite the Americans to explain their differences from the French theorists. Dimen suggests that the French err in seeing the body, thus the phallus, as being outside culture. "There's no place to stand outside [culture]" (p. 370). French culture, as French language, is more genderized than ours, Benjamin points out. Further, American child-rearing practices lead to an image of the bad mother who is more likely to be disappointing than controlling, like the French image.

Whatever the source of the differences between women analysts writing in French and those writing in English, this exposure to them makes exciting fare.

From these interviews one would conclude that the essential questions for feminist psychoanalysis are the following: (1) Is the mother in the unconscious a dangerous abyss unlimited and undefined, or a resource of comfort, strength, and creativity? (2) Does the father in the unconscious represent the pathway to individuation or the suppression of active strivings toward individuation and singularity? (3) Is hierarchy unavoidable, and possibly necessary for sexual tension? (4) Is change in the fundamental social/sexual relationship between men and women possible? (5) Are there symbols in language and in the unconscious which can express and sustain feminine agency and subjectivity? (6) Is the conflict between individuation and intimacy a cultural artifact, since any theory is a cultural description (Dimen, p. 375)?

These are questions that concern us all, irrespective of gender, analytic school, or attitude toward feminism. The interviews make clear how much we have to gain from the advent of new scholarship and the inclusion of scholars from other fields in our full analytic training programs.

Martha Kirkpatrick
988 Bluegrass Lane
Los Angeles, CA 90049-1433
FAX: 310 476 4862
e-mail: Bodicea@AOL.com

THE EGO AND ANALYSIS OF DEFENSE. By *Paul Gray*. Northvale, NJ: Aronson, 1994, 288 pp., $40.00.

Paul Gray emerged almost instantly at the forefront of psychoanalytic theoreticians and clinicians when his paper "Psychoanalytic Technique and the Ego's Capacity for Viewing Intrapsychic Activity" appeared in this journal in 1973. This paper has approached classic status, having become a staple on Institute reading lists. Essentially, its theme is psychoanalytic listening, or, as Gray described it, analytic perception. Gray noted at the time that this was one of the least well conceptualized aspects of our field, and one of the least discussed. His eloquently written paper seemed to have galvanized further interest in this area of our work.

Since then, Gray has extended the elaboration of his views in a series of papers on technique and on supervision. "The Ego and Analysis of Defense" is a compilation of these writings, nearly all of which had been previously published. Together with Samuel Ritvo's helpful foreword, summarizing the main chapters, and the author's own preface, orienting the reader to the evolution and development of his ideas, it offers a stimulating overview of the course of Gray's thinking.

In his 1973 paper, Gray differentiated between our mode of "free-floating" listening when the analyst is involved in attention to drive derivatives and that of a more purposeful stance when attending to *defense against drive* derivatives. The latter, he argued, drew upon a different aspect of the analyst's perceptual apparatus. Gray systematically illustrated the advantages in focusing attention on the ego's defensive operations as they take place within the hour. By offering the patient an opportunity for a more autonomous awareness of his or her own psychic processes, such listening minimized the likelihood of suggestion and persuasion substituting for the analytic work, Gray posited. Thus, he articulated a position for adjusting our focus so as to observe data limited to *inside* the analytic situation. This perspective did not mean confining attention only to transference manifestations, or omitting details of manifest content. He argued powerfully for the view that "the analyst's primary goal is always the analysis of the patient's psyche, not the patient's life (p. 9).

Gray laid particular stress on the minute and subtle manifestations of defense against emergence of aggressive impulses, observing that aggressive components in patients' associations are less likely to be sufficiently analyzed than erotic ideations. It is a different, perhaps more difficult, task for the analyst to achieve neutrality in the face of aggressive content, he wrote.

Noting further that he was not dealing with certain other concepts related to the analyst's observing functions, such as countertransference and empathy, Gray indicated that the latter would be considered in a later communication. This was not, however, the direction in which his subsequent writings moved.

Gray's (1982) next and also oft-cited paper is entitled, " 'Developmental Lag' in the Evolution of Technique." In this scholarly piece, he takes us through some of the theoretical underpinnings of his work, tracing the evolution and ambiguities in Freud's views about involving the patient's ego in the analytic effort. It was Anna Freud's (1936) monograph "The Ego and Mechanisms of Defense" which articulated the essential shift in technique and mode of observation from that of id to ego analysis—a shift which, Gray states, has been strongly resisted in clinical practice. Analysts' fascination with the id, predilection for an authoritative stance, preoccupation with external reality, and counterresistance to transference affects and impulses are among the reasons he cites for the occurrence of this "lag." He argues emphatically for the effort to counter the lag to enable analysis of resistance, rather than overcoming it via suggestion.

I very much agree with the author in his consideration of some of the difficulties and counterresistances met in monitoring the clinical material so closely. That we are ever unwittingly inclined toward an authoritative stance, and that we may pull back when patients' immediate affective experiences and impulses toward us are brought to the foreground, are vital matters consonant with views I have elsewhere expressed (cf. Schwaber, 1986, 1992, 1995). It does not seem, however, in these or in the ensuing papers, that Gray illustrates his full adherence to this position.

In discussing analysts' counterresistance, Gray writes,

> it is especially *because* the patient's "real" perceptions of the analyst will be *included* in the material, particularly as defenses against the act of perception are diminished, that the analyst's counterresistance to observing and analyzing the ego's activities is easily aroused. It is difficult for analysts to overcome narcissistic self-protection against having their actual characteristics—appearance, ways of speaking, ways of thinking . . . and so on—accurately perceived by the patient as a part of effective analytic process [p. 59].

While there is here an important observation regarding the analyst's difficulty with more immediately felt transference affects, one may see authoritarian implications (as well as epistemological questions) in the description of perceptions as "real" or "actual," suggesting that the analyst is making these assessments. Further, though I concur with the implication that the ego's activities include the patient's perception of the analyst's participation, the clinical illustrations do not demonstrate detailed attention to its elucidation. Consider the following vignette cited in the paper entitled "The Nature of Therapeutic Action in Psychoanalysis":

> [The patient] spoke briefly of wishing to know more about me than I revealed during our work together; he had long avoided

any active curiosity in this direction. He then paused briefly, almost imperceptibly, and his tone took on a different quality—a moment of "change of voice." He now spoke of the day he had first telephoned me (he has displaced to the past) and continued, "When I heard you saying, 'I can see you. . . . Will next week be alright, or is it more urgent?' I was so moved that tears came to my eyes" (in the displacement the conflicted active curiosity has given way to a more passive, dependent mode). At this point his feeling could be clearly heard. He paused very briefly and continued—now without the emotion (another "change of voice")—"It was a time when I was staying with my sister (a sibling with whom he was very close) . . . it was in the country, but I was so depressed, and something about your willingness to see me . . ." [pp. 95-96].

Gray's explication of this example focuses in an exemplary fashion on the details and shifts—verbal and nonverbal—occurring in the moment and on his efforts to draw the patient's attention to defensive processes he, too, could observe. In so doing, however, it allows us to see that there is no apparent regard given to the possibility that the analyst's silence—perhaps felt particularly at the time of the pauses—had a bearing on the patient's shifts, both with respect to affect as well as content. Indeed, the very fact that the patient returned to a memory of the analyst speaking—perhaps feeling the analyst had "revealed" himself thereby—might be a communication of what he was looking for and not feeling *now*. But to consider such a possibility or another would require attention to the patient's experience of the analyst's participation in the moment—and perhaps augment the analyst's self-reflection as well. This is not a direction of inquiry addressed here.

In Gray's efforts to help the patient observe his own defensive processes there is no explicit inclusion of the possibility that something in the patient's perception of the analyst—*still to be elucidated*—had a bearing on the emergence of a defense at that moment. Rather, the patient's stated perceptions are viewed as a priori expressions of his defensive activity. Indeed, Gray speaks of perceptions as *created*, by the child or patient, and of the patient "needing to distort the otherwise disturbingly unauthoritarian reality of the neutrality and permissiveness . . . the analyst provides" (pp. 122-133)—attributes the analyst apparently presumes to be more "real."

In his paper "Memory as Resistance, and the Telling of a Dream," Gray illustrates his approach to the defensive use of memory. The following instance is extracted from a longer case example:

Analyst: You sounded as if you were hesitating to speak critically about your mother, and then the memory of the dream interrupted.

Patient: Yes, I remember.

Analyst: Maybe it got unsafe to show me critical feeling toward your mother.

Patient: I don't want you to think I'm being unfair to her.

Analyst: In your memory of the dream you first pictured yourself as a judge and then took that away by making a white-robed, unshaven figure of yourself [p. 163].

In the ensuing elucidation, Gray carefully analyzes what he refers to as the "transferential authoritative influence, not leaving it in place for purposes of suggestion" (p. 166). Again, there is no evidence that the question of the analyst's contribution, seen from the patient's point of view, toward the emergence of that very transference experience—authoritative, unsafe, judgmental—is explored. Indeed, though he later tells the reader that he did not overlook this attribution, we can see the analyst himself shift away from the direct reference *to him, at that moment.*

Further, there is no evident consideration of the potential impact of the "suggestive power" introduced in "helping analysands observe intrapsychic activity." Gray carefully and explicitly asks analysands to venture this, explaining its rationale, and he is seemingly quite pleased when they succeed. He is very persuasive about the merits of his position, but what if an analysand were not persuaded, or were only persuaded? And what if these or other responses to it are hidden? Might the patient's seemingly more autonomous expression be in the service of an unrecognized dimension of the transference? I do not hear these questions addressed.

This apparent failure to regard the possibility of his own influence, in the moment, at least as communicated here, may bear upon a central dilemma in Gray's position. While he espouses a stance based on the importance of evidence reaching the patient's awareness, defensive meaning nonetheless remains inferred. He states, "these defensive activities are silent and invisible *to the patient*—that is why we refer to them as unconscious. They need not be so to the analyst if he is closely attentive to them, nor eventually to the patient if they are sufficiently demonstrated" (pp. 92-93; italics in original). The clinical stance here is evident: the analyst knows what the patient does not. Epistemologically, there is a further dilemma: how can the analyst know what is unconscious before it reaches awareness? We may first observe manifest phenomena and then call them to the patient's attention, but their meaning—defensive or otherwise—must await entry into consciousness before it can be known. Until then, it can be only inferred.

In summary, Gray's papers present a notable effort at integrating theory and practice. His theoretical discussions, particularly those tracing the evolution and vicissitudes in Freud's writings on the super-ego, are of special interest. His illustrative writings on his teaching philosophy and methodology offer a significant addition to the peda-gogical applications of our clinical stance. His emphasis on close-process monitoring is of central importance. In its focus and explica-tion of nuances of clinical data, the leaps of inference greatly re-duced, both for the patient as well as for the reader, its research potential is invaluable. The emphasis on the study of the patient's psychic processes, of his or her life *within*, serves as a vital reminder about the nature of the psychoanalytic enterprise.

A core difficulty, however, lies with the fact that though the effort is to reduce the analyst's authoritarian and suggestive influence, the impact of authority and suggestion—as may be experienced by the patient, whatever the intent of the analyst—is not addressed. Neither the exploration of the patient's perceptual experience nor the use of the analyst's self-reflections are illuminated here. The analyst teaches; one does not hear how he may learn from the patient.

But it is the consequence of Gray's candid and detailed contribu-tions that we are offered data permitting us to raise such questions. His work has significantly sharpened our clinical and theoretical dia-logue. "If you want to take the patient's ego along for the whole journey," he writes, "it's better to use data that both patient and analyst can corroborate. . . . Calling attention to these phenomena at the very moment they arise in the analytic hour provides the most convincing illustration of them for the patient (and for the analyst, too)" (p. 224). I would add, so too for the reader; Paul Gray shares what is vital for the continuing journey of our field. We are indebted to him.

REFERENCES

FREUD, A. (1936). *The Ego and the Mechanisms of Defense.* New York: Int. Univ. Press.
GRAY, P. (1973). Psychoanalytic technique and the ego's capacity for viewing intrapsychic activity. *J. Amer. Psychoanal. Assn.*, 21:474-494.
——— (1982). "Developmental lag" in the evolution of technique for psycho-analysis of neurotic conflict. *J. Amer. Psychoanal. Assn.*, 30:621-655.
SCHWABER, E.A. (1986). Reconstruction and perceptual experience: further thoughts on analytic listening. *J. Amer. Psychoanal. Assn.*, 34:911-932.

Book Reviews

————— (1992). Psychoanalytic theory and its relation to clinical work. *J. Amer. Psychoanal. Assn.*, 40:1039-1057.

————— (1995). The psychoanalyst's mind—from listening to interpretation: a clinical report. *Int. J. Psychoanal.*, 76:271-281.

Evelyne Albrecht Schwaber
4 Welland Road
Brookline, MA 02146
FAX: 617 632 7782

THE USE OF THE SELF. By *Theodore Jacobs*. Madison, CT: Int. Univ. Press, 1991, xxii + 238 pp., $27.50.

With the underlying premise that stalemated analyses occur because analysts "frequently overlook" all but the "surface layer" of "ordinary exchanges," Theodore Jacobs proceeds in *The Use of the Self* to show the influence of nonverbal communications, shifts in the transference, and secrets in the underlayers of analytic process. The clinical usefulness of countertransference (with emphasis on the analyst's discomfort) also gets prominent attention in this clearly written book illustrated with numerous case examples. Those familiar with Jacobs's work will be happy to have under one cover the three essays published here for the first time and the eight others that have appeared previously in journals or in other books.

The author frequently refers to, and implicitly decries, "ordinary" analysis and technique. It seems to me that the problems he is addressing arise less from technique being too ordinary than with the exclusivity of the domain to which any selected technique is applied: if that domain is restricted to the patient's psyche and verbal communications, for whatever reason, the analysis is less robust than if applied also to the analyst's own psyche—dreams, fantasies, associations, and interpretations.

The book is most solidly grounded in drive-defense theory, but also acknowledges and makes use of contributions from object relations theory and self psychology. Yet it must be said that Jacobs tends to confuse "difficult to recognize" with "has received little attention in the literature." To readers familiar with the work of Winnicott, Little, Reite, Schlesinger, Schwaber, and Jacob Jacobson, many of the admonitions and espoused principles in this book will not seem new: paying attention to one's countertransference reactions (verbal and behavioral) and translating them into comments or interpretations for oneself and the patient; avoiding disparagement of countertransference as only a distortion; seeing analyst and patient as an interregulating dyad, even at the level of the autonomic nervous system; and noting shifts in transference over time as representative of defensive changes in the patient's self- and object representations. Many of Jacobs's observations are directed at helping the analyst discover the *communication* in the *defense*—that is, at avoiding the trap of typing defensive acts and processes as mere "resistance."

The chapter "Notes on the Unknowable: Analytic Secrets and the Transference Neurosis" provides a good example of such a discovery. Rather than treat a patient's secret as only an obstruction, Jacobs applies a principle of Sandler's concerning analytic process, and in doing so opens up the process to its most intimate level. Sandler is paraphrased as saying that one motive central to process is the effort of *both* participants to impose an intrapsychic role relationship on the other. Jacobs then presents a patient, Mr. C, whose painful adolescent experiences had been warded off: disappointment in a father he felt had betrayed him. The author then ties his reactions with this patient to his ability to help him take a step:

> Clearly the difficulty of bringing to light so important a part of the transference neurosis was a two-way street. Like Mr. C, I experienced disappointment in my father in adolescence. . . . Mr. C's story resonated with my own history. . . . Patient and analyst . . . formed a conspiracy that had as its purpose the avoidance not only of current conflicts but of memories rooted in parallel life experiences.

Ironically, in some chapters we find ourselves in the position, criticized elsewhere in the book, of seeing process as the monadic emissions of the patient and his projective tendencies:

> Mr. A had two brothers, one several years older, the other a few years younger. Little material concerning them surfaced in the early months of treatment. Initially they remained, like the father, shadowy figures. In time, however, they came into view both in terms of Mr. A's current interactions with them and in the transference. The sibling transferences, in fact, had a special quality. Each gained prominence at particular, and ultimately predictable times in the analysis: when pronounced anxiety was stimulated in Mr. A by the emergence of threatening impulses connected with the prominent transference of the moment.

This unconscious maneuver, clearly used in the service of resistance, became initially most evident in terms of the older brother. . . .

Passages like this can jar the reader, because the author seems at odds with himself and his previously announced purposes. We are primed to hear him outline the *interaction* of the two players but, in this chapter at least, he focuses only on the patient's psyche, his "impulses."

But such lapses are few. At its best, this book rewards us with clear vignettes, replete with detail sufficient to provide us a good sense of what happened in the process and frankness in the author's approach and self-examination. The opening essay and the title essay are excellent examples of his creative use of himself and his reactions to complex patients. It is lamentable that our collective atmospherics remain such that a courageous author has to follow his open self-explorations with hesitant justification:

Ms. D's situation stirred up memories of certain troubling duplicities in my own family that must have stimulated in me wishes for her to face the truth as I had found useful to do.

Although my technique was influenced by these personal responses, I do not think that this was entirely a negative factor. . . .

On the contrary, it is precisely Jacobs's use of those personal responses that gains our interest, that makes us want to read the book, and that, in the end, makes this a book worth reading.

Michael G. Moran
National Jewish Hospital
1400 Jackson Street
Denver, CO 80206

THE MISUSE OF PERSONS: ANALYZING PATHOLOGICAL DEPENDENCY. By *Stanley J. Coen.* Hillsdale, NJ: Analytic Press, 1992, 341 pp., $43.95.

This book addresses the complex clinical and theoretical issues of analytic work with patients whose pathological dependency causes them to repeat self-defeating and destructive behavior patterns toward the analysis and the analyst. Work with this group of patients taxes the analyst's skill and tolerance, and frequently includes impasses and less-than-satisfactory outcomes.

Coen writes from the perspective of traditional psychoanalytic conflict theory integrated with an object relations perspective, so that for him drive and object relations fit together as a single entity. He describes both an intrapsychic and interpersonal perspective, emphasizing also that "interpersonal is to be understood in relation to intrapsychic. To a degree they cannot be separated and must at the same time be separated; that is, what goes on within our minds and between ourselves and others are parts of a whole" (p. 11).

Coen defines pathological dependency as "the felt inability to manage on one's own and to be alone" (p. 13). Further:

> The pathologically dependent person's fears of rage and destructiveness, in himself and in his vitally needed other, are so central to his conflicts . . . that multiple feelings and wishes are subsumed under rage and destructiveness including varying intensities of angry and hurtful wishes. The most frightening of these usually are those that most threaten to destroy the other or the relationship with the other. The more vitally one needs the other, the more dangerous rage and destructiveness become [p. 29].

He emphasizes that these wishes can take many forms, such as "cannibalism, evisceration, murder, robbery, castration, humiliation, rejection, disconnection, dehumanization, abandonment, contempt, belittling, spoiling, scorn, domination and so on" (p. 30).

"The patient needs to repeat such potentially dangerous and violent confrontations between self and other in the analytic transference to become convinced that his destructiveness can be felt, managed and contained" (p. 30). In this sense, Coen thinks of pathological dependency as a form of endless destructive engagement between the patient and the analyst; the need is to explore whether the patient can even move beyond this kind of impasse.

> Chronic hatred and pathological dependency intersect. Patients attempt to manage the immediate destructiveness of intense rage toward a vitally needed object by the containment of chronic hatred and chronically hateful relationships. This adaptive and defensive transformation of rage in the attempt to contain it within an object relationship is a central function of pathological dependency [p. 31].

Much of the rest of the book is an amplified and elaborated discussion of the manifestations of rage and hatred as seen in pathological dependency and in the behavior patterns that such patients enact and reenact with other individuals. The analyst of such patients needs to be capable of tolerating not only the patient's rage at himself or herself but also his or her own intermittent rage and hatred toward the patient. There are multiple potential countertransference responses that this interaction may induce.

These constructs and theoretical concepts are at times dense and difficult to unravel, and they require a detailed and careful reading. But there are many case vignettes scattered throughout the book which illustrate and allow the reader to understand from a familiar clinical perspective the theoretical constructs being addressed. Some of these vignettes are referred to multiple times and require rereading to refresh one's memory of the case, but the clinical material is well presented and helpful to the understanding of the basic constructs.

Another major hypothesis illustrated by Coen's clinical material is that such patients exhibit intense resistances to change. They manifest a felt need for endless reenactment and repetition, and concepts of change or renunciation of the sense of entitlement to the fulfillment of preoedipal wishes remain major and formidable resistances. The process of change is therefore extremely slow and uncertain, and unfortunately many such patients are unable successfully to conclude an analysis.

In describing the multiple manifestations of the pathological dependency itself or the many ways by which it is defended or expressed in derivative and compromised form, Coen ranges over a variety of other topics. These include manifestations of the patient's sense of defect, concepts of sexualization, and superego aspects of entitlement, as well as psychosomatic symptomology in the avoidance of awareness of psychic conflict. There is also an extensive discussion of sadomasochism with its excitement and its paradoxical qualities, as well as such issues as sexual perversion and pathological jealousy. Coen makes a plea for the active and persistent confrontation of these issues in the transference as a direct and immediate experience between patient and analyst, activating what he calls a "passionate analysis" as the only way that these patterns can ultimately be addressed and mastered.

There is also an appendix to the volume, which presents a summarizing guide to the literature on the topics of repetition, sexualization, and perversion; these are addressed from the point of view of the theoretical model of pathological dependency previously presented.

The book is not an easy one to read, and requires considerable concentration and critical thought as the reader goes through it. Because of the narrowness of its central thesis there is inevitably a significant degree of repetition that occurs as the major issue is focused upon from multiple different perspectives. And one may disagree with the all-encompassing nature of the basic hypothesis, recognizing that the same clinical data could be interpreted from alternative theoretical perspectives.

Nevertheless, the book adds to the understanding and the technical treatment issues for a significant group of patients. Coen emphasizes that they are individuals who initially in consultation appear to be neurotic in their personality structure and do not seem to be either borderline or psychotic patients. Because their dependency is transferred to the analyst, they appear cooperative and actively participate in the analysis during the early going. The pathological dependency comes to light when the analyst begins to recognize that despite the patient's continuing efforts to participate in the analytic experience, no change is occurring. Instead, the patient is involved in an endless reenactment and repetition of pathological behavior patterns, usually in an attempt to avoid progress and to effect the ultimate destruction of the analytic experience. It is when these issues or the ultimate prospect of termination become the focus of analytic scrutiny that the underlying conflicts and dynamics connected with the pathologically dependent patient make their appearance in the analytic material, in the transference-countertransference, where the analyst must now confront the previously avoided hatred, rage, and multiple manifestations of the patient's pathological dependency.

This book elucidates the understanding of a particularly difficult group of analysands. It will prove specifically useful to those analysts who have had experience with patients who, after an apparently appropriate early and middle phase of analytic treatment, become stalemated in an impasse that threatens to undo and destroy the analyst's work and with it the analyst's sense of confidence and self-esteem. It will also be of use to beginning candidates and therapists, although the intensity of the issues involved may be beyond their clinical experience. However, it can serve as an excellent guide and warning to the intensity of the problems and conflicts that such patients will sooner or later present.

Paul A. Dewald
4524 Forest Park Avenue
St. Louis, MO 63108
FAX: 314 361 6269

PSYCHOANALYSIS: SCIENCE AND PHILOSOPHY

PSYCHOANALYSIS AND ETHICS. By *Ernest Wallwork*. New Haven, CT:
  Yale Univ. Press, 1991, xiii + 344 pp., $35.00.

A household name to moral philosophers and clinical ethicists,
Ernest Wallwork is both a professional philosopher and a practicing psychoanalyst. This volume ranks with works such as Hartmann's (1960) and Rieff's (1959, 1966) on its topic. However,
despite its title, it deals almost exclusively with *Freud* and ethics.
I can only highlight most of Wallwork's book (Parts 2-4), and
limit any elaboration and critique to Part 1 (on determinism-
free will and morality), where we substantially disagree.

Psychoanalysis and Ethics is parsed into four parts. The first,
"Foundational Issues," consists of separate chapters (Chapters
2-4) on hermeneutics, determinism-free will, and psychic causality and moral responsibility. Part 2, "Psychological Egoism,"
comprises four chapters: "Overview of Psychological Egoism"
(Chapter 5), "The Pleasure Principle and Psychological Hedo-
nism" (Chapter 6), "Narcissism" (Chapter 7), and "Object
Love" (Chapter 8). The third part, "Normative Implications,"
contains two chapters—one on the love commandment (Chapter 9), the other on the normative dimensions of psychoanalytic
practice (Chapter 10). The fourth and final portion, "Foundations of Ethics in Freudian Theory," encompasses: "Toward
a Psychoanalytically Informed Ethic" (Chapter 11), "How Is
Practical Reason Guided? Happiness and the Basic Goods of
Life" (Chapter 12), "Normative Principles and Social Theory"
(Chapter 13), and the "Conclusion" (Chapter 14).

Wallwork's introduction (Chapter 1) explicates the book's
aim: to demonstrate the indispensability of moral philosophical
and psychoanalytical perspectives for one another. However,
his mutual analysis is complicated by the fact that each side
already contains presuppositions and implications generally
considered exclusive of the other (Wallace, 1990a, 1992b).
Moreover, ethical *and epistemological* unpacking of psychoanalytic concepts and practices must go hand-in-hand, as Wallwork
grasps and pursues.

"Psychological Egoism" (Part 2) is a masterful exegesis of Freud and significant items from the ethical literature. It demonstrates considerable reconcilability between aspects of Freud's "pleasure principle" and "narcissism" on the one hand, and Judeo-Christian desiderata of neighbor-love and altruism on the other. Though Freud often italicized the egoistic facets of motivation, he ignored altruism neither in theory nor in his personal and professional life. Like Hartmann (1960), Wallwork emphasizes the qualitatively different forms of pleasure in direct "instinctual" gratification, sublimation, and other-regarding and charitable behavior.

Parts 3 ("Normative Implications") and 4 ("Foundations of Ethics in Freudian Theory") are the moral-philosophical meat of the book. They are delightful, as well as informative and provocative. Wallwork contrasts Freud's balanced attention to the unconscious "instinctual"/passional roots of morality and the importance of ego operations, with the overrational and psychologically unrealistic approaches of philosophers such as Kant. Similarities and differences between Freud and great ethicists such as Aristotle, Hobbes, Hume, Kant, and Mill are itemized. Again, Freud's realism and balance are stressed throughout, including emphasis on the interdependence between the well-being of society and of its individuals (Freud, 1930).

Furthermore, as Wallwork affirms, Freud taught that overdetermination or multiple motivation also applies to the most ostensibly positive moral enactments. Coupled with Freud's famous accent on introspective honesty, this undercuts rationalization and pharisaism in the moral sphere. Nevertheless, as Wallwork warns, this suspicious unmasking can go too far; *its* motives and consequences must be scrutinized as well (p. 288).

His reconciling enterprise does for Freud's work what the great man could not stand back enough to do himself. Still, Wallwork realizes that there remain ambiguities, whether from Freud's limitations or our own.

Among the "normative" (i.e., morally prescriptive or programmatic) aspects of psychoanalysis, Wallwork underlines the concept of "analytic neutrality," based on ethical principles such as "respect for persons, truthfulness, keeping promises, and confidentiality" (p. 217). Hence, psychoanalysis is not value-free: "If it were, it would be a mere technology that could be used in the service of any values whatsoever, good or bad" (p. 217). But technologies themselves, and the sciences from which they derive, are hardly value-neutral. They have moral/ethical, social/political, cultural, and even cosmological dimensions and consequences, as history, anthropology, and philosophy preeminently show (Browning, 1987; Wallace, 1990a, 1992b). In this context, until the mid-nineteenth century, the term "moral" usually denoted what we now dissect into the "moral/ethical," "psychological," and "spiritual."

Finally, Wallwork enunciates the potential contributions of Freud's theories, methods, and findings to personal and social ethics, and to the pursuit of happiness. He argues that Freud integrated happiness as a normative and psychological principle with the objectives of social morality. This was achieved with Freud's version of Aristotelian harmony or balance: a psychologically necessary and morally justifiable measure of sensual and narcissistic gratification, limited by an optimal degree of the capacity for shame and guilt, and sublimated in personally satisfying and socially useful activities such as creativity, the acquisition of knowledge, productive work, aesthetic enjoyment, and affectionate love (pp. 288-289). Most individuals are so constituted, contends Wallwork, that they cannot be content if ignoring the interests of others, nor can they properly attend to others, if not attending to themselves.

Wallwork draws out Freud's moral-philosophical implications in a manner which, I suspect, Freud would have little opposed. Nevertheless, I doubt that he would have also endorsed Wallwork's claims that psychoanalysis per se is a "coherent ethical vision" (p. 291); Hartmann (1960, p. 66) clearly did not.

Other areas of *Psychoanalysis and Ethics*, which would likewise require lengthy treatment, are its rather aprioristic and monolithic treatment of religion and religious ethics—somewhat akin to Freud's own (Wallace, 1984, 1986a, 1990a); insufficient attention to the hyperindividualistic features of Freud's canon (see Rieff, 1959, 1966); overplaying of Freud's relatively scanty treatment of political-economic factors; downplaying of his politically conservative pronouncements and implications; and curious ignoring of Freud's (1921, 1930) ideas on the aggression-promoting and socially divisive consequences of unrestrained or unsublimated libido—particularly given today's progressively institutionalized usages of others as sensual part-objects, or even "selfobjects" (i.e., as means to one's ends, rather than Kantian ends in themselves).

Determinism / Free Will and Morality. Part 1 (Chapters 2-4) concerns determinism versus free (nonnecessitated or contracausal) will, and moral responsibility/accountability. Its author thinks this issue "central" and "foundational" to moral discourse, but I do not (Wallace, 1985, 1986a, 1986b, 1988, 1989a, 1989b), concurring with Milton's consigning it to Satan's lesser devils!

To begin with, there is no decisive empirical test of the matter of whether persons can ever do other than they actually do or did ("capability" applying to *all* aspects of mentation/behavior, from motivation to ego and superego operations). Such assessment would require either a Wellsian time machine or, what would amount to the same thing, reestablishment of precisely identical antecedent personal/environmental conditions. Hence, this controversy is ideal for obsessive vacillators, narcissistic perfectionists, moral masochists, and professional philosophers. Furthermore probably few, if any, can ponder it purely dispassionately.

A "compatibilist," Wallwork wants universal causation and yet also a notion of freedom transcending the necessity that is definitionally intrinsic to "causality" (see Taylor, 1967). With this mysterious causally-ensconced contracausal freedom, he can then have the libertarian version of moral evaluation he deems essential to the ethical enterprise. In seeking to bolster this contracausal freedom, he discusses Freud's perspective on causality, determinism, and intentionality in an imprecise and self-contradictory way, out of keeping with the logic of his study as a whole.

The problems with Wallwork's reasoning could be exemplified many times over. I can only glance at a few.

Consider, at the outset, the following: "To speak in terms of causes is not necessarily to speak in terms of *determining causes*. A cause may be any phenomenon that affects the occurrence of an outcome, even if its existence does not require that outcome" (p. 75; italics in original). To start with, I do not understand the difference between a "cause" and a "*determining cause.*" Wallwork tries to justify it, as did Collingwood (1939, 1946) before him, by distinguishing between ordinary causes (said to necessitate) and psychical causes or "motives" (said merely "to incline"). But causation is usually *multifactorial*—a mesh of conditions (i.e., the "cause"), each necessary, though by itself insufficient, for the particular effect. Both men also invoke the telic or purposeful aspects of motivation (e.g., Wallwork, p. 81) as if they circumvent the customary concept of causation, when they do not (see Mandelbaum, 1977; Bunge, 1979; Mackie, 1980; and Wallace, 1985, 1986b, 1989a, 1989b, for exhaustive elaboration). Nor does the necessitarian causation which Wallwork abrogates invariably require mediation through universal and ironclad covering laws (Mandelbaum, 1977; Bunge, 1979; Mackie, 1980; Wallace, 1985, 1986b, 1989a, 1989b; Chalmers, 1992).

With his idiosyncratic concept of causality, Wallwork misapprehends Freud's "overdetermination." He reasons from the correct premise that "the mere existence of a desire and beliefs regarding its satisfaction do not necessarily constitute a determining cause of action," to the incorrect conclusion that one "is free to [unnecessitat-edly] deliberate and choose which desire-belief set he will act on" (p. 76). In fact, it is the *entire constellation* of unconscious conflicting and converging motives and mental processes ("overdetermina-tion") that necessitates (i.e., "causes") the resultant behavior, *rather than any one of its interlocking components.* It is axiomatic that altering any of its constituents would yield a different outcome, however subtly so. Nevertheless, this is not enough for Wallwork. In effect, he desires the possibility of a different result (i.e., enacted choice), from *precisely the same* set of operative causal conditions!

Wallwork generally limits this contracausal freedom to ego func-tioning (pp. 76-83). And yet, at the same time, he acknowledges, "Of course, the ego is itself caused . . . anchored in a body, a history, and a surrounding milieu . . . function[ing] in terms of its own governing principles . . ." (p. 81)! He does not begin to explain how an organi-zation necessitated in its origin, capacities, and mode of operation (i.e., "governing principles") then comes to function acausally or contracausally. His invocation of a "decision-making" model is per-haps his nearest approach to doing so. But this is mere handwaving, for the existence of functions such as deliberation and choice among apperceived alternatives (discernible even in many animals) is not at issue, but whether they are nonnecessitated. (See Wallace, 1989a, 1990b, 1992a on mind-body issues pertinent to psychical causality.)

Were such contracausality possible, the whole psychoanalytic the-oretical and methodological apparatus, as Freud (1915-1916, p. 104) recognized, would collapse. A train of associations could be—or have been—divergent at any point, a parapraxis or symptomatic act as well not have occurred, and, for that matter, lifelong patterns of compromise formation, apperception/interpretation, and interper-sonal relations have been different at any instant!

Finally, the author's citations of Freud's ostensible oscillations on determinism-free will in no way support his argument in any philo-sophical, scientific, or clinical sense. There is more in Freud's corpus and theoretical system favoring or demanding universal determinism than otherwise (Wallace, 1985, 1986b). Many of Wallwork's refer-ences to Freud's supposed libertarianism are in fact ambiguous, while others do not imply or entail nonnecessitated willing: for example, "[analysis] does not set out to make pathological reactions impossi-ble, but to give the patient's ego *freedom* to decide one way or the other," and "[treatment] leaves the homosexual patient to choose whether . . . to abandon the path that is banned by society (Freud, in Wallwork, pp. 68, 68n; italics in original)."

It was deciding "*one way or the other* [italics added]" that such patients *could not* do—however strongly they *consciously wanted to*. They could *only* either waffle continuously and unsatisfyingly between apparent alternatives, or repeatedly enact ego-dystonic and maladaptive historically/situationally determined compromises. Psychoanalysis (i.e., the ongoing clinician-patient interaction, an instance of reciprocal "intersectional causation" [Wallace, 1985, 1986b, 1989a]) does not grant persons some nonnecessitating freedom to decide whether to return to their pretreatment modes of being—as if they would, *or could*, seriously want that anyway (see also Hanly, 1979)! Rather, analysis increases their appreciation of, and capacity to enact, "righter" choices—that is, less conflictual, ego-dystonic, and atavistic compromise formations.

In short, therapy moves one, not from determinism to acausal or contracausal freedom, but from less satisfactory modes of self-determination to more ego-syntonic, reality-oriented, and currently adaptive ones. What other kind of freedom could one need or want? Moreover, in acknowledging that our objective is not to make subsequent psychopathological reactions impossible, Freud was not implying that his successfully treated patients might later indeterminantly opt for sickness! Instead, he was accurately and modestly admitting (1) our inability to know, much less influence, all the relevant historical and ongoing psychobiological/interpersonal variables during the analysis itself; (2) that no analysis is complete or perfect; and (3) that we can hardly foresee the infinitude of possible posttermination events.

Regarding the issue's impact on concepts of moral responsibility, accountability, and evaluation, I reject Wallwork's (Chapter 4) protest that they are vitiated by universal causation or determinism. *If* one possesses the capacity for sufficiently consensual reality testing and rational operations, the ability to consider the likely consequences of present choices in light of prior experience, a reasonable degree of appropriate self-restraint, and a sufficiently intact internalized system of sociocultural values, *then* one may be deemed a morally responsible agent (Grünbaum, 1971; Nagel, 1979, p. 602; Wallace, 1985, 1986b). If, in addition, one is knowledgeable of the salient situational circumstances, then one is morally accountable for the consequences of one's behavior as well.

The agent's conscious intellectual position—pro, con, or vacillating—on contracausal freedom is largely beside the point. Whatever one believes on the matter, one's deliberations and actions will continue to flow from the ongoing intersections between one's constitutionally/historically conditioned personhood and the ambience.

"Even if a man has repressed his evil impulses into the unconscious, and would like to tell himself afterwards that he is not responsible for them, he is nevertheless bound to be aware of this responsibility as a sense of guilt whose basis is unknown to him" (Freud, 1915-1916, p. 331). The parallel with the plight of Oedipus is clear enough. Our clinical work bears out this tragic vision every day—that people are the products of the worst errors, perpetrated (by themselves and others) out of what are often the best conscious intentions, and because the actor, with his or her particular history, constitution, and circumstances, could not do otherwise.

Morality is a perspective on the beneficence and maleficence of one's intentions toward and, especially, impact upon, persons—including oneself, since one is a human being, and since one's welfare affects others as well. Moral evaluation can proceed quite independently of libertarian construals of responsibility and accountability. The assessment of motives, extenuating or mitigating circumstances, hazardousness to self or others, and remediability would continue much as before, and without ensnaring moral or juridical appraisal in the impossible task of discerning whether an action issued from some hypothetically contracausal freedom (Wallace, 1986b).

Moreover, moral appraisal is not moralism. The latter, I believe, is promoted by extravagant concepts of freedom, which, at worst, can engender savagely nonremediating responses toward the shortcomings of self and others. History is replete with instances of groups and individuals who have immolated themselves or others, ostensibly in the name of the highest morality. Propensities to projection and projective identification, and externalization of self-directed superego aggression and sadistic punitiveness, have produced phenomena such as the Inquisition and Naziism. No less a spiritual and moral teacher than Jesus warned against self-righteousness and vicious judgmentalness. And Paul, whose *caritas* ethic Freud (1921, p. 91) esteemed, bemoaned: "What I do is not what I want to do, but what I detest. . . . The good which I want to do, I fail to do, but what I do is the very wrong which is against my will . . ." (Romans 7:14, 19).

Finally, acknowledging both that our moral capacities are significantly determined by early constitutional/environmental factors beyond our ken, and that conscious moral positions may express or rationalize socially inimical unconscious or preconscious strivings, helps diminish that brand of immorality attending intolerance.

That our evolving moral careers are thoroughly determined—from deep within ourselves and through relations with others—makes us no less the authors of our behaviors, or any less causally
responsible for their impact, as Oedipus painfully divined.

> If I seek to classify the impulses that are present in me ac-
> cording to social standards into "good" and "bad," I must
> assume responsibility for both sorts; and if, in defense, I say
> that what is unknown, unconscious, and repressed in me is
> not my "ego," then I shall not be basing my position upon
> psychoanalysis . . . and I shall perhaps be taught better by the
> criticism of my fellow men, by the disturbance in my action and
> the confusion of my feelings. *I shall perhaps learn that what I am
> disavowing not only "is" in me but sometimes "acts" from out of me
> as well* [Freud, 1925, p. 133, italics added].

That, if may be, is enough, especially if one's task is laundering oneself, not others. One might then even remain indifferent to the irre-
solvable issue at hand—*if one can.*

REFERENCES

BROWNING, D. (1987). *Religious Thought and the Modern Psychologies.* Philadelphia:
    Fortress Press.
BUNGE, M.C. (1979). *Causality and Modern Science.* New York: Dover.
CHALMERS, A. (1992). *What Is This Thing Called Science?* (2nd ed.). St. Lucia:
    Queensland Univ. Press.
COLLINGWOOD, R. (1939). *An Essay on Metaphysics.* Oxford: Oxford Univ. Press.
——— (1946). *The Idea of History.* Oxford: Oxford Univ. Press.
FREUD, S. (1915-1916). *Introductory Lectures on Psycho-Analysis.* S.E., 15/16.
——— (1921). *Group Psychology and the Analysis of the Ego.* S.E., 18.
——— (1925). *Some Additional Notes on Dream Interpretation as a Whole.* S.E., 19.
——— (1930). *Civilization and Its Discontents.* S.E., 21.
GRÜNBAUM, A. (1971). Free will and the laws of human behavior. *Amer. Philos. Q.,*
    8:605-627.
HANLY, C. (1979). *Existentialism and Psychoanalysis.* New York: Int. Univ. Press.
HARTMANN, H. (1960). *Psychoanalysis and Moral Values.* New York: Int. Univ. Press.
MACKIE, J. (1980). *The Cement of the Universe: A Study of Causation.* Oxford: Oxford
    Univ. Press.
MANDELBAUM, M. (1977). *The Anatomy of Historical Explanation.* Baltimore: John
    Hopkins Univ. Press.
NAGEL, E. (1979). *The Structure of Science.* Indianapolis: Hackett.
RIEFF, P. (1959). *Freud: The Mind of the Moralist.* New York: Viking.
——— (1966). *The Triumph of the Therapeutic: Uses of Faith After Freud.* New York:
    Harper & Row.

Psychoanalysis: Science and Philosophy

TAYLOR, R. (1967). Causation. In *Encyclopedia of Philosophy*, ed. P. Edwards. New York: Macmillan, Vol. 2, pp. 56-66.

WALLACE, E. (1984). Freud and religion. *Psychoanal. Study Society*, 10:113-161.

——— (1985). *Historiography and Causation in Psychoanalysis: An Essay on Psychoanalytic and Historical Epistemology*. Hillsdale, NJ: Analytic Press.

——— (1986a). Freud as ethicist. In *Freud: Appraisals and Reappraisals*, ed. P. Stapansky. Hillsdale, NJ: Analytic Press, pp. 83-141.

——— (1986b). Determinism, possibility, and ethics. *J. Amer. Psychoanal. Assn.*, 34:933-974.

——— (1988). Psychoanalytic causation revisited. *Psychiat. Forum*, 14:1-21.

——— (1989a). Toward a phenomenological and minimally theoretical psychoanalysis. *The Annual of Psychoanalysis*, 17:17-69.

——— (1989b). Pitfalls of a one-sided image of science: Adolf Grünbaum's *Foundations of Psychoanalysis*. *J. Amer. Psychoanal. Assn.*, 37:493-529.

——— (1990a). Psychiatry and religion: toward a dialogue and public philosophy. In *Psychoanalysis and Religion*, ed. J. Smith & S. Handelman. *Psychiatry and the Humanities*, 11. Baltimore: Johns Hopkins Univ. Press, pp. 295-330.

——— (1990b). Mind/body and the future of psychiatry. *J. Med. Phil.*, 15:41-73.

——— (1992a). Freud and the mind/body problem. In *Freud and the History of Psychoanalysis*, ed. T. Gelfand & J. Kerr. Hillsdale, NJ: Analytic Press, pp. 231-269.

——— (1992b). Psychiatry: the healing amphibian. In *Does Psychiatry Need a Public Philosophy?*, ed. D. Browning & I. Evison. Chicago: Nelson-Hall, pp. 77-120.

Edwin R. Wallace, IV
Center for Bioethics
Institute of Public Affairs
University of South Carolina
Columbia, SC 29208

BETWEEN HERMENEUTICS AND SCIENCE. By *Carlo Strenger*. Madison, CT: Int. Univ. Press, 1991, xv + 234 pp., $30.00.

If nature is indivisible, as many scientists assume, then the analyst's mental functioning during an analytic hour must have something in common with similar kinds of listening and reasoning in nonanalytic situations. It is to Carlo Strenger's great credit that he has started to build a bridge between what the analyst sometimes succeeds in doing and other kinds of mental achievements. In the process, he shows up the flaws in the traditional argument that only *analyzed* critics could properly understand the analytic attitude. By showing that the practicing analyst is frequently functioning in familiar ways, Strenger opens the way toward better understanding of the analytic task, toward the planning of more enlightened research, and (we would hope) toward increased sympathy from other disciplines.

How does the analyst listen? Strenger presents us with what he calls a "rational reconstruction" of the process, which includes the following stages: (1) Establish the object of interpretation, which frequently reduces to "listening for subjectively determined, ideosyncratic patterns in the patient's way of acting, feeling, and thinking" (p. 78). (2) Provide a "narrative which gives intelligibility to the patient's previously inexplicable patterns of action, thought, and emotion" (p. 86). (3) Listen for ways in which the tentative narrative produces new patterns of response (which brings us back to point 1 and thence to point 2; the cycle is repeated until the treatment comes to a close).

Throughout this discussion (the heart of Chapter 4), Strenger is intent on adhering to what he calls the Continuum Principle, which takes the following form: "It must be possible to show that the claimed capacities [of the practicing analyst] are refinements of ordinary human capacities, and it must be made plausible why under specified circumstances such refinements can actually occur" (p. 95). In the course of explicating the range of material to which the analyst is sensitive, Strenger repeatedly underlines the necessary distinction between what is directly observable—terms of clinical description—and the fruits of genetic and other kinds of speculation. He concludes that "only if this differentiation . . . is taken seriously can the epistemological value of clinical material be defended" (p. 104). It goes without saying that a systematic focus on, and elaboration of, the terms of clinical description will reinforce the continuum principle; conversely, too much emphasis on speculation can only reinforce the idea that analytic work is a species of mumbo jumbo that is largely mystical, subjective, and impossible to clarify or refine.

But there is an interesting difficulty that faces us once we take the next step, and this is a problem not directly addressed by Strenger. Consider a parallel problem in music. Strenger reminds us that the fourth movement of Brahms's 4th Symphony "consists of 31 variations on the theme of the first 8 bars" (p. 95), and once this fact is brought to the attention of a listener with average musical gifts, he can identify the lion's share of the variations. But this move is made possible only because we have a terminology that lets us define theme and variation and because the composer (Brahms) was working within a framework that assumed these distinctions. Comparable terms for analytic distinctions still need to be created, as do the names for the appropriate units of analysis. We have nothing comparable to the bar line in music; we have no agreement on a possible family of key signatures; and we have no available narrative theory to tell us when various pieces of the patient's associations turn into a theme (this is the problem of narrative coherence to which Strenger devotes a fair amount of space—see pp. 188-193) or when Theme A becomes Theme B. Pattern matching, the skill we use when we identify similarities of form or content in the patient's discourse, is still a largely intuitive art, and the ingredients of good and bad timing are still a matter of speculation and argument. Strenger might easily devote his next book to working out some of these details, and a fuller description of these issues would have significantly strengthened his account of the analyst's mind at work.

As lawfulness in the clinical material becomes more widely documented, we will begin to discover what might be called general principles of listening that many, if not most, analysts probably subscribe to without knowing it (for one sample of such a pattern, see Spence, Mayes, and Dahl, 1994). As lawfulness in our listening and interpretative habits becomes more generally established, we will be well on our way toward closing what Strenger calls the gap between hermeneutics and science. In hindsight, we may discover that hermeneutics is what we call something when we don't fully understand its workings (see Rorty, 1979, for a similar argument). As awareness grows and new terms develop for identifying its important distinctions, its mystical features drop away and it becomes part of normal science.

But this kind of evolutionary approach, which emphasizes continuity and gradualness, is difficult to maintain in the face of Strenger's either/or argument. In choosing to frame his overall argument as a choice "between hermeneutics and science" (the book's title) or in declaring that the book "can be viewed as an attempt to mediate between the hermeneuticist conception of psychoanalysis and the requirement for stringent experimental truth" (p. 194), Strenger tends to reinforce the black/white argument that has come to preoccupy psychoanalysis in recent years. It leads to papers like Blight's (1981) "Must Psychoanalysis Retreat to Hermeneutics?"; to questions such as "Which side are you on?"; and to similar kinds of political maneuverings. Not only is *science* becoming less and less of a single thing and ever harder to define, but *hermeneutics* is even harder to pin down, both as a concept and as an approach to clinical work. It, too, is evolving. But the fuzziness of either *science* or *hermeneutics* is belied by Strenger's tendency to use these words as clearly defined opposites that mark the two ends of the clinical continuum. Indeed, a constant reference to these terms tends to give them an epistemological status that they do not presently deserve.

In similar fashion, Strenger tends to reify the evils of relativism and pluralism and make the presence of multiple theories a larger problem than may in fact be the case (see Chapter 6). The fact that we are currently beseiged by a host of different analytic schools based on a number of quite different theories may also be nothing more than a sign of growing pains, a sign that we do not have at hand the necessary terms to accurately and exhaustively describe any given clinical happening. If we think of theories as essentially after-the-fact attempts to explain certain kinds of clinical events, then it is not surprising (1) that different analysts come up with different stories, (2) that these stories will change over time, and (3) that the final, mature explanation of the analytic process, 100 years from now, will resemble none of them. Current theory seems to function as a set of provisional laws that reassure the therapist and provide him or her with an intellectual home; it remains to be seen whether they provide much in the way of insight into the analytic process. As Strenger extends his "rational reconstruction" of how the analyst's mind works, he may find that theory tends to fall by the wayside; as we learn better how to define theme and variations, moments of interpretative opportunity, pockets of miscommunication and the like, we may find that many of our concepts are dispensable, a kind of modern-day phlogiston, and that our thinking goes better without them.

But these are minor variations on a secondary theme. Strenger is to be congratulated for cutting to the heart of our present crisis and making it plain that we are desperately in need of a new language to describe what we hear and what we do with it without being able to translate these actions into words (because, I would argue, our theories have little or nothing to do with clinical phenomena). And he is undoubtedly right in believing that analytic work shares many features of other kinds of pattern-finding and theme-building operations. The sooner we discover these bridges, the quicker we will benefit.

REFERENCES

BLIGHT, J. (1981). Must psychoanalysis retreat to hermeneutics? Psychoanalytic theory in the light of Popper's evolutionary epistemology. *Psychoanal. Contemp. Thought*, 4:147-205.
RORTY, R. (1979). *Philosophy and the Mirror of Nature*. Princeton: Princeton Univ. Press.

Psychoanalysis: Science and Philosophy

SPENCE, D.P., MAYES, L.C. & DAHL, H. (1994). Monitoring the analytic surface. *J. Amer. Psychoanal. Assn.*, 42:43–64.

Donald P. Spence
University of Medicine and Dentistry of New Jersey
Robert Wood Johnson Medical School
Department of Psychiatry
675 Hoes Lane
Piscataway, New Jersey 08854-5635
FAX: 908 235 5158
e-mail: Spenced@Pucc.Princeton.edu

THE MIND AND ITS DEPTHS. By *Richard Wollheim.* Cambridge, MA: Harvard Univ. Press, 1993, x + 214 pp., $24.95 (hardcover), $14.95 (paperback).

Professor Richard Wollheim is not only a substantial contributor to psychoanalytic thinking, he is also something of an intellectual rarity. Philosophers in the logical-analytic or empirical-analytic tradition (sometimes called "Anglo-American" in contrast to the Continental tradition) have only infrequently been interested in psychoanalysis; when their interests have turned in this direction, it has often been with a disdainful and ill-informed attitude, or with the careerist ambition to expose our multitude of shortcomings, even to proclaim the "death" of the discipline. By contrast, Wollheim has devoted a major portion of his career to the study of psychoanalytic thinking, and has done so in a manner that is consistently knowledgeable, lucid, and respectful, while not being uncritical. Yet he is an eminent British philosopher with rigorous training in the Anglo-American tradition, and he enjoys a strong reputation for his work on matters of art and topics in moral philosophy, much of which has been directly or indirectly enriched by his psychoanalytic knowledge.

Throughout his career Wollheim has contributed to the philosophical literature with distinction, producing several books on art and painting, a text on F. H. Bradley's ethical philosophy, and numerous lectures on issues of moral deliberation. Many psychoanalysts are familiar with Wollheim's 1971 text, *Sigmund Freud,* written for the "Modern Masters" series. It remains an outstanding introduction to its subject, a model of brevity, clarity, and well-balanced exposition.

Similarly, the anthology he edited in 1974, *Freud: A Collection of Critical Essays*, has retained its value. Beyond these explicitly psychoanalytic writings, Wollheim's more general work has focused on recurrent themes that bridge his philosophical and psychoanalytic interests: the nature of expression, in art and elsewhere; the "corporealization" of thought (the tendency of infantile thinking to represent itself as something bodily); and the basis of "higher" functions such as morality on drive and instinct. He is articulate and adamant in condemning the view that philosophy and psychology are totally independent disciplines. Rather, he believes that "there are many philosophical questions that cannot be answered unless we know the relevant psychology, and there are many psychological questions whose answers await the relevant philosophy" (p. 159).

In many respects, the volume under review is a sequel to *On Art and the Mind* (1973), which collected various papers written by Wollheim prior to 1972. Similarly, *The Mind and Its Depths* is a miscellaneous collection of twelve essays from the years 1975 to 1989. While many of these essays originated as lectures which have been subsequently revised, and most have been previously published, few are available in print at this time. There is much in this book that will please philosophically minded psychoanalysts, especially those inclined to the mode of philosophy characteristic of the Anglo-American tradition.

For example, Wollheim offers an essay examining Freud's injunction that "the ego is first and foremost a bodily ego" (Freud, 1923, p. 26), which goes to the fundament of the mind-body problem as it is encountered in psychoanalytic theorizing. The thesis of the bodily ego specifies the relationship between the body and representational states, between the material and the phenomenological. Wollheim adroitly elucidates this relationship in terms of the idea that certain mental states are self-representing, and proceeds to analyze the questions that arise from this in terms of Freud's position that beliefs (directed to whether something is true or false) are anticipated by "proto-beliefs" (directed to whether something is good or bad). This then leads Wollheim into an interesting discussion of the character of "internal objects" (the sense in which they are *internal*, the sense in which they are *objects*) and their formation through "phantasy" (spelled in the manner of the English school), which involves the psychic mechanisms of introjection and projection in a manner that is both causal and intentional.

The influence of Kleinian ideas on Wollheim's writings is conspicuous, for he finds in Klein and Bion a cogent account of a topic over which philosophers flounder: the origins of thinking. It may be hard to imagine Kleinian psychoanalysis rendered concordant with the austerity and sobriety of British philosophy, but Wollheim achieves nothing less. For example, his fascinating essay "The Good Self and the Bad Self" compares the moral psychology of British idealism (mostly Bradley) with the English school of psychoanalysis (mostly Klein), and exemplifies Wollheim's scholarship at its most creative. Admitting that philosophical "idealism and psychoanalysis may seem an incongruous pair" (p. 39). Wollheim proceeds to show how each complements and strengthens the other, and thus offers a convincing demonstration of his belief that philosophy needs psychoanalytic psychology, and vice versa.

In a final note of appreciation, I would like to highlight Wollheim's essay entitled "Desire, Belief, and Professor Grünbaum's Freud." This is one of the few pieces in this collection that has not appeared previously, and I believe it deserves the widest possible readership. It begins by describing the two major attitudes that conventional philosophies of mind hold toward Freudian perspectives (either Freud concocted his concepts entirely *de novo*, in which case they are trivialized as unrelated to previous modes of explanation, or Freud's concepts are merely an extension of common sense, in which case their novelty only resides in their divergences from such common modes of explanation). Wollheim proceeds to delineate, in terms of the concepts of desire and belief, the various forms of psychological explanation and the ways in which Freud deepened such explanations by producing three major variations and contextualizing the schema of such explanation. Wollheim then examines the arguments in Adolf Grünbaum's 1984 book, *The Foundations of Psychoanalysis: A Philosophical Critique.* Although Wollheim's essay cannot be replicated here, suffice it to indicate that he persuasively demonstrates how Grünbaum tendentiously restricts his arguments exclusively to matters of clinical testability. Wollheim next skillfully exposes the ways in which Grünbaum systematically misunderstands Freudian thinking, particularly the contextual character of its explanations and the location of its explanations within a structure of theorizing. In sum, the "crucial feature" of the misconception of Freudian theory that underlies Grünbaum's inquiry "is that it leaves out the psychological structure that Freud was at such pains to reconstruct. Furthermore, Grünbaum leaves it out as though it were the obvious thing to do, or as though there were no need for structure within a science of the mind" (p. 110). Finally, addressing Grünbaum's repeated cry that "suggestibility" might well enough explain anything that clinical psychoanalysis might achieve, Wollheim deftly points out that "for all the serious attention that Grünbaum asks *us* to give to this alternative theory, he never for a moment thinks that its plausibility requires *him* to give an account of how suggestion by the analyst would engage with the patient's psychological structure" (p. 111). As of the date that I write this review, Grünbaum has not replied to Wollheim's critique.

This collection of essays has much to recommend it. Much as philosophy has to learn from psychoanalysis, there can be no question that psychoanalysis urgently needs the aid of mature philosophical inquiry. In this anthology, Professor Wollheim offers us a sampling of the best of his work in this direction.

REFERENCES

FREUD, S. (1923). The ego and the id. *S.E.*, 19.
GRÜNBAUM, A. (1984). *The Foundations of Psychoanalysis: A Philosophical Critique.* Berkeley: Univ. California Press.
WOLLHEIM, R. (1971). *Sigmund Freud.* London: Collins.
——— (1973). *On Art and the Mind.* London: Allen Lane.
——— (Ed., 1974). *Freud: A Collection of Critical Essays.* Garden City, NY: Anchor Press/Doubleday.

Barnaby B. Barratt
7480 Greenwich East
Bloomfield, MI 48301-3920

PSYCHOANALYSIS AND THE SCIENCES. By *André Haynal.* Berkeley, CA: Univ. California Press, 1993, xii + 290 pp., $30.00.

André Haynal is a Swiss psychoanalyst of Hungarian origin who has written extensively about the intellectual history of psychoanalysis and its epistemology. Under his aegis, the Bálint Archive has been established at the University of Geneva, so he deserves much of the credit for the ongoing publication of the basic documentation of the Freud-Ferenczi collaboration. At the same time, Haynal is one of the leaders shepherding psychoanalysis into the "postmodern" world: at once an ecumenicist, a progressive, an intellectual preservationist, and a partisan of the Budapest school. I should probably add that, if push came to shove, I might describe myself in the same terms.

The volume under review is a collection of Haynal's essays on the scientific status of contemporary psychoanalysis and on the historical circumstances that determined the course of the Freudian enterprise. Earlier versions of some chapters were written for specific occasions; although Haynal has clearly tried to produce a coherent book, he has been unable to avoid some repetitiveness as well as some disjunctiveness in terms of subject matter. Elizabeth Holder's translation from the French is generally felicitous: the book is gracefully written and easy to follow, so few readers will be bothered by the fact that it is not a monograph. Haynal himself acknowledges that the epistemological and historical sections of the book lack a unifying focus.

From an American vantage point, what distinguishes Haynal's work is its placement within the internal discourse of French psychoanalysis. His viewpoint is of particular interest because, in almost every respect, Haynal takes an anti-Lacanian position. However, aside from Freud and Ferenczi, most of his references are to francophone authors, and Americans are notably underrepresented in his bibliography. (This is especially striking because many Americans he cites, like Sylvan Tomkins or Howard Gardner, are not psychoanalysts but contributors to cognate fields.) It is somewhat sobering to see how well our European colleagues can get along without our contributions!

One sign of Haynal's implantation among the French is the shape of most of his essays: by "Anglo-Saxon" standards (as they put it in Paris), it is very difficult to define their subject matter. An account of the Freud-Jung-Sabina Spielrein triangle takes a detour into the history of psychoanalysis in Russia and the Soviet Union, the fate of émigré Russian analysts, and the parallels between Spielrein's history and that of the heroine of D. M. Thomas's *The White Hotel.* It all goes down as easily as champagne, but I have the disquieting feeling that I often miss Haynal's point. Perhaps the problem is simply mine: I am not as postmodern as I need to be in the age of deconstruction. At the same time, I cannot forget that postmodernism is largely a movement to restore French hegemony over Western intellectual life—as one Parisian colleague confessed, it is now bad form to write in a manner too easy to follow. Some of the time, I fear that I am unable to follow Haynal's thesis because it seems to answer arguments with which I am not familiar.

Most often, Haynal seems to espouse positions with which I agree, along with the great majority of Americans: Freud tried to articulate scientific propositions about mental functions, based on his clinical experiences, and encoded in a loosely defined vocabulary designed to keep the system relatively open. In his lifetime, none could challenge his authority without deserting the psychoanalytic movement, and he felt free to appropriate many ideas first proposed by his disciples. The appropriate parameters of the analyst-analysand relationship were only gradually clarified; in the meantime, they were often confused with those of teacher-pupil transactions—even with those of friendship and love. Under the circumstances, none of the protagonists had a monopoly on virtue and wisdom, or their opposites. Freud neglected therapeutic considerations in favor of overarching psychological theories; Ferenczi acted as a counterweight to this tendency.

I part company with Haynal when he asserts that matters can be "elucidated" without systematization—in my view, even postmodern science must articulate a well-defined set of propositions. Haynal approves of Melanie Klein's contributions; I find them unserviceable because of her failure to integrate them into psychoanalytic theory in a coherent way. Haynal uses concepts such as "narcissism" and "death instinct," although he advocates a change from basing theory on the concept of energy to that of information. Yet these Freudian terms are either based on vicissitudes of psychic energy or they are meaningless panchrestons. In the French context, Haynal usefully insists on the need to keep psychoanalysis within the boundaries of science; from the shores of Lake Michigan, what he espouses as science does not seem to have sufficient empirical underpinnings and more closely resembles a rationalist philosophical system. It is very sophisticated, but it is alien to our "Anglo-Saxon" heritage. And thus do Hungarian émigrés take on the coloring of their new surroundings. . . .

Yet Haynal and I preserve enough of our common roots in Central Europe to agree on extending the therapeutic tradition of Ferenczi, with its emphasis of experience in the here and now and its focus on the actualities of analyst-analysand transactions. I suspect that Haynal is more inclined than I to believe that Ferenczi's actual procedures of the early 1930's are still serviceable. In contrast, I think that these measures were necessitated by the unanalyzed analyst's disabling difficulties; in a contemporary context, persons as vulnerable to profound influence from their patients as was Ferenczi should not undertake to do psychoanalytic work. It is one thing to take the mutual influence of the participants in analysis into account—it is quite another utterly to alter the observational field by yielding to the psychological pressures emanating from analysands.

Of course, it is precisely because he expects such views from analysts trained in the United States that Haynal expresses his disagreement with the American psychoanalytic ethos that honors scientific clarity. He may urge Europeans to be more scientific, but he is not unaffected by the French preference for viewing psychoanalysis not as a healing procedure but as an avant-garde way of life.

If psychoanalysis is akin to a philosophical dialogue, it is only natural that its dyadic context is regarded, as it is by Haynal, as the norm of human mental life. (In this sense, Haynal's loyalty to Ferenczi and his assimilation in Geneva have conspired to pull him far away from Freud's "one person psychology.") What Americans tend to view as a therapeutic alliance, Haynal describes as (mutual) seduction. This is an excellent illustration of the difference between a tradition that absorbed ego psychology and one that has largely rejected it. At any rate, the most serious disagreement I have with Haynal's thesis concerns his neglect of what Arnold Modell (1992) has called "private space." Human psychological life does not take place in a dyadic context exclusively. *Mais, après tout, vive la différence!*

REFERENCE

Modell, A. (1992). The private self and private space. *The Annual of Psychoanalysis*, 20:1-14. Hillsdale, NJ: Analytic Press.

John E. Gedo
680 N. Lake Shore Drive
Chicago, IL 60611
FAX: 312 944 6485

HIERARCHICAL CONCEPTS IN PSYCHOANALYSIS: THEORY, RESEARCH AND CLINICAL PRACTICE. Edited by *Arnold Wilson* and *John E. Gedo*. New York: Guilford Press, 1993, 333 pp., $39.95.

Psychoanalysis is in a period of transition, confronted on the one hand by alternate models of psychic functioning and new data on child development and on the other by the renaissance in understanding brain function. Psychoanalytic theory has become less insular, and practitioners and theorists alike have attempted to broaden their understanding by integrating multiple models. This volume is an attempt to place psychoanalysis in the mainstream of science from the point of view of both psychology and, to a lesser degree, neuroscience. From this perspective, Wilson and Gedo attempt to transcend the fragmentation of psychoanalysis imposed by multiple models—conflict theory, ego psychology, object relations theory, and so on—in this multiauthor volume that emphasizes hierarchically ordered psychological experiences originating in early life as constant influences on adult functioning. Although this theme integrates the volume, the authors have been encouraged to present their own perspective, and no attempt is made to offer a unified model without contradictions. The data of modern cognitive psychology, linguistics, and neurobiology are utilized. The volume is divided into three sections: Research, Theory and Historical Perspectives, and Clinical Applications. Many of the authors are scholars of psychoanalysis and present views expounded in greater detail elsewhere, often condensing their work in ways that make reading more difficult.

A central theme dominates: this is a systems theory of psychological development transposed to psychic functioning in the adult. Gedo's "eclectic" model is the unifying structure, strongly seconded by Lichtenberg's very imaginative and interesting view of development, carefully supported by empirical data generated by child developmental studies. The attempt at integration with knowledge of brain function, a chapter contributed by Levin, is highly condensed but buttressed by extensive references to Levin's own work. One might view this book as an attempt to put meat on the bones of Engel's (1977) biopsychosocial model. In this light there is an emphasis on the earliest organization of the regulation of physiological functions: first by the nurturing object, followed by movement toward self-regulation and development of psychological functions, initially primitive, then more complex.

The volume begins with an excellent chapter by Bucci, who is interested in operationalizing the study of psychoanalytic process so as to address one of the central problems of psychoanalysis, namely, the development of meaning. She develops a model of the mind that posits the verbal system as the code of language and logic and the nonverbal system as including all sensory modalities; motoric activity as well autonomic, visceral, and somatic experience; and, in particular, emotional events. The emotional events are organizing factors in development laid down in the context of relationships with others. Central to her model is what she calls the referential process, namely, the relationships between these two systems, which are by no means simply related to primary and secondary processes, since both systems may have conscious and unconscious determinants. Bucci develops a scoring system that permits the microanalysis of verbal, nonverbal, and referential connections so as to permit the examination of the evolution of these processes in analysis. Movement in analysis implies the increased elaboration of meaning as the verbal and nonverbal areas become connected through association. Intellectualization is defined by Bucci as "the articulation of meanings based on connections within the verbal system only" (p. 43). Conversely, in acting out, "connections to motoric activation occur within maladaptive emotional structures without mediation by the logic and reality filters of the verbal code" (p. 43).

Grand, Finer, and Reisner present a scale for an epigenetic hierarchy of developmental function as it relates to pathology. Although their success in clarifying distinctions between schizophrenic and borderline patients is interesting, it is not likely to be helpful in the clinical situation. Wilson and Passik, in an elaborate and complicated chapter that requires careful reading, develop an Epigenetic Assessment Rating System (the EARS) that is designed to provide empirical reference for psychoanalytic concepts that define the progressive and regressive movement of clinical phenomenon within a particular theoretical hierarchy of personality organization. They present an elegant discussion of the epigenetic hypothesis, and their thinking is clearly influenced by new theories of complexity and, in particular, by what they call emergent properties, a concept developed from chaos theory. The EARS uses the TAT to analyze narration and to understand it from the point of view of a five-level hierarchical scheme ranging from primitive preverbal to high-level functioning. This is a very complex chapter that will be of greatest interest to researchers in psychopathology and psychoanalytic process.

Gedo's and Lichtenberg's chapters in the theoretical section are rich, and one cannot do justice to them in a brief review. Clearly they are the central and organizing chapters of the volume, and the details of their concepts have been published extensively elsewhere. Essentially, they present parallel hierarchical schemes, Lichtenberg's from a developmental point of view and Gedo's from a point of view directed to adult psychopathology. Lichtenberg develops an interesting theory of stranger anxiety that involves an elaboration of his previous concept of imaging capacity, now subsuming what he calls "affect referencing" (the infant's increasing capacity to differentiate affective responses in the maternal figure that suggest a range of pleasure and unpleasure and the associated security or danger). He emphasizes that maturation of central nervous system capacities permits the infant to respond not simply to visual perception but also to the affective climate that surrounds the visual perceptions; such affect referencing represents a central organizing feature in the response of the infant to his environment. This conceptualization is consistent with our knowledge of child development and offers an explanation of why maturational growth generates anxiety during transitional phases.

Levin's theoretical presentation would be easier to assimilate were it less condensed. Of special interest is his description of the plasticity of the brain in development. Particularly intriguing was his discussion of how environmental processes affect the capacity of the deaf to develop or to fail to develop capacities for abstract thought and language.

Grossman, in his predictably elegant and scholarly way, demonstrates Freud's approach to theory building as "an account of a person observing his own mental processes and arriving at a picture of the mind and of his world" (p. 173). Striking is the modernity of Freud's view of the nervous system, with interconnected chains of associations and parallel chains of associations, as they relate to both language and sensory input. Grossman demonstrates how Freud's method of theory building can be constructed from his early monograph *On Aphasia* (Freud, 1953).

The clinical section of this volume is somewhat less satisfying. Although there appear to be insights in the articles by Robbins (on primitive personality) and by Khantzian and Wilson (on drug addiction) their views, stated much too boldly, are reductionistic. Clearly, primitive psychopathology and drug addiction are very complex phenomena with multicausal etiology. Although there is merit in Khantzian and Wilson's view that drug abusers use drugs to deal with dysphoric affects and that drug use thus represents an attempt at self-regulation, the generalization is much too broad to encompass the behavior of all drug addicts. Similarly, the concept of alexithymia, discussed by Robbins, though useful in some situations, is hardly a unicausal factor in severe psychopathology. This idea originated with the French psychosomaticians in the concept of "*pensée operatoire*" and was used by them to describe psychosomatic disease. We now recognize in the extensive work by Weiner (1977) that the seven "psychosomatic diseases" that Alexander thought were primarily products of specific intrapsychic conflicts are highly heterogeneous illnesses that have a variety of pathophysiological mechanisms and are variably influenced by genetic, psychological, and social factors.

Psychoanalysis: Science and Philosophy

Clearly, this pertains as well to drug abuse and severe primitive personality disorders, although the concept of alexithymia may have some merit in individual cases. Overall, the idea that there is a failure of development from the primitive expression of affect and conflict through somatic channels to a higher stage of psychological expression is valuable and is much in keeping with the theme of this volume.

This is a very complex and difficult book written by individuals immersed in theory and in research. Hopefully it will offer a substrate for further research in psychoanalysis and as such will be of special interest to researchers who may apply these concepts and instruments in their own endeavors.

This book will be of interest to a wide variety of analysts, who can focus on the chapters related to their areas of expertise.

REFERENCES

ENGEL, G.L. (1977). A need for a new medical model: a change for biomedicine. *Science*, 196:129-136.
FREUD, S. (1953). *On Aphasia*, tr. E. Stengel. New York: Int. Univ. Press.
WEINER, H. (1977). *Psychobiology and Human Disease*. New York: Elsevier.

Milton Viederman
New York Hospital
525 E. 68th St., Box 208
New York, NY 10021
FAX: 212 746 8529

Book Reviewers *JAPA 43/4*

BARNABY B. BARRATT, Lecturer, Michigan Psychoanalytic Institute; Director of Behavioral Sciences and Associate Professor of Family Medicine, Psychiatry and Behavioral Neurosciences, Wayne State University.

PAUL A. DEWALD, Training Analyst Emeritus, Supervising Analyst, St. Louis Psychoanalytic Institute; Clinical Professor of Psychiatry, St. Louis University School of Medicine.

JOHN E. GEDO, Former Book Review Editor, *Journal of the American Psychoanalytic Association*; contributed over 120 reviews to the psychoanalytic literature.

MARTHA KIRKPATRICK, Clinical Professor of Psychiatry, University of California, Los Angeles; Senior Faculty, Los Angeles Psychoanalytic Society and Institute; Training and Supervising Analyst, Institute of Contemporary Psychoanalysis, Los Angeles.

MICHAEL G. MORAN, Associate Professor of Psychiatry, University of Colorado; Director, Adult Psychiatry, National Jewish Center for Immunology and Respiratory Medicine, Denver.

JOSEPH REPPEN, Editor, *Psychoanalytic Books: A Quarterly Journal of Reviews*.

EVELYNE ALBRECHT SCHWABER, Training and Supervising Analyst, Psychoanalytic Institute of New England, East; Faculty, Boston Psychoanalytic Society and Institute.

DONALD P. SPENCE, Professor of Psychiatry, Robert Wood Johnson Medical School, Piscataway, New Jersey.

MILTON VIEDERMAN, Professor of Clinical Psychiatry, Cornell University Medical College; Training and Supervising Analyst, Columbia University Center for Psychoanalytic Training and Research.

EDWIN R. WALLACE, IV, Professor of Psychiatry, Medical College of Georgia; Research Professor of Bioethics, University of South Carolina.

1245

February 23, 1995

The Analyst's Theorizing

In "Critical Notes on the Psychoanalyst's Theorizing" (*JAPA*, 42/3) Barnaby Barratt raises some very important and provocative psychoanalytic questions. Nevertheless, his position presents some difficulties as well, and I would like to elaborate what I see these to be. I also want to clarify my own position (Ehrenberg, 1992b, 1993, 1994a, 1994b, 1994c, 1995. Note also that *The Intimate Edge: Extending the Reach of Psychoanalytic Interaction*, which contains most of my papers published between 1974 and 1991, was published by W. W. Norton in 1992, not by "Contemporary Psychoanalysis Publ.," as listed in Barratt's references).

Barratt begins by stating "the central questions might be articulated as follows: When, or under what criteria, might the psychoanalyst's theorizing activity during a psychoanalytic session be considered resistive or facilitative to the psychoanalytic process itself? And how might the psychoanalyst, in the moment-to-moment of the clinical encounter, know the difference?" (p. 698). He then goes on to argue that three different approaches, which he labels the "computational," the "engaged," and the "cadaverized," "foster or fixate the psychoanalyst's illusions, and are therefore resistive to the psychoanalyst's radical responsibility to interrogate free-associatively his or her own suppositions and discursive maneuvers" (p. 697).

The first question, about how we might know whether the analyst's theorizing activity during a session is resistive or facilitative to the psychoanalytic process, seems fairly straightforward and, of course, is extremely important. If we recognize our own vulnerability to unconscious influence, no matter what our theory, and if we believe in the power of countertransference and the inevitability of varying degrees of unwitting enactment and unconscious collusion, however, then the suggestion implicit in the second question, that we can actually determine if our thought process is resistive or facilitative at any given time, seems problematic. How can we ever be sure that our very efforts to make such an assessment do not themselves involve some form of unconscious enactment, however conscientious we may be striving to be?

The same concern, of course, applies with regard to Barratt's call for us to interrogate free-associatively *our own suppositions and discursive maneuvers*. His argument about the way the analyst's approach might fixate the analyst's illusions makes quite clear the dangers of theory getting in our way rather than being helpful. The problem is that the kind of effort he suggests as a solution seems in and of itself insufficient to solve the dilemmas he astutely delineates, precisely because such efforts are as vulnerable to unconscious influence as the suppositions and discursive maneuvers in question.

Barratt's depiction of the psychoanalyst's theorizing as involving a striving "toward an 'understanding' of what the patient says and does" (p. 708) is also problematic from my perspective. As I read this, his focus on the analyst's "*covariational judgments*, which are beliefs as to 'what meaningfully belongs with what' " (p. 708), reflects the very model of psychoanalytic thinking he sets out to challenge. How can we ever be sure our judgments are not influenced by unconscious factors? How can we trust that the premises of our theory are not interfering with rather than facilitating our ability to grasp the issues? How can we ever control for our own impact in shaping whatever we "see." This section of his paper seems inconsistent with his own position, stated in *Psychoanalysis and the Postmodern Impulse: Knowing and Being since Freud's Psychology* (Barratt, 1993), that "psychoanalysis becomes a process that interrogates the very act of . . . ideological impositioning, freeing the subject from the alienation entailed by the systematization of interpretative positing and repositing" (p. 16), that "the trajectory of free-associative movement . . . eludes all efforts at interpretative summation and semiotic capture" (p. 26), and that "the psychoanalyst is not some sort of agent of computation, seated above the patient and making 'observations and inferences' about the patient's 'material' " (p. 29).

All of the concerns raised above apply to each of the "positions" he addresses himself to, as well as to his own. The interpretation of the computational analyst, for example, has interactive meaning and impact apart from its content, and apart from the analyst's conscious intent. Gill (1994), Hoffman (1991), Levenson (1972), and many others besides myself have made similar points over the years. An interpretation may be experienced by the patient as empathic, holding, containing, gratifying, manipulative, seductive, controlling, competitive, coercive, invasive, evasive, a form of mental rape, whatever, irrespective of the analyst's conscious intent. It also may *be* any of these whether or not analyst or patient recognizes the degree to which this may be so.

The same of course is true for the participation of the cadaverized psychoanalyst. Any form of analyst participation will be experienced and construed differently by different patients, no matter what the analyst's conscious intent, and the analyst can never control for what he or she conveys and responds to nonverbally, without conscious intention or awareness. To assume we can ever work without memory or desire is even more problematic, but I will not take that up here.

In Barratt's discussion of what he calls the engaged psychoanalyst, he suggests a common thread between points of view that actually are extremely divergent. Analysts of the diverse points of view he includes here, incompatible as they may be, are equally vulnerable to unconscious collusion and enactment.

Although Barratt locates my own work in the "engaged" category, in my view it is useless to argue the merits of the analyst being engaged or not engaged. We are all engaged, like it or not. It is *how* we engage, and whether and how we use our awareness of the nature of this engagement, that distinguishes different ways of working. The critical question is what defines *psychoanalytic* engagement, since we are all well aware that too often analyst and patient can be engaged without an analytic process taking place, whether or not the participants realize this is so (Ehrenberg, 1992b, 1993).

Based on my own concerns with some of the very dilemmas Dr. Barratt raises, I have argued that because we are always vulnerable to unconscious influence, and to interactive enactments without awareness, no matter how conscientiously we may try to question ourselves, a radical shift in how we define "analysis" is required. Also required are new perspectives on how we might best use ourselves as psychoanalytic instruments, and on how we understand the nature of psychoanalytic data—i.e., the data of psychoanalysis must include not only the patient's dreams, associations, etc., but everything that goes on between patient and analyst, as well as within each of them in relation to each other, or crucial interactive issues may never be recognized or analytically engaged.

As I have argued elsewhere (Ehrenberg, 1993, 1994b), in some instances failure to attend to interactive considerations, no matter what our "theory," becomes a basis for impasse. By the latter I refer not only to situations involving ruptures in treatment, but also to those treatments that go on for years with no substantial analytic result. Failure to attend to interactive considerations is often also the basis for so-called "negative therapeutic reaction." In many such instances these "negative" reactions are iatrogenic responses to some aspect of the analysts' participation of which neither patient nor analyst may be consciously aware. Though we can never transcend our own involvement and our own vulnerability to unconscious influence, recognizing the power of what goes on interactively, and that there will always be levels of involvement we will not be able to be consciously aware of, enables us to be alert to interactive dangers of manipulation, seduction, and collusion, and to bring more of those elusive aspects of the interaction that are often neither recognized nor addressed into analytic focus.

In considering Barratt's important question as to how, if at all, the psychoanalyst is to "use" conscious, deliberative theorizing while engaged with the patient, I believe it is essential to be clear about the level of theory and level of abstraction at which we are operating. Theory of psychopathology and theory of cure as internal (intrapsychic) issues must be distinguished from theory of treatment and cure as interactive process (even if the analyst is silent), and from theory regarding how we might best use ourselves as a psychoanalytic instrument (which we might perhaps think of as theory of technique). In addition, from my perspective, the issue is not only how to use conscious, deliberative theorizing, but also how to be affectively present in the most optimal way. Theorizing can be a defense against a more affectively sensitive way of participating, and vice versa. Perhaps the critical point here is that what we do (and toward what end) and what defines analytic process are not easily agreed upon by analysts, even among those within a single one of Barratt's categories. Similarly, even among those who agree about the importance of attending to the subtleties of the analytic interaction, the question of *how* we might do this most advantageously remains controversial.

I will not pursue any of these points here. I will simply note that, as I emphasized at the Classics Revisited session at the American Psychoanalytic meetings in December 1992, focusing on Eissler's "The Effect of the Structure of the Ego on Psychoanalytic Technique" (1953), it is increasingly clear that following all the rules about what is "correct" analytic procedure and what is a correct analytic stance, as traditionally defined, does not guarantee an analytic process. It may at times be counteranalytic. For this reason, in my view, a more meaningful definition of analytic process must take into account what kind of working process actually is facilitated, and what is achieved by the patient, not just what the analyst does. As I have argued elsewhere (Ehrenberg, 1992a, 1992b), to define "analysis" by whether the analyst follows standard procedure, and/or to

Letters

view patients as "unanalyzable" when they are not responsive to standard technique, rather than questioning our own technique instead, prevents us from learning from the work how to refine and revise our theory and our technique and prevents us from taking psychoanalysis forward. These comments, by the way, were not included in Kevin Kelly's summary of discussion from the floor in his *JAPA* (42/3) report on the Eissler panel.

I believe Barratt's stimulating comments help to focus some of the most critical issues we must all attend to, and know how difficult the challenge here is. I appreciate this opportunity to clarify my own position.

REFERENCES

BARRATT, B.B. (1993). *Psychoanalysis and the Postmodern Impulse: Knowing and Being since Freud's Psychology.* Baltimore: Johns Hopkins Univ. Press.

EHRENBERG, D.B. (1992a). On the question of analyzability. *Contemp. Psychoanal.*, 28:16–31.

——— (1992b). *The Intimate Edge: Extending the Reach of Psychoanalytic Interaction.* New York: Norton.

——— (1993). On impasse as a result of failure to attend to the psychoanalytic interaction. Presented at American Psychological Association, New York, April 1993.

——— (1994a). Reply to reviews of *The Intimate Edge: Extending the Reach of Psychoanalytic Interaction. Psychoanal. Dialogues*, 4:303–316.

——— (1994b). On the importance of attending to the psychoanalytic interaction: enactment vs. analytic use of countertransference. Presented at American Psychological Association, Washington, D.C., April 16, 1994.

——— (1994c). Vulnerability, experience and desire in the psychoanalytic relationship: new perspectives on the analyst's use of self. Presented at the Chicago Association for Psychoanalytic Psychology, Chicago, October 15, 1994.

——— (1995). Countertransference disclosure. *Contemp. Psychoanal.*, 31, in press.

EISSLER, K.R. (1953). The effect of the structure of the ego on psychoanalytic technique. *J. Amer. Psychoanal. Assn.*, 1:104–143.

GILL, M. (1994). *Psychoanalysis in Transition.* Hillsdale, NJ: Analytic Press.

HOFFMAN, I.Z. (1991). Discussion: towards a social-constructivist view of the psychoanalytic situation. *Psychoanal. Dialogues*, 1:74–105.

LEVENSON, E.A. (1972). *The Fallacy of Understanding.* New York: Basic Books.

Darlene Bregman Ehrenberg
11 East 68th Street
New York, NY 10021

Letters

September 1995

Letter from Germany

Two kinds of political issues have preoccupied German psycho-analysts lately: (1) the relationship between psychoanalysis, the German insurance system, and its implications on training; and (2) the importance of the Nazi regime and the national socialist militancy of some of the "founding fathers" of the postwar German psychoanalytic movement.

1. German health insurance is a comprehensive system that covers practically the whole population of the country. It was conceived by Bismarck in the last century when he took measures to counter social unrest and demands for better living and working conditions. In the beginning it only covered the working classes on matters of physical illness, but with time it evolved. Since the end of World War II it has become an all-embracing health system covering all health risks except psychological ones, which only became subject to insurance payments after 1967 as a result of prolonged talks with all psychotherapeutic societies and institutions. The insurance system agreed to pay for a psychoanalytic treatment of four weekly hours of 50 minutes up to a total of 300 sessions (with some elasticity above this total number if justified by a report). Candidates were paid for their training cases if supervised by a training analyst. Nonmedical candidates and practitioners were part of the system if they were supervised or had their patient delegated by a psychoanalyst with a medical degree.

As with all health systems that started by being generous and comprehensive, time has produced a financial erosion and has made the insurance institutions look for ways to save money. These savings have targeted, amongst others, psychotherapy and psychoanalysis, and have led to attempts to restrict payments for these procedures by trying to restrict the frequency of analytic sessions to three weekly hours and certainly not finance any sessions beyond 300. If the patient and the analyst agree about the necessity and desirability of a fourth or a fifth session, there have been attempts to make it illegal for the patient to pay out of his own pocket for these extra sessions. Candidates have encountered greater difficulties with these extra sessions even if they offer them for free.

There have been long and at times acrimonious discussions be-tween analysts and the insurance system, including attempts to take the insurance system to court, which so far have been inconclusive leaving everyone to seek his or her own solution. This situation has also caused internal difficulties since the insurance system has always employed senior psychoanalysts to assess the confidential reports which every analyst has to send for approval by the insurance system before starting a therapy. These assessors have tried in some cases to ease the situation but in other cases have left analysts with the impression of taking sides with the insurance system and betraying psychoanalysis. This situation has led to extended discussions about the validity of high-frequency treatments (4 or 5 weekly hours) and their efficacy when measured against low frequency treatments (2 or 3 weekly hours).

Candidates have brought their problems to Psychoanalytic Soci-ety meetings stating their difficulties in finding patients prepared to come four times a week even without extra payment for their fourth session. Practical and theoretical arguments plus anger have been exchanged to no avail and little result.

Lately, the officers of the Psychoanalytic Society have adopted a negotiating stance and assembled a committee of senior analysts who are or have been insurance assessors to confront the insurance system in a positive way and try to solve what has become an impasse.

2. The maturation of the older postwar German generation (in-cluding psychoanalysts) and the fiftieth anniversary of the ending of World War II, have promoted a movement toward reviewing the historical past and assessing the rôle played by Nazi ideology and its influence on present-day Germany. During the last couple of years, hardly a day has passed without a TV program or a newspaper article dealing with the atrocities of the Third Reich and their conse-quences. This spirit of revision has not bypassed psychoanalysis, and for the past couple of years, every sixth monthly meeting of the German Psychoanalytic Association has included a workshop, a ma-jor paper, or the guest speaker dealing with the events of 1933 to 1945 and their relevance (conscious or unconscious, personal or collective) to the present.

Soul searching, "conscience," guilt, and reparation have been the contents of programs, discussions, and meetings. The revision of the stance of the first German postwar psychoanalysts, the "founding fathers," who trained the present "older generation," has begun to be assessed. Some revered figures from the past have been questioned, with some difficult facts emerging. Doubts, accusations, and lengthy papers in bulletins and information letters have promoted major discussions. Upheaval, claims, and disclaimers, attacks and defenses, questions and explanations have followed. The result has been perhaps to create a more open atmosphere amongst German psychoanalysts, without the unconscious and the not so unconscious taboos that determine a good deal of the denial that was present before. Today it has become not only acceptable but is seen as necessary to ask patients about the position of their parents or grandparents during the Nazi regime and to discuss their feelings and thoughts about these matters.

The two above points have had an effect on the German psychoanalytic scientific scene. Publications concerning these discussions have appeared along with discussion of other issues which have also preoccupied German psychoanalysis; for example, the uses of transference and countertransference. Until some years ago German psychoanalysis was a unitarian institution, mostly oriented toward ego psychology. But interest in new developments has taken over, and Kleinians, Kohutians, hermeneutitians, empiricists, biologicians, etc., are now very much on the scene. This is reflected in the variety of papers in the specialized journals, so that it is almost impossible to sum up the latest publications and talk about themes. The cultural aspects of psychoanalysis are also strongly represented, and together with papers from foreign analysts give the present-day literature a multicolored aspect.

German psychoanalysis is in a state of ferment and renewal in which it is interesting to participate.

Klaus Fink, M.D.
Im Zeitlett 25
89081 ULM

Journal of the  JAPA 43

American **P**sychoanalytic Association

Scientific Papers

Salman Akhtar
A THIRD INDIVIDUATION: IMMIGRATION, IDEN-
TITY, AND THE PSYCHOANALYTIC PROCESS 1051

Richard Almond
THE ANALYTIC ROLE: A MEDIATING INFLUENCE
IN THE INTERPLAY OF TRANSFERENCE AND
COUNTERTRANSFERENCE 469

Fred Busch
BEGINNING A PSYCHOANALYTIC TREATMENT:
ESTABLISHING AN ANALYTIC FRAME 449

Fred Busch
DO ACTIONS SPEAK LOUDER THAN WORDS? A
QUERY INTO AN ENIGMA IN ANALYTIC THEORY
AND TECHNIQUE 61

Rita W. Clark
THE POPE'S CONFESSOR: A METAPHOR RELAT-
ING TO ILLNESS IN THE ANALYST 137

Judith Dupont
THE STORY OF A TRANSGRESSION 823

Gerald I. Fogel
PSYCHOLOGICAL-MINDEDNESS AS A DEFENSE 793

Allan Frosch
THE PRECONCEPTUAL ORGANIZATION OF
EMOTION 423

Glen O. Gabbard
THE EARLY HISTORY OF BOUNDARY VIOLA-
TIONS IN PSYCHOANALYSIS 1115

Robert M. Galatzer-Levy
PSYCHOANALYSIS AND DYNAMICAL SYSTEMS
THEORY: PREDICTION AND SELF SIMILARITY 1085

Vol. 43

1995

Contents   *JAPA 43*

Karen Gilmore
GENDER IDENTITY DISORDER IN A GIRL: IN-
SIGHTS FROM ADOPTION   39

Robert G. Goldstein
THE HIGHER AND LOWER IN MENTAL LIFE: AN
ESSAY ON J. HUGHLINGS JACKSON AND FREUD   495

Michael I. Good
KARL ABRAHAM, SIGMUND FREUD, AND THE
FATE OF THE SEDUCTION THEORY   1137

Stanley Grand
A CLASSIC REVISITED: CLINICAL AND THEORET-
ICAL REFLECTIONS ON STONE'S WIDENING
SCOPE OF INDICATIONS FOR PSYCHOANALYSIS   741

James W. Kern
ON FOCUSED ASSOCIATION AND THE ANA-
LYTIC SURFACE: CLINICAL OPPORTUNITIES IN
RESOLVING ANALYTIC STALEMATE   393

Lucy LaFarge
TRANSFERENCES OF DECEPTION   765

Elizabeth Lloyd Mayer
THE PHALLIC CASTRATION COMPLEX AND PRI-
MARY FEMININITY: PAIRED DEVELOPMENTAL
LINES TOWARD FEMALE GENDER IDENTITY   17

Barbara Milrod
THE CONTINUED USEFULNESS OF PSYCHO-
ANALYSIS IN THE TREATMENT ARMAMENTARIUM
FOR PANIC DISORDER   151

David L. Raphling
INTERPRETATION AND EXPECTATION: THE
ANXIETY OF INFLUENCE   95

Gail S. Reed
CLINICAL TRUTH AND CONTEMPORARY RELA-
TIVISM: MEANING AND NARRATION IN THE PSY-
CHOANALYTIC SITUATION   713

Contents

Owen Renik
THE ROLE OF AN ANALYST'S EXPECTATIONS IN CLINICAL TECHNIQUE: REFLECTIONS ON THE CONCEPT OF RESISTANCE   83

Steven P. Roose and Robin Horwitz Stern
MEDICATION USE IN TRAINING CASES: A SURVEY   163

Herbert J. Schlesinger
THE PROCESS OF INTERPRETATION AND THE MOMENT OF CHANGE   663

Donald P. Spence
WHEN DO INTERPRETATIONS MAKE A DIFFERENCE? A PARTIAL ANSWER TO FLIESS'S *ACHENSEE* QUESTION   689

Lisa A. Uyehara, Susan Austrian, Letitia G. Upton, Rebecca H. Warner, and Roberta A. Williamson
TELLING ABOUT THE ANALYST'S PREGNANCY   113

Milton Viederman
THE RECONSTRUCTION OF A REPRESSED SEXUAL MOLESTATION FIFTY YEARS LATER   1169

Panel Reports

Linda S. Altman
CLASSICS REVISITED: LEO STONE'S *THE PSYCHOANALYTIC SITUATION*   197

Boyd L. Burris
CLASSICS REVISITED: FREUD'S PAPERS ON TECHNIQUE   175

Fredric N. Busch
AGORAPHOBIA AND PANIC STATES   207

Seth Eichler
FREUD IN AMERICA   835

Contents

Lawrence Friedman
CLASSICS REVISITED: INTRODUCTION   171

Lawrence Friedman
TWO PANELS ON INTERACTION: AN INTRO-
DUCTION   517

David M. Hurst
TOWARD A DEFINITION OF THE TERM AND CON-
CEPT OF INTERACTION   521

Salley S. Jessee
CLASSICS REVISITED: HEINZ KOHUT'S *THE ANAL-
YSIS OF THE SELF*   187

Margaret C. Keenan
ENACTMENTS OF BOUNDARY VIOLATIONS   853

Stephen D. Purcell
INTERPRETIVE PERSPECTIVES ON INTERACTION   539

Plenary Addresses

Henry F. Smith
INTRODUCTION: GEDO AND FREUD ON WORK-
ING THROUGH   331

John E. Gedo
WORKING THROUGH AS METAPHOR AND AS A
MODALITY OF TREATMENT   339

Dale Boesky, Marianne Goldberger, Arnold
H. Modell, Arnold Rothstein, Morton
Shane, Estelle Shane, and Arthur F.
Valenstein
COMMENTARIES   356

John E. Gedo
ENCORE   384

Howard Shevrin
IS PSYCHOANALYSIS ONE SCIENCE, TWO SCI-
ENCES, OR NO SCIENCE AT ALL? A DISCOURSE
AMONG FRIENDLY ANTAGONISTS   963

Contents   *JAPA 43*

Lawrence Friedman, Wilma Bucci, Arnold
Goldberg, William I. Grossman, Paul E.
Meehl, Robert Michels, Richard C. Simons,
and Mark Solms
COMMENTARIES   986

Howard Shevrin
AMAGANSETT REVISITED   1035

Editorials

Donald Meyers— TRIBUTE TO BERNARD L.
PACELLA   957

Kenneth Calder— TRIBUTE TO LEO STONE   7

Arnold D. Richards— IT'S ALL IN THE TIMING   9

Opinions

Joseph   Schachter— THE   ANALYST   UNDER
STRESS: ISSUES OF TECHNIQUE   11

Sandra   K.   Cohen— PSYCHOANALYSIS   AND
PSYCHOTROPIC MEDICATION   15

John Munder Ross— THE FATE OF RELATIVES
AND COLLEAGUES IN THE AFTERMATH OF BOUND-
ARY VIOLATIONS   959

Samuel Abrams— COMMON BELIEFS, GROUND,
HOPES, ILLUSIONS, AND ARGUMENTS   327

Book Essay

John Munder Ross
KING OEDIPUS AND THE POSTMODERNIST PSY-
CHOANALYST   553

Book Reviews

Salman Akhtar and Henri Parens, Editors— BEYOND THE SYMBIOTIC ORBIT: AD-
VANCES IN SEPARATION-INDIVIDUATION THEORY:
ESSAYS IN HONOR OF SELMA KRAMER
reviewed by Moisy Shopper   923

Contents

Salman Akhtar— BROKEN STRUCTURES: SEVERE
PERSONALITY DISORDERS AND THEIR TREATMENT
reviewed by Glen O. Gabbard   627

Lewis Aron and Adrienne Harris, Editors— THE LEGACY OF SANDOR FERENCZI
reviewed by Stephen A. Mitchell   228

Elaine Hoffman Baruch and Lucienne J. Serrano— WOMEN ANALYZE WOMEN
reviewed by Martha Kirkpatrick   1201

Wilfred R. Bion— COGITATIONS
reviewed by Lucy LaFarge   610

Eva Brabant et al., Editors— THE CORRESPONDENCE OF SIGMUND FREUD AND SANDOR FERENCZI: VOLUME 1, 1908–1914
reviewed by Lewis A. Kirshner   873

Sylvia Brody and Miriam G. Siegel— THE
EVOLUTION OF CHARACTER: BIRTH TO EIGHTEEN
YEARS, A LONGITUDINAL STUDY
reviewed by Francis Baudry   258

Stanley J. Coen— THE MISUSE OF PERSONS: ANALYZING PATHOLOGICAL DEPENDENCY
reviewed by Paul A. Dewald   1216

Jody Messler Davies and Mary Gail Frawley— TREATING THE ADULT SURVIVOR OF CHILDHOOD SEXUAL ABUSE: A PSYCHOANALYTIC
PERSPECTIVE
reviewed by Bonnie J. Buchele   282

R. Horacio Etchegoyen— FUNDAMENTALS OF
PSYCHOANALYTIC TECHNIQUE
reviewed by Otto F. Kernberg   601

Kay Field, Bertram J. Cohler, and Glorye
Wool, Editors— LEARNING AND EDUCATION:
PSYCHOANALYTIC PERSPECTIVES
reviewed by Stefan Stein   915

Merton M. Gill— PSYCHOANALYSIS IN TRANSITION: A PERSONAL VIEW
reviewed by Robert S. Wallerstein   595

Contents

JAPA 43

Sander L. Gilman— THE CASE OF SIGMUND
FREUD: MEDICINE AND IDENTITY AT THE FIN DE
SIÈCLE
    reviewed by John E. Gedo   889

Sander L. Gilman— THE JEWS' BODY
    reviewed by Harold P. Blum   891

Arnold Goldberg, Editor— THE WIDENING
SCOPE OF SELF PSYCHOLOGY: PROGRESS IN SELF
PSYCHOLOGY, VOLUME 9
    reviewed by Brenda Clorfene Solomon   245

Dodi Goldman— IN SEARCH OF THE REAL: THE
ORIGINS AND ORIGINALITY OF D. W. WINNICOTT
    reviewed by Patrick J. Casement   223

Paul Gray— THE EGO AND ANALYSIS OF DE-
FENSE
    reviewed by Evelyne Albrecht Schwaber   1208

André Green— LA DÉLIAISON
    reviewed by Theodore Cherbuliez   267

André Green— LE TRAVAIL DU NEGATIF
    reviewed by André Lussier   263

Jay Greenberg— OEDIPUS AND BEYOND: A
CLINICAL THEORY
    reviewed by Donald M. Kaplan   618

Leon Grinberg— GUILT AND DEPRESSION
    reviewed by Vamık D. Volkan   938

J.S. Grotstein et al., Editors— THE BORDER-
LINE PATIENT: EMERGING CONCEPTS IN DIAGNO-
SIS, PSYCHODYNAMICS, AND TREATMENT
    reviewed by Sonia Kulchycky and Rich-
    ard L. Munich   623

James S. Grotstein and Donald B. Rinsley,
Editors— FAIRBAIRN AND THE ORIGINS OF OB-
JECT RELATIONS
    reviewed by Peter Buckley   241

Ilse Grubrich-Simitis— ZURÜCK ZU FREUDS
TEXTEN
    reviewed by Lore Schacht   583

Contents   *JAPA 43*

André Haynal— Psychoanalysis and the Sciences
    reviewed by John E. Gedo   1236

Virginia Hunter— Psychoanalysts Talk
    reviewed by Joseph Reppen   1197

Theodore J. Jacobs— The Use of the Self
    reviewed by Michael G. Moran   1214

Michael A. Jenike, Editor— Obsessional Disorders
    reviewed by Aaron H. Esman   629

Helmut Junker— Von Freud in den Freudianern
    reviewed by Maria V. Bergmann   586

Joseph D. Lichtenberg, Frank M. Lachmann, and James L. Fosshage— Self and Motivational Systems: Toward a Theory of Psychoanalytic Technique
    reviewed by Jules Glenn   236

Zvi Lothane— In Defense of Schreber: Soul Murder and Psychiatry
    reviewed by George H. Allison   573

Murray Meisels and Ester R. Shapiro, Editors— Tradition and Innovation in Psychoanalytic Education: Clark Conference on Psychoanalytic Training for Psychologists
    reviewed by Salman Akhtar   909

Arnold H. Modell— The Private Self
    reviewed by Fred M. Levin   232

Darius Gray Ornston, Editor— Translating Freud
    reviewed by Wolfgang Berner   580

Joel Paris, Editor— Borderline Personality Disorder: Etiology and Treatment
    reviewed by Henry J. Friedman   276

Contents JAPA 43

R. Andrew Paskauskas, Editor— THE COM-
PLETE CORRESPONDENCE OF SIGMUND FREUD AND
ERNEST JONES, 1908–1939
 reviewed by Leo Rangell 877

Jean-Michel Petot— MELANIE KLEIN: VOLUMES
I & II
 reviewed by Lucy LaFarge 606

Saul Rosenzweig— FREUD, JUNG, AND HALL
THE KING-MAKER: THE HISTORIC EXPEDITION TO
AMERICA
 reviewed by Nathan M. Kravis 576

Elisabeth Roudinesco— JACQUES LACAN &
CO.: A HISTORY OF PSYCHOANALYSIS IN FRANCE,
1925–1985
 reviewed by Joseph H. Smith 615

Leonard Shengold— "FATHER, DON'T YOU SEE
I'M BURNING?"
 reviewed by Marvin Margolis 898

Leonard Shengold— "THE BOY WILL COME
TO NOTHING!"
 reviewed by Jorge Schneider 895

Ulrich Streeck and Hans-Volker Werth-
mann, Editors— LEHRANALYSE UND PSYCHO-
ANALYTISCHE AUSBILDUNG
 reviewed by Johann Michael Rotmann 918

Carlo Strenger— BETWEEN HERMENEUTICS
AND SCIENCE
 reviewed by Donald P. Spence 1229

Edward Timms and Ritchie Robertson, Editors— PSYCHOANALYSIS IN ITS CULTURAL CON-
TEXT: AUSTRIAN STUDIES III
 reviewed by George J. Makari 903

Silvan S. Tomkins— AFFECT IMAGERY CON-
SCIOUSNESS: VOLUME 3. THE NEGATIVE AFFECTS:
FEAR AND ANGER
 reviewed by Rainer Krause 929

Contents

Henri and Madeleine Vermorel— SIGMUND
FREUD AND ROMAIN ROLLAND: CORRESPON-
DENCE, 1923–1936
    reviewed by Françoise Bouchard   883

George E. Vaillant— EGO MECHANISMS OF DE-
FENSE: A GUIDE FOR CLINICIANS AND RE-
SEARCHERS
    reviewed by Lawrence H. Rockland   255

George E. Vaillant— THE WISDOM OF THE EGO
    reviewed by Jerome B. Katz   251

Robert S. Wallerstein, Editor— THE COM-
MON GROUND OF PSYCHOANALYSIS
    reviewed by Paul A. Dewald   591

Ernest Wallwork— PSYCHOANALYSIS AND
ETHICS
    reviewed by Edwin R. Wallace, IV   1221

Arnold Wilson and John E. Gedo, Edi-
tors— HIERARCHICAL CONCEPTS IN PSYCHO-
ANALYSIS: THEORY, RESEARCH AND CLINICAL
PRACTICE
    reviewed by Milton Viederman   1239

Richard Wollheim— THE MIND AND ITS
DEPTHS
    reviewed by Barnaby B. Barratt   1233

Frank E. Yeomans, Michael A. Selzer, and
John F. Clarkin— TREATING THE BORDERLINE
PATIENT: A CONTRACT-BASED APPROACH
    reviewed by Salman Akhtar   270

Books Received   287

Obituary

Jerome A. Winer— MERTON M. GILL, M.D.   635

Letters   295, 641, 1247